THE
BLACK HAWK WAR
OF 1832

Campaigns and Commanders

THE
BLACK HAWK WAR
OF 1832

Patrick J. Jung

University of Oklahoma Press : Norman

Library of Congress Cataloging-in-Publication Data

Jung, Patrick J., 1963–
   The Black Hawk War of 1832 / Patrick J. Jung.
     p.   cm. — (Campaigns and commanders ; v. 10)
   Includes bibliographical references and index.
   ISBN 978-0-8061-3811-4 (alk. paper)
     1. Black Hawk War, 1832. 2. Black Hawk, Sauk chief, 1767–1838.
   3. Sauk Indians—Wars. I. Title.
   E83.83.J86 2007
   973.5'6—dc22   2006024462

The Black Hawk War of 1832 is Volume 10 in the Campaigns and
Commanders series.

1 2 3 4 5 6 7 8 9 10

To my wife, Rochelle

CONTENTS

Illustrations

Maps

ACKNOWLEDGMENTS

There are many people who have been instrumental in assisting me with this project over the course of the past several years. I developed many of my initial ideas for this book while researching and writing my doctoral dissertation, and members of my dissertation committee provided tremendous insight and expertise. I want to thank James Marten, Alice Kehoe, Steven Avella, Robert Hay, and Reginald Horsman for serving on my committee. I also wish to express my gratitude to the Arthur J. Schmitt Foundation for providing generous financial assistance that allowed me to complete my dissertation. Marquette University was also a generous benefactor during my years of graduate study. I am extremely grateful to the faculty and administration at Marquette for bestowing upon me a graduate student assistantship, a graduate student teaching fellowship, the Reverend John P. Raynor, S. J. Fellowship, and the Reverend Henry J. Caspar, S. J. Fellowship.

I extend my sincere thanks to Joanne Dyskow, Karl David, Nancy Oestreich Lurie, and the Reverend Francis Paul Prucha, S. J., for reading early drafts of this book. I also wish to extend my appreciation to the anonymous reviewers assigned by the University of Oklahoma Press to assess this book while it was still in manuscript form. The comments and suggestions made by these distinguished scholars were invaluable. The editorial staff at the University of Oklahoma Press was also extremely supportive, professional, and patient during the time that I worked on this book, and I wish to thank Ron Chrisman, Charles E. Rankin, Bobbie Canfield, Jay Dew, Jay Fultz, and Emmy Ezzell for all of their assistance. I am also very grateful to Cindy Burish for her graphic art skills and for turning what were my very rough sketches into the best maps of the Black Hawk War that have ever been produced. Special thanks also must go to all of my colleagues at the Milwaukee School of Engineering, particularly the members of the General Studies Department. I have thoroughly enjoyed their collegiality and friendship for the past several years. I also wish to express my gratitude to Jeffrey Chown of Northern Illinois University for featuring me in his recent documentary, *Lincoln and the Black Hawk War.*

The staffs at several archives and libraries were critical to the successful completion of this book. I extend my appreciation to the National Archives, the Marquette University Library System, the Wisconsin Historical Society, the Milwaukee Public Library, the University of Wisconsin-Milwaukee Golda Meir Library, the Illinois State Archives, the Abraham Lincoln Presidential Library, the University of Wisconsin-Green Bay Area Research Center, the University of Wisconsin-Platteville Area Research Center, the Burton Historical Collection of the Detroit Public Library, the Chicago Historical Society, the Missouri Historical Society, the Kansas State Historical Society, the Minnesota Historical Society, and the National Anthropological Archives.

Finally, I am very grateful to my mother, Georgia Lee Winter Jung, and my father, Robert Joseph Jung, for the encouragement they have given me throughout my academic career. I am also grateful to my three children—Katherine, Aloysius, and Francis—for their unconditional love and inspiration. Most of all, I thank my wife Rochelle for her years of love and support. I would not have been able to complete this book without her selfless devotion.

THE
BLACK HAWK WAR
OF 1832

INTRODUCTION

The red men looked on with amaze,—
They would not, could not change their ways
Of living in a few brief days
And grudgingly gave place:
Though here and there heroic bands
Sought to retain their best loved lands,
Perforce they heeded the demands
Of an all-conq'ring race.
—AMER MILLS STOCKING

During the spring of 1832, about eleven hundred Indians joined a Sauk warrior named Black Hawk and defied an order by the federal government to leave Illinois and settle on the west side of the Mississippi River. They did not intend to make war against the United States, but a series of events turned what was supposed to be a peaceful demonstration of resolve into an armed conflict. The fighting raged during the summer months of 1832, and after the final, grisly battle along the Mississippi on August 2nd, only about half of the Indians in Black Hawk's band remained alive.

This conflict known as the Black Hawk War has generated a tremendous amount of scholarly interest, particularly in the Midwest. The first books concerning the Black Hawk War began to appear shortly after the conflict ended, and there has been a steady stream of published work since. The participants, including Black Hawk, penned many of the first books on the war. These early works fall into two general categories: those that blame the Indians for

3

starting the conflict, and those that blame the whites. Later works produced during the late nineteenth and early twentieth centuries simply tend to rehash these earlier arguments.

Studies of the Black Hawk War written since World War II are more interdisciplinary and use ethnographic data to examine how Black Hawk and his rival Keokuk both rose to positions of prominence among the confederated Sauk and Fox tribes despite neither man coming from a clan that provided hereditary leadership. These works are the most influential today because they are better researched and more balanced than the earlier works, many of which are blatantly ethnocentric.[1] The one thing that all these works have in common is that they generally tell the same story. The facts that comprise the main historical narrative of the Black Hawk War have been established for generations. Historians have known the principal events of the war since the guns went silent during the waning days of that sweltering summer in 1832.

So why a new book on the Black Hawk War? Although no new study of the conflict will significantly alter the facts, a fresh one can reconsider its causes and consequences. Scholarship on the nature of Indian resistance during this period, for example, provides an important new context in which to understand the war. Of particular importance is the work of Gregory Dowd concerning Native-American communities in the trans-Appalachian West during the eighteenth and early nineteenth centuries. The various Indian tribes of the region during this period experienced an "awakening" of nativistic spirit accompanied by millennial religious messages promising a new, golden age. This awakening gave Indians a sense of racial solidarity they had not had before. The overtly anti-white and particularly anti-American attitudes produced by this awakening provided the ideological foundation for a variety of Indian resistance movements, culminating in those led by the Shawnee chief Tecumseh and his brother Tenskwatawa, or the Shawnee Prophet. The brothers united the disparate tribes of the trans-Appalachian West into a confederation that forcibly resisted the United States and attempted to turn back the tide of white settlement. While the defeat of Tecumseh's confederation during the War of 1812 greatly diminished this ideology of resistance, it did not destroy it. Indeed, the Black Hawk War was proof of its continued existence almost twenty years later.[2]

Another factor that had a significant impact upon the course of the Black Hawk War was the escalation of intertribal warfare among the Indian communities of the upper Great Lakes and upper Mississippi River Valley. In the years immediately preceding the conflict, the tribes of this region had coalesced into two loosely organized alliance systems that fought with increasing frequency and intensity. Fearing that an even larger and more destructive conflagration could erupt, federal officials stepped in on numerous occasions to halt the incessant warfare. The fighting gave military commanders and Indian agents a tremendous opportunity, however, and both exploited these divisions during the Black Hawk War by using the enemies of the Sauks and Foxes to engage Black Hawk's band. The allies of the Sauks and Foxes did not rush to Black Hawk's aid because he represented only a faction of the two tribes, and a relatively small faction compared to that of Keokuk, who successfully urged the majority of the Sauks and Foxes and their allies to remain peaceful. Once the war began, Black Hawk and his followers found themselves alone, squeezed between their Indian enemies and white soldiers, with virtually no Indian allies.

These two forces—resistance to American expansion and intertribal warfare—came together in an awkward embrace in the years immediately preceding the Black Hawk War. They were not completely unrelated, for white settlement had pushed many tribes farther to the west and forced them to compete with other Indian communities for new lands and hunting grounds. Tecumseh and Tenskwatawa had urged the tribes to put aside their differences and embrace pan-Indian unity, but by the 1830s this idea was only a shadow of what it had been twenty years earlier, and the lingering notion of resistance to American expansion was not potent enough to resurrect it. Nonetheless, it was still strong enough to produce uprisings against the United States on two occasions, first during the 1827 Winnebago Uprising, and five years later during the Black Hawk War. However, it was not able to unite diverse Indian nations as it once had, and in the two decades after 1815, intertribal warfare continued unabated. The ideology of resistance was not even potent enough to spark unity within communities. Indeed, only factions initiated and undertook revolts after 1815, not entire tribes.

Thus, Black Hawk was heir to a weakened and fractured resistance movement coupled with a vigorous interest among the tribes in fighting one another. It was the collision of these two forces that insured the failure of any insurrection against the United States and its citizens. The Winnebagos had discovered this stark reality during the 1827 Winnebago Uprising, a fact generally overlooked by historians. The Winnebagos had a much stronger, widespread, and well-organized resistance movement than that of Black Hawk, but even this was not enough to ensure success, and their attempt to rise up against the United States in 1827 ended shortly after it began. More relevant to the history of the Black Hawk War is the fact that the Winnebagos inadvertently helped sow the seeds of Black Hawk's destruction. In the aftermath of the Winnebago Uprising, the United States Army increased its presence in the region and took other measures to insure that it could respond quickly to future Indian revolts, actions that generally proved effective during the Black Hawk War.

Although many works deal with the Black Hawk War, a number of books and essays (particularly the earlier ones) have been based on sources of questionable veracity and provenance. As a result, many of these works contain errors, some serious, that have found their way into later works. Even the more scholarly works on the Black Hawk War do not examine adequately the effect that intertribal war had on the conflict, and none discusses the pan-Indian resistance movement. This book is therefore based on original primary sources. My endeavor has been made easier by the fact that, in the 1970s, Ellen C. Whitney of the Illinois State Historical Library edited and published the most important primary source documents of the Black Hawk War. Whitney's volumes are, by far, the most significant ever published on the conflict, and her excellent editorial work has done much to uncover the errors of previous scholars.[3]

Perhaps the most compelling reason for examining the Black Hawk War is that it provides an excellent example of how Indian wars came about and how they were conducted. Thus, by learning about the Black Hawk War, students of history will gain a firm understanding of the various conflicts that occurred between Indians and whites throughout the course of American history. First, strong anti-white (and, more specifically, anti-American) sentiments provided an ideological foundation for the war. Related to this was the fact that the Black Hawk War was a product of a pan-

Indian revitalization movement that took traditional religious and cultural elements and molded them into a new political expression seeking to unite various tribes against white expansion. Both of these elements were characteristic of earlier and later Indian wars. Second, Black Hawk sought an alliance with the British in Canada in order to strengthen his hand against the United States. He was not the first Indian leader (nor was he the last) to seek the assistance of a Euro-American imperial power such as France, Britain, or Spain to fight against a white foe. Third, whites used a similar strategy, and this was also a facet of the Black Hawk War that was characteristic of other Indian wars. Pan-Indian unity was undermined by inter-tribal disputes, and whites exploited these divisions, using friendly tribes as allies in their armed conflicts with hostile Indian communities. Fourth, intra-tribal disputes between tribal leaders and the factions that they led in part caused the Black Hawk War, and this typified other Indian wars as well. Black Hawk and Keokuk headed separate factions that had differing notions concerning how the Sauk and Fox tribes should manage their relationship with the United States. Black Hawk chose the path of resistance while Keokuk chose the path of accommodation. Fifth, the dispute between the two men arose principally because of the 1804 treaty that the Sauks and Foxes signed with the United States. The federal government employed dishonesty and chicanery when negotiating the treaty, and the two tribes were essentially swindled out of their lands as a result. This was complicated by the encroachment of white settlers upon lands claimed by both native communities and the United States. These occurrences were common in other Indian-white conflicts as well. Finally, white politicians, commanders, and soldiers frequently demonstrated sheer incompetence as well as morally repugnant behavior during the Black Hawk War. Black Hawk did not intend to make war, but poor decisions, ineffective leadership, and irresponsible statements and actions on the part of white leaders led to misunderstandings and ultimately violence. Moreover, the untrained and undisciplined frontier militia volunteers who did the bulk of the fighting hated Indians and sought nothing less than their extermination. Thus, the Black Hawk War at many times resembled a massacre rather than a war, particularly since women, children, and elders were needlessly and viciously killed. Sadly, such massacres were common to many Indian wars during the course of American history.

Several explanations concerning terms and usage are necessary. The words *Indian, Native American, American Indian,* and *native peoples* will be used interchangeably to designate collectively the aboriginal inhabitants of North America. Admittedly, there were tremendous cultural and linguistic differences among various Indian groups and, when appropriate, specific tribes will be named. The words *tribe* and *nation* will be used interchangeably as well, although it should be remembered that Indian tribes in the Great Lakes region, while sharing common languages and cultural traits, were usually not well integrated politically but instead consisted of many semi-autonomous bands and villages that were loosely allied. The tribes themselves often have had a confusing number of labels attached to them throughout their histories. The French, for example, referred to the Fox tribe as *Renards,* other tribes called them *Outagami,* and they called themselves *Mesquakie.* To avoid confusion, the most common names and spellings are used for each tribe unless another source that uses an alternate designation is quoted directly. This same system is used for the names of individual Indians. Although whites used spellings such as *Decoret* and *Decori,* the most frequent spelling of this Winnebago name is *Decorah.* Whenever possible, Indian names are provided in their native languages using the most common spellings. English translations are used when the Indian pronunciation is unavailable and also when discussing certain well-known Indians such as Black Hawk and Red Bird, who are better known by their English names.

The short passages at the beginning of each chapter require a brief explanation. In 1926, Amer Mills Stocking (who was of Wampanoag Indian descent) produced an epic poem about the Black Hawk War. In it, Stocking sought to present a version of the Black Hawk War that was complete, accurate, impartial, and in meter and verse. He hoped his work would be "more vivid and interesting" than standard histories of the war.[4] Although Stocking's poem should not be relied upon as a scholarly resource, and some of its perspectives go against modern sensitivities, it reflects the intense regional interest in the Black Hawk War that existed in Stocking's day. Many of the poem's passages admirably succeed in capturing the spirit of the various phases of the Black Hawk War, which, I would argue, makes it worthy of quotation. The excerpts are incidental to a book that, I hope, presents a more complete understanding of what remains one of the last Indian wars fought in the upper Great Lakes and upper Mississippi Valley.

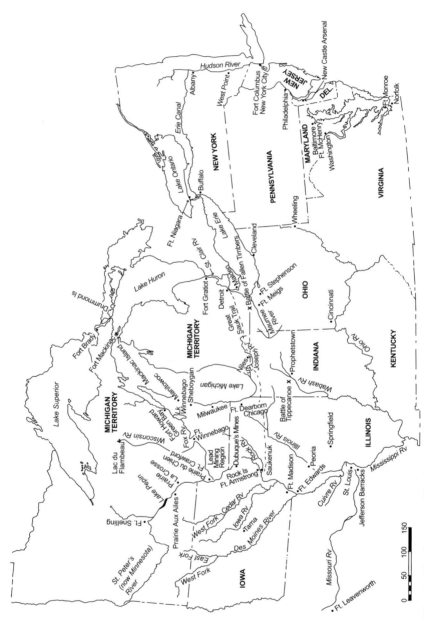

Map 1. Northeastern North America

IO

1

Sowing the Seeds of Fury

The hearts of the Sauks and the Foxes were fired,
And a home in that eden they greatly desired.
They gathered their forces, and with one consent
With all they possessed down the Rock River went.
Arriving, they drove the Kaskaskias away,
Took the land for their own, and determined to stay
As long as the trees of the forest should grow,
The flowers should bloom and the great waters flow.
— AMER MILLS STOCKING

In autumn of 1833, an aging Sauk warrior recounted the story of his life and recent troubles to Antoine LeClaire, the government interpreter at Fort Armstrong at Rock Island, Illinois. LeClaire translated the Sauk's story while John B. Patterson, a local newspaper editor, prepared it for publication. The Sauk was Ma-ka-tai-me-she-kia-kiak, whose name translated literally as "Black Sparrow Hawk" but who was better known among whites as Black Hawk.

The year before, Black Hawk had led a brief war against the United States. After federal troops took him captive, they transported Black Hawk and the other leaders of the revolt to Jefferson Barracks near St. Louis, where they remained incarcerated for the winter. In spring, Black Hawk and his comrades went east as prisoners. In addition to meeting with President Andrew Jackson, they toured Norfolk, Baltimore, Philadelphia, and New York. After a return journey through the Great Lakes, Black Hawk and his compatriots returned to their homes. Black Hawk was sixty-seven years old when he related his autobiography, and although not born into a leadership clan that provided civil chiefs, he had attained great influence

among the Sauks because of his courage and charismatic personal-
ity. Now, near the end of his life, he stood vanquished. His attempt
to stop the United States from acquiring his beloved homeland had
ended in failure, and the once-proud warrior found himself without
influence in his tribe. Toward the end of his narrative, Black Hawk
waxed philosophic about the rebellion he led. He no longer talked of
war but of peace. "We will forget what has past," he stated, "and
may the watchword between the Americans and the Sacs and Foxes,
ever be—'Friendship!'"[1]

Black Hawk spoke these words with sincerity, for he had learned
a terrible lesson during the short war that he fought against the
United States. He lived for six years after the conclusion of the conflict and established a new home in Iowa, where he was noted for
receiving white guests with hospitality. In his final years he directed
his bitterness toward Keokuk, his rival among the Sauks. Black
Hawk was present at two treaty councils in 1836 and 1837 when his
tribe sold millions of acres of land to the United States. He offered
no resistance to either transaction. Thus, the great warrior who earlier had fought to preserve his homeland had been driven into
silence and obscurity as more of his tribe's domain slipped into the
hands of the federal government. About three months before he died
in October 1838, he was the guest of honor at an Independence Day
celebration at Fort Madison in Iowa. His words to the assembled
crowd of white settlers summed up his sentiments: "I was once a
great warrior. I am now poor. Keokuk has been the cause of my present situation."[2]

Black Hawk's words reflected what had been a long and stormy
relationship with Keokuk, or the Watchful Fox, who, like Black
Hawk, had come to prominence despite not being born into a leadership clan. Black Hawk had not always blamed Keokuk for the difficulties that he and his tribe faced. He may have made peace with
white Americans in his later years, but he also knew that they had
cheated the Sauks and their confederates, the Foxes, out of their
tribal domain. Although the feud between Keokuk and Black Hawk
certainly helped precipitate the Black Hawk War, the split between
them and the tribal factions they led arose because of the treaty that
the Sauks and Foxes signed with the United States in 1804. He
acknowledged this in his autobiography when he stated that the
1804 treaty "has been the origin of all our difficulties."[3]

The story of how the two tribes came to sign that treaty, which ceded much of present-day Illinois, Wisconsin, and Missouri to the United States, began almost two centuries earlier. The Sauks and Foxes, like most tribes in the Great Lakes and the upper Mississippi River Valley, developed diplomatic and political relationships with the four great imperial powers that claimed sovereignty over this region: France, Great Britain, Spain, and the United States. Most tribes developed strong ties to the French and later the British. The Sauks and Foxes were unusual in that they resisted both powers at various times, although they, too, developed strong ties when it suited their purposes. Like all tribes, the Sauks and Foxes intensely mistrusted the Americans, but whereas most tribes stopped fighting against the United States after the War of 1812, the Sauks and Foxes under Black Hawk's leadership continued their resistance into the 1830s.

Given the propensity of the Sauks and Foxes to resist political and cultural domination, their conflicts with the imperial powers—particularly the United States—were not surprising. When the French established themselves in eastern Canada during the early 1600s, the Sauks lived in the vicinity of the Saginaw River Valley of Michigan, while the Foxes lived nearby in southern Michigan and northeastern Ohio. Both tribes spoke the same language within the Algonquian linguistic family and had been united as a common people centuries earlier. In the 1640s and 1650s, both the Sauks and Foxes fled west to escape the onslaught of the tribes of the Iroquois League, which, from their villages in New York, launched a war of annihilation against Indian communities in the Great Lakes region. By the end of the seventeenth century, the Sauks and Foxes were located in present-day northeastern Wisconsin. New problems for the Foxes began when a faction of the tribe that had returned to southern Michigan became embroiled in conflicts that ultimately led to a twenty-year war with the French at Detroit and the tribes allied to them. About one thousand Foxes died in the initial skirmish at Detroit in 1712, and a few who managed to escape fled to the Fox villages in northeastern Wisconsin. From there, the Foxes launched raids against the French and their Indian allies. The French countered with a series of campaigns that culminated in the 1730 siege of a palisaded fort built by the Foxes in central Illinois. The French sought nothing short of genocide, and by 1732 they had almost achieved their goal, for only about two hundred Foxes remained alive. In desperation, the remaining Foxes sought refuge with the Sauks at Green Bay in 1733, thus beginning the era of confederation between the tribes that would last until the 1850s. Members of the two tribes had intermarried heavily, and thus, the Foxes had many bonds of kinship with the Sauks. Union with the Sauks was a wise decision, for the French commenced a final campaign of extermination against the Foxes in 1733. After a brief skirmish near Green Bay, the two tribes moved west toward the Mississippi and established themselves in Iowa. Following a failed campaign in the winter of 1734–35, the French sought and achieved a full reconciliation with the two tribes by 1742.[4]

In the wake of the Fox Wars, the Sauks and Foxes settled in the Mississippi River Valley and established villages from the mouth of the Des Moines River north to Prairie du Chien. One of the largest villages, Saukenuk, stood at the junction of the Mississippi and Rock Rivers. It was here that Black Hawk was born in 1767. The tribes remained confederated, and despite frequent intermarriage between their members, both retained distinct tribal and political identities. By the early nineteenth century, the Sauks numbered about 5,300 persons and the Foxes about 1,600.[5]

The British replaced the French and took control of the trans-Appalachian West as the French and Indian War entered its final stages in 1759. Many tribes, including the Sauks and Foxes, initially harbored a strong resentment toward the British. By 1763, this hostility led to a series of loosely coordinated Indian uprisings commonly known as Pontiac's Rebellion. The famed Ottawa chief from Detroit actually led only a regional revolt, although Pontiac's actions certainly encouraged resistance to the British elsewhere. A group of Sauks joined the Ojibwas in slaughtering the British garrison at Michilimackinac, but the revolt did not move any farther west, and the Sauks and Foxes had no further involvement. Indeed, they later joined with other tribes in the region such as the Menominees, Santee Sioux, Winnebagos, and Ottawas and pledged peace to the British. This was due in large part to the efforts of a British officer stationed at Green Bay who had successfully established peaceful relations with the interior tribes.[6]

The Sauks and Foxes eventually became British allies after Pontiac's Rebellion because the British restored the system of diplomacy and trade with the Indians that had existed under the French.

Both tribes fought on the side of the British during the American Revolution and took part in the attack against St. Louis in May 1780. Although the population was predominantly French, St. Louis and the rest of Louisiana had been transferred to Spain after the French and Indian War. While the British fought a war with their thirteen restive colonies in the East, they also had a conflict with Spain. The Spanish and Americans engaged in a common cause against the British in the Mississippi Valley, and the British sought to end these intrigues by capturing St. Louis in 1780 with a force composed almost entirely of Indian warriors and fur traders from the upper Great Lakes. The Sauks and Foxes, however, had stronger ties to Spanish traders in St. Louis than to the British in the upper Great Lakes. Thus, they were the most reluctant contingent and joined largely due to British coercion. Sauk and Fox warriors mounted only a half-hearted effort, and their mediocre performance doomed the attack against St. Louis. Their participation, poor as it was, did not please the Spanish or Americans either, and in retaliation a polyglot Spanish, American, and French force attacked Saukenuk a month later.[7]

Despite these occasional instances of friction, the Sauks and Foxes generally had sporadic and relatively inconsequential relations with the imperial powers after the Fox Wars. Of far more importance were the wars both tribes fought against their Indian enemies. During the century between the end of the Fox Wars and the Black Hawk War, the Sauks and Foxes focused far more attention and resources on fighting other Indians. From the 1780s onward, the two tribes expanded their hunting grounds west of the Mississippi and clashed with Siouan-speaking tribes. From the 1780s until the 1820s, the Sauks were involved in almost continual warfare with the Osages. Later, as warfare with the Osages waned, both the Sauks and Foxes began to battle other tribes in the trans-Mississippi West—the Santee Sioux, Omahas, Otos, and Yankton Sioux—for new hunting grounds.[8]

The tribes in the region of the upper Great Lakes and upper Mississippi Valley, including the Sauks and Foxes, generally never developed strong diplomatic ties with the Americans as they had with the French, British, and Spanish. The reasons were complex, and every tribe had a unique relationship with the United States. The Americans took a radically different approach: unlike France, Britain, and Spain, the United States ultimately wanted the Indians' land for its expanding population. The Northwest Ordinance of 1787 became the key document for guiding American Indian policy, presented in innocuous and even benevolent language. The United States promised only to purchase Indian lands that the tribes consented to sell in the present-day Midwest, but the ordinance also clearly stated the United States' intent to purchase all Indian lands. From the 1780s onward, the United States learned that when the Indians did not consent, they could be manipulated, deceived, and coerced into selling land. The United States hoped to avoid conflict, but a land cession treaty, once made, even if not in good faith, was considered legal, and the federal government would, if necessary, use force to implement it.[9]

This policy created the conditions that led to several conflicts, including the Black Hawk War and the earlier Northwest Indian War of the 1790s. Sauk and Fox warriors fought alongside the Ohio tribes during the Northwest Indian War, which the United States initiated in order to enforce treaties negotiated during the 1780s. Why Sauk and Fox warriors went east to fight in this conflict is uncertain. The young republic was certainly no threat to either tribe, for it was the Indian confederacy in Ohio made up of tribes such as the Miamis, Shawnees, Weas, Delawares, and Wyandots that was under pressure from the United States to cede lands. Most likely, the American attack upon Saukenuk in 1780 generated anti-American sentiments among the Sauks and Foxes and prompted members of both tribes to fight in Ohio in the 1790s. Their numbers were small, and more significantly, Black Hawk mentioned nothing about the Northwest Indian War anywhere in his autobiography. Nevertheless, this limited participation following the earlier attack on Saukenuk produced a nascent distrust of Americans among the two tribes. Indeed, after federal troops arrived at St. Louis in March 1804 to take control of the upper districts of the Louisiana Purchase, Black Hawk noted that "we had always heard bad accounts of the Americans from Indians who had lived near them!"[10] Anti-American sentiments among the Sauks and Foxes would increase from 1804 onward.

The Northwest Indian War ended in 1794 with the victory of General "Mad Anthony" Wayne at Fallen Timbers (near present-day Toledo). The Treaty of Greenville the next year transferred to the United States present-day southern and eastern Ohio and also established what was to be a permanent boundary line between the

Americans and the regional tribes. Over the next decade, federal Indian policy underwent a subtle shift, particularly under the presidency of Thomas Jefferson, who not only wanted to acquire additional land from the Indians but also sought to change their way of life. Jefferson believed that the Indians could be convinced to give up their "savagery" and live instead like "civilized" white men who farmed the land. Indeed, Jefferson believed that once the Indians adopted white husbandry and domestic manufactures, they would willingly sell their excess land to the United States. While Jefferson sincerely sought to imbue federal Indian policy with a moral purpose, his assessment was overly optimistic and naive, for the Indians had no desire to abandon their cultures and live like whites. Nevertheless, in Jefferson's mind, the "civilization" of the Indians and the acquisition of their land for America's growing population became thoroughly intertwined.[11]

The Sauks soon became targets of Jefferson's policy. After Ohio entered the union in 1800, the remainder of the Northwest Territory was reorganized as Indiana Territory, and William Henry Harrison became the territorial governor. Harrison was, like Jefferson, a firm believer in American expansion, but unlike Jefferson, he cared little for dealing fairly with the Indians and instead sought to acquire their lands aggressively. Although the Indians technically consented to all sales, Harrison often negotiated with tribal leaders who did not have the authority to sell land. His underhanded activities generated much hostility among the Indians, particularly since it soon became apparent that the Greenville Treaty line was not the permanent boundary that the federal government had promised it to be. Moreover, Napoleon Bonaparte of France, seeking to create a new French empire in North America, purchased Louisiana from Spain in 1802, and Jefferson and his secretary of war, Henry Dearborn, sought to acquire territory on the east bank of the Mississippi River to counter possible French aggression. Harrison followed their instructions and purchased southwestern Illinois from the Kaskaskias in 1803. Jefferson concluded the Louisiana Purchase in 1803, and while this ended any potential French threat, Jefferson wanted to insure that no other tribes had claims to the lands ceded by the Kaskaskias. To that end, Dearborn wrote to Harrison in June 1804: "It may not be improper to procure from the Sacks [sic] such cessions on . . . the southern side of the Illinois [River] and a considerable tract on the other side."[12]

The opportunity presented itself when Harrison arrived in St. Louis in October 1804 to administer the upper districts of Louisiana Territory that Congress had temporarily placed under his jurisdiction. Several recent events had strained relations between the Sauks and Foxes and the United States. In March 1804 a garrison of United States soldiers took possession of St. Louis, thus replacing the Spanish (the French had never taken formal possession after purchasing Louisiana from Spain). The Sauks and Foxes had enjoyed strong relations with the Spanish since the 1760s, and their sudden departure caused no small amount of consternation, particularly since they were being replaced by the Americans, against whom both tribes already harbored strong suspicions, if not enmity. Even worse, federal officials appeared to favor their enemies, the Osages. Indeed, the new federal Indian agent at St. Louis, Pierre Chouteau, belonged to a powerful fur trading family that had long enjoyed close ties with the Osages. Another sign of American favoritism occurred in August 1804 when federal troops at St. Louis prevented a three-hundred-man Sauk and Fox war party from going to war against the Osages. Many young Sauk and Fox warriors advocated making war against the United States and the Osages. The older chiefs argued instead that tribes who enjoyed good relations with the United States, such as the Osage, had received abundant presents. The chiefs proposed pursuing a similar policy, but these voices of conciliation were silenced abruptly. Once the Americans took control of Louisiana, a number of white settlements began to spring up on the Sauk and Fox hunting grounds in present-day southern Illinois and Missouri, one of which was about thirty miles northwest of St. Louis on the Cuivre River. It was here in September 1804 that a party of four Sauks killed three white settlers who were trespassing on what they claimed were Sauk hunting lands. Certain histories have suggested that the murders were in revenge for sexual advances and indignities that Sauk women had suffered at the hands of white settlers, but there are no primary sources attesting to this. The extant sources make it clear that the warriors who committed the murders did so primarily to challenge the faction that favored conciliation with the Americans. According to several of the chiefs, the young warriors responsible for the killings threw the scalps of the dead whites at their feet and taunted them by saying, "Now you that make the land to smile, go cry with the whites."[13]

The killings set off a panic in the American settlements in Missouri as rumors abounded that the Sauks and other tribes were determined to make war against the United States. A panic also prevailed among the Sauks as the chiefs rightly feared retaliatory attacks by whites. A delegation of two Sauk chiefs journeyed to St. Louis to meet with federal authorities, calm the situation, and voice official disapproval of the war party's actions. They met with the commander of the U.S. Army garrison stationed at St. Louis, who ordered the murderers to be surrendered to the United States for punishment. The chiefs agreed to cooperate but noted that they had no power to force their tribe to give up the accused.[14]

The chiefs were not lying, for traditionally they had very little power over their tribal members. Like most tribal communities in the region of the upper Great Lakes and upper Mississippi Valley, the Sauks and Foxes had very loose systems of government. Civil chiefs inherited their positions and managed the day-to-day affairs of village life. In both tribes, clan membership was patrilineal (or through the father), and among the Sauks, members of the Bear and Fish clans provided civil chiefs; the Bear clan alone provided them among the Foxes. The civil chiefs sat in tribal councils composed of lesser chiefs, clan elders, appointed speakers, and secretaries who memorized speeches made in council. Tribal civil chiefs had to come from the proper leadership clans and also had to be acceptable to other members of the council. Moreover, the civil chiefs could not dictate decisions. Members of the councils arrived at decisions through consensus, but these decisions were not binding since the councils had no mechanisms to enforce them. The civil chiefs and other council members could only use their influence to persuade other tribal members.[15] This explains why the young Sauk warriors attacked white settlements despite the fact that their tribal council preferred conciliation with the Americans. Indeed, the nature of tribal government among the Sauks and Foxes led to the emergence of factions that promoted contrary policies, and the split between anti-American and pro-conciliation factions would characterize the two tribes for the next thirty years.

The limitations of tribal leadership also explain why the chiefs could not force the warriors who committed the murders at the Cuivre River to surrender themselves to federal authorities. Their persuasion did bear some fruit, for in October 1804 one Sauk warrior

agreed to surrender himself as a *"peace offering* for his nation."[16] He
was accompanied by a delegation comprised of four Sauks and a Fox
that arrived in St. Louis hoping to free the warrior who had surrendered himself and gain pardons for the rest by "covering the blood"
(also called "covering the dead"). This was an Indian custom by
which the lives of those who had been killed were purchased with
goods and money as a means of gaining pardon. Although this custom would have sufficed if the victims had been members of other
tribes, the delegation soon discovered that Americans had no such
custom; Americans demanded the lives of the murderers instead.
Harrison had arrived in St. Louis about two weeks before the Sauk
and Fox delegation. The members of the delegation, anxious to gain
pardons and freedom for their young warriors, met with Harrison to
discuss the matter.[17]

What happened during the course of these talks is sketchy. The
delegation, headed by the Sauk chief Pashipaho (The Stabbing Chief)
and another Sauk chief named Quashquame (Jumping Fish), had
been authorized by the Sauk tribal council (and probably by the Fox
council as well) to free the prisoner and gain pardons for the others;
the council did not authorize the delegation to sell land. Nevertheless, Harrison saw that he had a great deal of leverage over the delegates and used it to his advantage. He agreed to request a
presidential pardon for the prisoner and would not pursue convic-
tions for his accomplices in exchange for a land cession from the two
tribes. The manner in which Harrison conducted the talks was
highly irregular; he did not keep a journal of the talks, a practice that
was considered standard at the time. According to Quashquame,
Harrison also dispensed liberal amounts of whiskey and kept the
delegation "drunk the greater part of the time they were in St.
Louis."[18] Moreover, the negotiation of land cession treaties usually
involved the entire leadership of a tribe, not a small, five-man delegation. On November 3, 1804, the delegates signed the treaty, the
most significant article of which stipulated that the two tribes ceded
most of what is today western Illinois, southwestern Wisconsin, and
a strip of eastern Missouri to the United States. In exchange for
these fifteen million acres of land, the Sauks and Foxes received
$2,234.50 worth of goods on the spot and an annuity, or annual pay-
ment, of $1,000 in goods in perpetuity.[19]

When the delegates arrived in St. Louis, they received an invitation to meet with Harrison from Pierre Chouteau for the purpose of

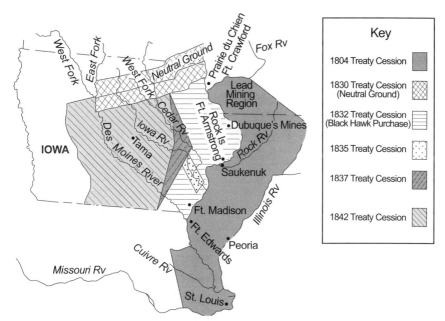

Map 2. Land Cessions of the Sauks and Foxes

settling the matter of the murders at the Cuivre River and establish-
ing peace; Chouteau mentioned nothing about the sale of land. Nevertheless, the five delegates almost certainly knew they were selling
some land when they signed the treaty. Moreover, if Harrison had,
indeed, kept the delegates drunk, it would have been easy to misrep-
resent the true nature of the treaty and convince them to sign it. The
available evidence suggests that Harrison told the delegates that they
were selling at least some land in exchange for pardoning the prisoner but that he intentionally failed to reveal the extent of the cession. Quashquame stated on returning from St. Louis that he and the
other delegates had sold only small amounts of land on the west and
east banks of the Mississippi in the region north of St. Louis. This
area was actually a small part of the total cession; it contained no
permanent village sites and had generally been used by the Sauks
only as hunting grounds. Thus, Quashquame and other delegates
most likely signed the treaty thinking they were merely selling what
amounted to superfluous land with which the tribe could easily part,
particularly since it was well worth the price of an annuity and the
freedom of the imprisoned Sauk warrior and pardons for the rest.
Over the next thirty years, Quashquame consistently asserted that

they had not intended to sell any land north of the Rock River. Harrison kept his promise and secured a pardon for the Sauk warrior, but shortly before it arrived, the warrior was fatally shot in May 1805 during an escape attempt from the jail where he was held.[20]

The two tribes only gradually came to understand how much land the treaty ceded to the United States. Indeed, they made no complaints about the cession the next year; their complaints initially focused upon the annuity rather than the sale itself. In July 1805, the Sauk and Fox chiefs noted to James Wilkinson, the new territorial governor at St. Louis, that prior to the treaty they had "never before Sold Land, and . . . did not know the value of it . . . we have given away a great Country . . . for a little thing, we do not say we were cheated, but we made a bad bargain . . . yet the bargain Stands, for we never take back what we have given."[21] Later that year, the chiefs' most significant complaint continued to be the "smallness" of the annuity. Relative to similar land cession treaties, the annuity outlined in the 1804 treaty was rather small, and it consisted only of goods and not cash. The first year's gifts arrived at St. Louis in a "ruined condition" according to the territorial governor "and of a selection & quality entirely unacceptable to the Natives of this Quarter."[22] Between 1806 and the War of 1812, a few Sauks and Foxes made a few vague references to disliking the treaty because it transferred land to the United States, but they did not indicate that they knew how much land the cession involved.[23]

The Sauk and Fox leaders probably did not discover the true extent of the cession until after the War of 1812. William Clark, the federal superintendent of Indian affairs at St. Louis, noted in July 1815 that several Sauks forcefully asserted that their tribe would never relinquish the lands ceded by the 1804 treaty. In 1817, the Foxes noted that they would "live on roots rather than part with their lands."[24] Evidence also suggests that some tribal members had no idea that the treaty ceded any land to the United States, although it would appear that such persons were in a definite minority. The federal Indian agent to the two tribes, Thomas Forsyth, noted that until 1818 several tribal leaders had assumed that the annuity goods were simply presents rather than payment for land. The cession also overlapped with the claims of other tribes, and the Illinois River Potawatomis, the Sauks' and Foxes' neighbors, learned only in 1815 that the two tribes had sold land, some of which they also claimed. Even as the Sauks and Foxes learned more about the extent of the cession, there was considerable confusion for many years as to what the treaty specified. Sauk leaders noted in 1821 that the 1804 delegation had never intended to sell any land north of the Rock River, and other chiefs, including Quashquame, repeated this argument several more times in the 1820s. Even by 1830, William Clark noted that many Sauks and Foxes still did not fully understand the extent or nature of the land cession. The 1804 treaty allowed the two tribes to continue residing on the ceded land until it was sold by the United States to white settlers. When this process began in the late 1820s, the federal government stepped up efforts to remove the Sauks and Foxes from the ceded land, and, not surprisingly, the two tribes became more vocal about the illegitimacy of the cession.[25]

While the 1804 treaty generated intense anti-Americanism among the Sauks and Foxes, it was not the only source of such sentiments. From 1804 until 1815, the two tribes (along with every other Indian community in the trans-Appalachian West) became engulfed in a mass movement that culminated during the War of 1812. It was a movement that began in the late 1730s as Indian peoples in the region east of the Mississippi developed a nascent sense of racial solidarity, or an "awakening" of nativistic spirit. This produced significant cultural, intellectual, and religious shifts within the tribes, for although tribal rivalries remained, Indians began to see themselves as racially distinct from whites and even annunciated the belief that Euro-Americans had sprung from a separate (and often diabolic) creation. Although often preached by Indian religious leaders (usually labeled "prophets" by whites), Indian leaders in the political arena drew from these new ideas. Most importantly, the increase in intertribal contacts during this period laid the ideological foundation for a militant pan-Indianism directed at those Euro-Americans who posed the greatest threat during any given period. In the 1760s, Neolin, or the Delaware Prophet, and his political counterpart, Pontiac, preached that the French, not the British, were the true friends of the Indians. As white settlement of the trans-Appalachian region increased after the 1760s, the idea of racial distinction became wedded to the idea of limiting white expansion. Indeed, this was the dynamic behind the pan-Indian alliance of the Ohio tribes of the 1790s during the Northwest Indian War, and expansion, from the 1780s onward, meant American expansion. Thus, by the early nineteenth century, pan-Indianism took on a decidedly anti-American tone.[26]

This anti-Americanism, already evident among the Sauks and Foxes before the 1804 treaty, became more pronounced with the arrival of a new prophet the next year. Tenskwatawa, or the Shawnee Prophet, had lived a dissolute life prior to receiving a vision in 1805 from the Master of Life, who promised all Indians a paradise after death if they would abandon their evil habits and live more virtuous lives. The Shawnee Prophet urged Indians to return to the traditional cultures they practiced before contact with whites. Except for firearms, white trade goods were to be eschewed, and a strict prohibition of alcohol was to be observed. The Shawnee Prophet, in contrast to the Delaware Prophet, shifted the focus of pan-Indianism toward the United States and preached that the French and British were allies who would help fight the Americans. This message was carried to the Sauks, Foxes, and every other Indian community in the trans-Appalachian West.[27]

The Shawnee Prophet led his movement from 1808 onward from his village, named, appropriately, Prophetstown, which was located near the confluence of the Tippecanoe and Wabash Rivers in Indiana. Thousands of Indians, some from as far away as the Lake Superior basin, visited him, while others served as messengers and took his teachings of spiritual renewal to other Indian villages, including those of the Sauks and Foxes. At its height, as many as 3,000 Indians resided at Prophetstown. The Sauks and Foxes sent delegations to Prophetstown to hear the Shawnee Prophet's message. How many Sauks and Foxes visited Prophetstown between 1808 and 1811 is impossible to calculate, but the number was significant. Indeed, a party of 240 Sauks and Foxes passed through Prophetstown on their way to British Canada in May 1810, and in June 1810 a party of 1,100 Sauks, Foxes, and Winnebagos visited the village. Afterward, many Sauks and Foxes left Prophetstown to recruit Indians into the growing pan-Indian confederation. Surprisingly, Black Hawk expressed ambivalence toward the Shawnee Prophet's message, most likely because he viewed the Americans as a rather remote threat to the Sauks and Foxes at the time. Nevertheless, he admitted the popularity of the Shawnee Prophet's message among the two tribes.[28]

The Shawnee Prophet annunciated the religious foundation of the growing pan-Indian movement, and it was his brother, Tecumseh, who gave it a political and military structure. Tecumseh participated in the Northwest Indian War and became a vociferous opponent of "government chiefs" who consistently acceded to the United States' demands for land. Tecumseh preached that tribal lands belonged to all Indians, and that all the tribes of the region had to agree to any land sales. Tecumseh's message took effect after the Treaty of Fort Wayne in 1809, when the Delawares, Miamis, and Potawatomis sold three million acres of land in Indiana. Enraged by yet another cession, Tecumseh began to forge a confederation of tribes throughout the trans-Appalachian region. Aside from the religious message annunciated by his brother, only military and political cooperation among the tribes would prevent further American expansion. Tecumseh made several tours among the tribes in the Great Lakes, the South, and along the Mississippi, including the Sauks in April 1809.[29]

In addition to the Shawnee Prophet and Tecumseh, there were lesser prophets as well. Among the Sauks and Foxes, the most significant was Main Poc, a Potawatomi who claimed to be a wabeno: a type of Indian sorcerer who possessed the power to handle fire without being burned. Main Poc, who fought in the Northwest Indian War, was staunchly anti-American and became attracted to the Shawnee Prophet's message. He visited him in 1807 but had several strong reservations. Unlike the Shawnee Prophet, Main Poc continued to drink whiskey, and despite Tecumseh's desire for all tribes to put aside their differences in order to unite against the Americans, Main Poc continued to fight with the Sauks and Foxes against the Osage. Nevertheless, he still recruited other Indians for Tecumseh's confederacy, particularly among the Sauks and Foxes, and preached resistance to American expansion. Main Poc exemplified the prevalence of anti-Americanism and its many forms. Although many Indians disliked the United States and readily accepted the Shawnee brothers' message, they did not accept all of their teachings. As the message articulated by the Shawnee Prophet and Tecumseh filtered into Indian communities, it was not necessarily accepted in its entirety, and there were wide variations in the specific doctrines that individual Indians accepted.[30]

However, this did not mean the message lacked efficacy. The pan-Indian movement from 1805 to the close of the War of 1812 became a politicizing agent for a whole generation of Indians in the trans-Appalachian West. The set of anti-American beliefs articulated by leaders such as the Shawnee Prophet, Tecumseh, and Main Poc are best defined as an ideology: a systematic set of ideas that advocate a particular policy or set of policies. Like any ideology, the ideology of anti-Americanism promulgated by the movement's leaders was received in an endless variety of forms and often became infused with older, traditional cultural elements. Regardless of how the message was received, it created a wide-spread, anti-American ideology among the Indians of the trans-Appalachian West. As noted, not every Indian accepted it.[31] This explains why during this time the Sauks and Foxes remained split between those factions favoring a conciliatory approach to the United States and those favoring war. It also explains how a warrior like Black Hawk, who showed little interest in the pan-Indian movement led by the Shawnee Prophet and Tecumseh, could still absorb much of its rhetoric and beliefs.

The effects of this movement quickly became evident. Every tribe in the region soon possessed large factions generally composed of younger warriors who supported the pan-Indian movement and its anti-American ideology. Between 1805 and 1812, young warriors among all tribes expressed their sentiments by committing depredations against and even murdering white Americans. Sauk and Fox warriors killed three whites in the autumn of 1805. Afterward, members of the two tribes threatened to attack an American military detachment from St. Louis that had arrived at Saukenuk in an unsuccessful attempt to apprehend the perpetrators. The 1804 treaty had required the federal government to establish an instructional farm for the Sauks and Foxes as a means to "civilize" them, and by 1805 the farm stood along the east bank of the Mississippi above the Des Moines River. In the fall of 1806, a party of young Sauk and Fox warriors descended upon the farm and killed all the cattle and horses. The next year, in 1807, a Sauk warrior killed a French trader at Portage des Sioux in Illinois, while a group of Iowas killed three French traders the following year. The Winnebagos had been particularly zealous adherents of the Shawnee brothers and, along with Kickapoo, Iowa, and Potawatomi warriors, stole horses, killed livestock, and murdered white settlers in Illinois and Missouri.[32]

Federal officials placed the blame for this unrest squarely upon the British in Canada. Despite the fact that Jay's Treaty a decade earlier had settled the final disputes that had arisen from the American Revolution, Britain and the United States began to drift toward war from 1807 onward. Given this heightened state of affairs, Americans believed that British agents were responsible for inciting the Indians against the United States and encouraging the activities of the Shawnee Prophet and Tecumseh. This belief was reinforced by the fact that many Indians from the United States visited British posts in Canada to receive gifts that included arms, ammunition, and gunpowder. Sauk parties ranging from 50 to 300 warriors regularly visited the British posts, particularly Fort Malden across the river from Detroit. The reality was that the tribes, rather than being pawns, pursued policies that paralleled those of the British. Both the British and the Indians wanted to contain American expansion: the Indians to preserve their tribal lands, and the British to protect Canada. Both drifted toward war with the United States, and, not surprisingly, they found an alliance to be convenient. It was not always an enthusiastic alliance, for the British had abandoned their Indian allies after the American Revolution and during the Northwest Indian War.[33] Nevertheless, the tribes believed the only hope for retaining their lands was through an alliance with Great Britain.

The Indian confederation was the first to go to war. In the autumn of 1811, William Henry Harrison took advantage of Tecumseh's absence and led an army of regular troops and militia against Prophetstown. By early November, Harrison had moved his army within a few miles of the village in order to provoke a battle. On the morning of November 7, 1811, Winnebago warriors at Prophetstown fired upon the American force. In what was known as the Battle of Tippecanoe, Harrison's army routed the Indian warriors, a large number of whom were Winnebagos. Although the battle itself was indecisive, the Indians who fled from Prophetstown dispersed to their villages and took with them an even more intense hatred toward Americans. While Congress did not declare war against the British until June 18, 1812, the Battle of Tippecanoe set in motion an undeclared Indian conflict six months prior to the declaration of war. The number of Indian depredations against American frontier settlements increased dramatically. William Clark recorded over fifty instances where Sauk and Fox warriors stole or destroyed livestock, crops, homes, and other property.[34]

A group of Winnebagos, carrying scalps they had taken from American settlers, visited Black Hawk's village and persuaded many Sauks to join them in an attack against Fort Madison. Established in 1808 twenty-five miles north of the confluence of the Des Moines and Mississippi Rivers, Fort Madison was strategically important, for it was the northernmost outpost of American military power in the Mississippi Valley. The Sauks had resented its presence from the time it had been built, and several, including Black Hawk, took part in a failed attempt to launch a sneak attack upon the garrison in 1809. With the commencement of hostilities at the Battle of Tippecanoe, subterfuge became unnecessary, and the Sauks openly attacked the post. Sporadic attacks began in the spring of 1812 and culminated in a three-day siege in September that involved about two hundred Indians, mostly Winnebagos. Black Hawk and other Sauks joined the Winnebagos in the attack and killed and scalped one American soldier and destroyed many buildings outside the palisade. They failed to force the garrison's surrender, but nevertheless, Fort Madison's days were numbered.[35]

After the attack upon Fort Madison, Robert Dickson, a Scottish trader who was the principal British recruiter among the tribes of the upper Mississippi, persuaded Black Hawk to join the British. Black Hawk did so because, unlike the Americans who made many promises and never kept them, "the *British* made but few—but we could always *rely upon their word!*"[36] In early 1813, Black Hawk fought as part of a British and Indian force near Detroit in the Battle of Frenchtown and later in the unsuccessful sieges against Forts Meigs and Stephenson in Ohio. While many Sauks and Foxes fought against the United States during the War of 1812, others continued to counsel peace and thus reinforced the division between the anti-American and pro-conciliation factions. By 1813, a significant number of the young men had joined the Indian confederation that fought alongside the British despite the fact that the tribal councils had officially voiced neutrality. This angered those who favored conciliation, particularly since the absence of the young men left the tribes open to the possibility of attack by the Americans.

In September 1813, about 1,550 Sauks (or a quarter of the tribe) split off from those living in the Mississippi Valley and placed themselves under the protection of the United States. They relocated along the Missouri River, where they were safe from both American and British attacks. Some later returned to the Mississippi Valley, but most stayed, and over time the Missouri River Sauks became a distinct group.[37] The exodus of the Missouri River Sauks had a disruptive effect, for without their voices urging restraint in tribal councils, the balance tipped decidedly in favor of the anti-American faction, which consisted of almost all of those who remained in their villages along the Mississippi River by late 1813. Events the next year served only to increase anti-American sentiments among this faction.

The Indian-British alliance had maintained a strong hold over the upper Great Lakes and upper Mississippi River Valley since the start of the War of 1812; the American garrisons at Mackinac Island and Chicago fell during the summer of 1812, and in the autumn of 1813 the U.S. Army finally abandoned Fort Madison. Until 1814, the Sauks and Foxes of the Mississippi Valley had not wholly committed themselves to the alliance, and thus, the number of Sauk and Fox warriors who, like Black Hawk, fought alongside the British probably did not exceed three hundred. The United States made several attempts to regain possession of the upper Mississippi Valley in 1814, and in the process as many as one thousand Sauks and Foxes joined in the attacks to repulse the American invasions. This deepened their anti-American sentiments. The United States established a small fort at Prairie du Chien in May 1814 in order to reassert its power in the upper Mississippi Valley, but a force composed of over five hundred Indians and British volunteers defeated the garrison in July 1814. An American relief column sent that same month from St. Louis to Prairie du Chien was subsequently attacked by four hundred Sauks, Foxes, and Kickapoos and forced to retreat. Sauk women even joined in the attack by jumping on the flatboats and assaulting the American soldiers with hoes. The next month, in August 1814, an expeditionary force under the command of Major Zachary Taylor, the future president, ascended the Mississippi to burn Saukenuk and build a new fort at the mouth of the Des Moines River. However, Taylor's small, 320-man detachment was turned back by a force of thirty British volunteers from Prairie du Chien and a force of about 1,200 Indians composed mostly of Sauks (including Black Hawk) and Foxes, as well as a few Kickapoos, Winnebagos, and Santee Sioux. Taylor retreated and built a fort at the Des Moines but was forced to abandon it in October.[38]

The Indian-British alliance consistently defeated the United States in every major military operation in the upper Great Lakes and upper Mississippi Valley, and the Indians and British naturally assumed that the area would be retained by Great Britain. However, they were gravely disappointed. The British commissioners who met with their American counterparts in August 1814 to negotiate a final settlement proposed that the entire region become an independent

Indian state that would act as a barrier to protect Canada from any future American aggression. The American commissioners, stunned by this proposal, were even more incredulous when the British went so far as to suggest that the 1795 Greenville Treaty boundary be reestablished. As the talks dragged on, however, the British commissioners softened on this demand, particularly since the situation in Europe was not stable. The British were anxious to end their war in North America, and they dropped the idea of an Indian barrier state and replaced it with watered-down language that recognized American sovereignty over the region and merely demanded that the United States end all hostilities with the tribes and restore them to their prewar possessions and territories. The Treaty of Ghent, signed on December 24, 1814, ended the war and was yet another betrayal of the Indians by their British allies. British officers in the region were stunned at the news. Robert McDouall, the British commander at Mackinac Island who had fought alongside the Indians during the last year of the war and who had worked so hard to defend the region against the Americans, was "penetrated with grief" and "mortified" upon hearing that the forts at Mackinac Island and Prairie du Chien would be given back to the Americans.[39] Officers such as McDouall had the unenviable duty of informing their Indian allies of the treaty. McDouall remarked that all of the Indians displayed "haughty indignation" at the idea of being "deceived and abandoned . . . by the British Govt."[40]

In accordance with the Treaty of Ghent, the United States appointed commissioners and initiated peace talks with Indians in May 1815. The commissioners sent invitations to the tribes of the upper Mississippi Valley and upper Great Lakes and asked them to assemble at Portage des Sioux about twenty-five miles north of St. Louis. The commissioners noted that several tribes refused to end their hostilities and even believed that the news of the war's end was a ruse and that they would be killed if they went to Portage des Sioux. The commissioners noted that the Sauks and Foxes were particularly hostile, and in addition to continuing their depredations against white frontier settlements, they even killed the messenger sent by the commissioners. That year the Sauks sent only a single civil chief, Namoett (who possessed no authority to negotiate a treaty) and about fifty Sauk and Fox warriors who swaggered about the council grounds, treated the American commissioners contemptuously, and stated that no peace would exist between them and the

Americans. Moreover, Namoett and the members of this delegation flatly stated that the Sauks and Foxes would never abide in the land cession outlined in the 1804 treaty.

Even as Namoett attended the council, Sauk and Fox warriors were engaged in hostilities against whites. The Battle of the Sink Hole in May 1815 was one of the most significant of these clashes, and Black Hawk led the war party that fought in this skirmish. In 1813, Illinois volunteers in federal service captured and executed a young Sauk man hunting in southern Illinois. Two years later, Black Hawk sought revenge and raised a thirty-man war party that attacked a body of Illinois volunteers of roughly the same size about thirty miles northwest of St. Louis; Black Hawk and his warriors killed seven white volunteers during the engagement. General Andrew Jackson, commander of the army's Southern Division, deemed the situation so grave that he advocated a military expedition against the Sauks and Foxes. Although this did not occur, War Department officials believed that such a course should be considered if the two tribes refused to make peace.[41]

By October 1815, the commissioners had concluded thirteen treaties of peace with various tribes, most of which had either small or inconsequential anti-American factions. The Sauks along the Mississippi were one of the most obstinate Indian nations and one of the last to make peace. Like the Sauks, the Foxes had a sizeable number of warriors who fought against the United States during the war, but unlike the Sauks, the faction favoring conciliation remained within the tribe, and for this reason the pro-conciliation faction among the Foxes retained its influence. Thus, even as many of their warriors joined the Sauks in committing depredations, the Fox chiefs signed a treaty of peace with the United States on September 14, 1815. As part of its postwar plan to bolster frontier defenses, the United States in the autumn of 1815 sent troops up the Mississippi to the mouth of the Des Moines River, where they established Fort Edwards. The next spring, in May 1816, another post named Fort Armstrong was constructed at Rock Island. The United States built both forts in the heart of the Sauks' country in order to send the message that continued hostilities would not be tolerated but met with force. The Sauk leadership realized that continuing a policy of hostility toward the United States served no purpose, particularly without British support, and they decided to sign a treaty of peace in May 1816. William Clark knew that despite official professions of peace, there were large numbers of individuals in both tribes who would continue to resist the United States. He noted almost prophetically in a letter to the War Department that "it would not be a matter of surprise if we should find our Country engaged in new difficulties with them."[42]

Black Hawk signed the treaty of peace. However, neither he nor any of the Sauk chiefs were told that the first article of the treaty stated that the Sauk fully accepted the land cession outlined in the 1804 treaty without reservation. This was about the time that many of the Sauks began to learn the full extent of land ceded by the 1804 treaty. When they learned that the 1816 treaty of peace reconfirmed the land cession, they felt doubly deceived. According to Black Hawk, the 1816 treaty was "the first time, I touched the goose quill to the treaty—not knowing, however, that, by that act, I consented to give away my village."[43] In the immediate postwar years, as the Sauks and Foxes gradually came to understand both treaties, they developed an intense distrust of federal officials and the documents they bore. Thomas Forsyth, the Indian agent at Rock Island, was required to have the Indians sign receipts for the annuity goods they received as part of the 1804 treaty, but the Indians refused to sign them or any other papers. Indeed, they even posted guards to insure that no one signed the annuity receipts. According to Forsyth, the Sauks in particular believed that the papers "might come back to them in another shape . . . alluding . . . that their lands would be claimed."[44]

The seeds of the Black Hawk War had been sown with the 1804 treaty, but the events that transpired between 1804 and 1816 did much to fertilize the ground where the seeds of fury could germinate. The Sauks and Foxes were not the only tribes that harbored large numbers of persons with intensely anti-American sentiments. Virtually all of the Winnebagos were staunchly anti-American as well. Not surprisingly, all three Indian nations would clash with the United States, but the young republic would not be the easy target it had been during the War of 1812. After 1815, the United States significantly extended its political, military, and economic power in the region of the upper Mississippi Valley and upper Great Lakes. This restricted, but did not completely stop, the ability of the Indians to resist American hegemony. Although Tecumseh died at the Battle of the Thames in 1813, his spirit lived on, and Indian resistance continued. However, for the tribes of this region, the Americans were simply one enemy, and not always the most important.

2

THE STORM CLOUDS
GATHER

Red Bird and some others, in cabins
By stealthy attack slaughtered four,
But as that only equaled the culprits
Other means were adopted for more.
Two boats going down from Fort Snelling
Were attacked by a party of braves:
Four white men were slain in the action,
And eight Winnebagoes found graves.
—AMER MILLS STOCKING

Immediately after the War of 1812, the United States sought to strengthen its military presence in the Mississippi Valley and upper Great Lakes. It had been practically nonexistent before the war and consisted of three undermanned posts: Fort Mackinac with eighty-eight men, Fort Dearborn with fifty-three, and Fort Madison with forty-four. Thus, a mere 185 troops had the impossible mission of defending a four-hundred-mile-long frontier. Moreover, these three garrisons were either captured, massacred, or abandoned during the war. The War Department believed that the key to reasserting and maintaining American sovereignty was to control the principal river routes. The most important of these was the Fox-Wisconsin waterway, and for this reason the army built new posts at Green Bay (Fort Howard) and Prairie du Chien (Fort Crawford). In order to control entry into the Rock and Illinois Rivers, the army established Fort Armstrong and reestablished Fort Dearborn. Fort Snelling at the confluence of the St. Peter's (now the Minnesota) and

Mississippi Rivers served as the bulwark to prevent British fur traders of Canada's North West Company from penetrating into the Mississippi Valley. These five forts constituted the largest military force that any imperial power had ever stationed in the region. Indeed, by the end of 1822, their combined strength stood at 769 men and officers. This was more than four times the number of soldiers that the United States had in the region before the War of 1812.[1]

Nevertheless, these troops had a vast area to secure, and large numbers of them were often not available for military duties. Of the 769 men stationed in the region in 1822, 207 were not available for duty because they were sick, under arrest, absent, or building the forts. This equaled about one-quarter of the total strength. The number of troops decreased even more in the late 1820s when the War Department pushed the army farther west; Congress had fixed the size of the army at a mere 6,183 troops, and thus any new forts had to be manned with soldiers from other garrisons. To make the most of its manpower, the army abandoned Fort Dearborn in 1823 and Fort Crawford three years later. By 1826, only Forts Howard, Armstrong, and Snelling remained with a total of 680 soldiers. The army was also hobbled by the myriad of non-military duties that constituted the routine of the frontier army. Each post grew much of its own food, and this required commanders to excuse soldiers from all other duties so that they could spend their time farming. At some posts twenty-five to almost forty percent of soldiers were occupied with constructing and maintaining the buildings and structures around the forts. One commander noted in 1828 that the constant repairs made "anything like instruction to the Troops . . . entirely out of the question, and the Officers are in very little better Employment than *merely overseers.*"[2]

Poor equipment and training also had a negative impact upon the frontier army. Colonel George Croghan, the inspector general, complained that no one at most posts knew his duties and if attacked by an enemy, officers needed half a day's preparation to ready their soldiers for an assault. At Fort Howard, Croghan found no officer proficient in firing the post's lone artillery piece, which was in a poor state of repair from being continually exposed to the weather. When he ordered a young lieutenant to fire the gun, it took several hours to prepare the fuses, and when he finally fired about a dozen shells, only two burst. Croghan found a similar lack of knowledge regarding the artillery piece at Mackinac Island. Officers at Fort Snelling admitted to little military training, and at Fort Armstrong officers had not conducted military drill with their troops in over four years. Fort Brady at Sault Ste. Marie was so poorly constructed that Croghan could not understand "why this place is dignified with the name of Fort." He reached similar conclusions concerning Forts Howard and Mackinac.[3]

Commanders were well aware of these shortcomings, and they developed strategic principles that took them into account. The War Department itself never formally developed or disseminated such principles; that responsibility devolved down to frontier commanders who, by necessity, had to develop effective means to subdue recalcitrant Indian nations. Frontier army officers formulated a military policy that revolved around two broad strategic principles. First, the very presence of troops at the forts served to "awe" the Indians into submission and keep them peaceful. The forts built by the army, poor and often undermanned as they were, were symbols of the federal government's military power, not manifestations of it. Second, if hostilities occurred, the small isolated forts were supposed to withstand an attack only long enough for reinforcements to arrive from other posts, and, if possible, local militia volunteers would be called up as well. In areas lacking white settlers, Indian warriors from friendly tribes would be employed against hostiles. These two principles made for a less-than-perfect frontier military policy; nevertheless, it was the only one that the frontier army had.[4] Both principles were utilized in various Indian conflicts, including the Black Hawk War.

The fact that every tribe continued to harbor anti-American factions virtually guaranteed that further conflicts would occur, as did British efforts to maintain their alliances with the tribes. The United States and the British never fought again for control of the upper Great Lakes and upper Mississippi Valley after the War of 1812, but things were far less clear to those who resided on opposite sides of the United States–Canadian border in 1815. The British in Canada, the Indian tribes, and the United States believed another conflict was a definite possibility. For the first few years after the war, the Indians felt that the British had once again abandoned them by returning the region—and thus, their homelands—to the United States. Despite this initial hostility, the British slowly rebuilt their relationships with the tribes. After 1815, the British shifted their operations in the upper Great Lakes from Mackinac Island to Drummond Island forty-five miles to the northeast. Here, they distributed abundant goods to the Indians from the United States in order to maintain their alliances. Indeed, presents were an important part of Indian diplomacy. The Indians called the British (and before them, the French) their "fathers." This did not mean that the Indians viewed themselves as inferior or subordinate (as the imperial powers often thought). Instead, a "father," whether real or metaphorical, was not stern and demanding but was beneficent and generous. The British continued to perform this paternal role after 1815 by distributing presents to Indians who resided in the United States from their post at Drummond Island as well as from Fort Malden opposite Detroit. The United States after the War of 1812 also tried to be a "father" to the Indians, but the British did a far better job since the security of Canada depended upon it. The tribes, despite their initial postwar resentment, believed it was necessary to renew their ties to the British. The United States, seeing another British-Indian alliance forming, remained wary.[5]

The gatherings at Fort Malden and Drummond Island attracted ever-increasing numbers of Indians. In 1816 at least 1,500 men, women, and children assembled on Drummond Island to receive presents. In 1818, that number swelled to almost 3,000 while that same year another 4,500 went to Fort Malden. By 1820, the number of Indians receiving presents reached 3,800 at Drummond Island and 5,685 at Fort Malden, and most of the recipients came from lands under American sovereignty. Tribes such as the Winnebagos, Menominees, Ottawas, Potawatomis, Sauks and Foxes, Santee Sioux, and Ojibwas regularly made pilgrimages to Canada. Of the 5,906 Indians who received presents at Fort Malden in 1827, 4,409, or about seventy-five percent, resided within the borders of the United States. The British spent a tremendous amount of money on presents. Indeed, the British Indian Department in Upper Canada (now Ontario) distributed £23,000 worth of presents per year in 1823 and 1824. This equaled $102,120 in United States currency. The United States, by comparison, spent far less money on presents due to the parsimonious nature of Congress. During this same period, the United States Indian Department distributed only $11,000 worth of presents in 1823 and about $18,000 in 1824, and this was to the tribes

in all regions, not just those in the upper Great Lakes and upper Mississippi Valley. The Indians definitely noticed. In 1823, a group of
visiting Sauks and Foxes told Thomas Forsyth, the Indian agent at
Rock Island, that the Americans were not the "real Father" of the
Indians because they did not give as many presents as the British.[6]

When the Indians visited Drummond Island and Fort Malden to
receive presents, they also listened to speeches from British Indian
agents. The British used presents to keep the Indians within their
diplomatic orbit in case of a war, but at the same time they wanted
to prevent another conflict with the United States. British agents
had to walk a fine line that kept their Indian allies ready for a war
without provoking them into committing hostilities. British agents
also listened to the concerns of the Indians, and they were quick to
denounce the United States whenever the federal government
engaged in policies that the Indians found repugnant. The British
ultimately sent an ambiguous message, and the Indians who traveled to the posts often came away with different interpretations of
what the British actually promised. A common problem caused by
this vagueness was that many Indians believed frequent, although
inaccurate, rumors that Britain and the United States were soon to
engage in yet another war. In such cases, anxious British agents
emphatically denied such rumors and implored the native peoples
assembled at the posts to remain at peace. Far more problematic
were those Indians who left the British posts believing that the
British would provide them with military aid if they rose up against
the United States. This expectation led to violence on more than
one occasion and was a precipitating factor that encouraged Black
Hawk to resist the United States.[7]

In addition to inflammatory speeches by British agents, the
American desire for land kept the fires of anti-Americanism burning.
After 1815, white miners swarmed onto the rich mineral lands of
what is today northwestern Illinois and southwestern Wisconsin.
The federal government leased these lands to private individuals, and
throughout the 1820s the region began to attract increasing numbers
of miners from Missouri, Illinois, Kentucky, and Tennessee, most
of whom worked illegally without leases. Galena, Illinois, perched
on the banks of the Fever (now the Galena) River, became the principal town in this burgeoning trade, and soon miners swept north up
the Fever River and its tributaries and established dozens of small

mining and smelting operations. The white population of the Fever River district exploded from 150 in December 1825 to 540 by August 1826. Some estimates put the number of whites as high as 1,000 to 1,500 by the end of 1826. This influx created a great deal of friction with the Sauks, Foxes, and Winnebagos, all three of which mined considerable amounts of lead and used it to procure goods from white traders. In 1811 the Sauks and Foxes alone mined 400,000 pounds of the mineral. Not surprisingly, they saw the white miners as economic competitors. Miners entering the country without leases posed a grave problem, but even more serious was the fact that many were extracting lead on Indian lands. As early as 1822, the Foxes complained that whites were mining lead from their lands on the west side of the Mississippi at Dubuque's Mines, one of the richest veins in the entire region, while to the east, whites were spilling over into the Rock River Valley and taking the mineral off Winnebago lands.[8]

The British posts in Canada and the presence of white miners on Indian lands proved to be a volatile combination that led to further Indian resistance. From 1815 until the 1827 Winnebago Uprising, the Indian communities of the upper Great Lakes and upper Mississippi Valley did not engage in open warfare as they did during the War of 1812; such a course would have been futile without British support. Instead, the Indians shifted their tactics and resorted to a form of guerrilla warfare that relied upon random, often deadly assaults against Americans. In effect, Indians simply committed further depredations. While federal officials and white settlers usually labeled these as criminal acts, the Indians who committed them did so for political and ideological reasons, not with criminal intent.[9] Thus, crimes against Americans became the new modus operandi for the Indian resistance movement, but, as the Winnebago Uprising illustrated, the line between such resistance and open rebellion could be very thin.

The first depredations came in the summer of 1819, shortly after British Indian agents at Fort Malden and Drummond Island made speeches that were particularly critical of the United States. Although it is not known what they said, many of the assembled Indians believed that Britain would support a general Indian uprising the next spring. Soon after leaving the British posts, several Winnebago warriors engaged in a variety of defiant actions. In two incidents in August and September 1819, parties of armed warriors shot at federal soldiers and American traders crossing Lake Winnebago in boats. No one was killed in either incident, but the Winnebagos had made their sentiments readily known. The next month, a party of Winnebagos at the Fox-Wisconsin portage met up with two U.S. Army surgeons. No violence occurred, but according to one of the surgeons, the Winnebagos forcibly entered their tent, rummaged through their goods, and treated the surgeons and their entourage with so much insolence that he wrote, "I could scarcely prevent my men from committing violence on them."[10] A few months later, in January 1820, Ojibwas at Manitowoc raided a group of Americans delivering a herd of cattle to the troops at Fort Howard. No one was killed, but the Ojibwas took one man's clothing and saddle bags, as well as a straggling cow. Later that spring, several Menominees at Green Bay assaulted a soldier and took the whiskey he was carrying in his canteen.[11]

While virtually every tribe had some members who partook in such acts, the Winnebagos, more so than any other, developed a clear and conscious program of resistance to the United States. This was not surprising, for the Winnebagos had been some of the strongest supporters of the Shawnee Prophet and Tecumseh. One old chief, distressed at how the Shawnee brothers had undermined his authority, lamented in 1810 that his young warriors "breathed nothing but war against the United States."[12] This intense anti-Americanism carried over into the postwar years. William Clark noted in 1827 that the Winnebagos were the most staunchly anti-American of the tribes and that two-thirds harbored strong opposition. Certainly, not all did; but they were a minority within their tribe. During 1819, several Winnebagos sent messages and war belts to the Santee Sioux and the Ojibwas asking for assistance in any hostilities against the United States the next year.[13] It did not come to pass because anti-American tribal leaders did not automatically condone violence against Americans because such acts threatened to bring down the wrath of the federal government upon their communities. Such dissent existed among all the tribes west of Lake Michigan, and among the Winnebagos this stymied the efforts of the most vehemently anti-American members of the tribe who wanted to coordinate a general Indian uprising in the spring of 1820. Nevertheless, this did not stop at least a few Winnebagos from committing additional crimes against the United States and its citizens.

The focal point of Winnebago resistance shifted to Fort Armstrong, where in April 1820 three Winnebagos killed and scalped two unarmed soldiers outside of the fort on a wood-cutting detail. The murderers, members of the Rock River bands, acted without the consent of their chiefs, who, in order to prevent unnecessary conflict with the United States, surrendered the three men to the army in June 1820. The leader, Chewachera, claimed that his sister and her husband had been killed by American soldiers two years earlier, and he murdered the soldiers in revenge. Chewachera's claim was of uncertain veracity, particularly since one witness, a Métis (a person of mixed Indian and European descent), buried Chewachera's sister and stated that she and her husband had fallen through ice and drowned and had not been assaulted. Nevertheless, Chewachera believed that American soldiers had killed his sister and brother-in-law, and his beliefs were undoubtedly shaped by his anti-American bias. Colonel Henry Leavenworth of Fort Snelling detained Chewachera and his principal accomplice, Whorahjinka, so that they could be tried for murder. The Rock River Winnebago chiefs balked at the idea of imprisoning and trying the two men. They had hoped that by voluntarily handing over the men, the United States would look favorably upon the act and grant pardons. However, neither Leavenworth nor the secretary of war was in so magnanimous a mood. Chewachera and Whorahjinka remained in confinement for a year under terrible conditions. An all-white jury in Edwardsville, Illinois, found them guilty. Chewachera died while in jail, and Whorahjinka was later hanged.[14] The deaths deepened the already pervasive anti-Americanism among the Rock River Winnebagos.

The next murders by Winnebagos had little to do with resistance against the United States, but they were a precipitating factor in the 1827 Winnebago Uprising. In March 1826, a group of Winnebagos from the Wisconsin River bands (and probably a few members of the Mississippi River bands as well) killed members of a Métis family near Prairie du Chien. Although the Winnebago chiefs initially dragged their feet and refused to surrender the perpetrators, they ultimately gave up two men, Wau-koo-Kau and Man-ne-tah-peh-keh. The evidence suggests that the principal motive was to loot the family's campsite. Like the confinement of Chewachera and Whorahjinka six years earlier, the arrest of Wau-koo-Kau and Man-ne-tah-peh-keh created much ill-will among the Winnebagos. The army confined the two men to the guardhouse at Fort Crawford in the summer of 1826. It was during this time that the army decided to abandon Fort Crawford. The post was in poor physical condition due to the annual flooding of the Mississippi River, which inundated the buildings and made many of them uninhabitable for long periods of time. The garrison took the two Winnebago prisoners when it withdrew in October 1826 to Fort Snelling. Michigan Territorial Governor Lewis Cass, who strongly disagreed with the decision to abandon the post (particularly since Fort Dearborn at Chicago had been abandoned three years earlier), stated that the post was necessary to "overawe and restrain the Indians."[15] Cass's statement turned out to be prophetic, for the Winnebagos interpreted the abandonment of Fort Crawford as a sign of American weakness. This already volatile situation became worse when, during the summer of 1827, the Winnebagos heard that Wau-koo-Kau and Man-ne-tah-peh-keh had been handed over to local Ojibwas and killed. While this hearsay turned out not to be true (it had actually been two Santee Sioux who suffered this fate), it further enraged the Winnebagos.[16]

This rumor came at a time when white miners were pouring onto the Winnebagos' mineral lands, and many Winnebagos felt justified in leading a general Indian war against the United States. Throughout 1826 and 1827, the members of the Winnebago bands of the upper Mississippi River Valley, along with warriors of the Wisconsin River bands, spearheaded the effort to forge an Indian alliance against the United States and sent war pipes to the Santee Sioux and the Foxes, although only the Santee Sioux evinced any interest. Among the Santee Sioux, the principal actor was a warrior of Chief Wabasha's band named Wawzeekootee, who promised the Winnebagos that if they would strike the Americans, the Santee Sioux would follow their lead and join them in a war against the United States. The Rock River Winnebago bands, having witnessed the fate of Chewachera and Whorahjinka seven years earlier, were reluctant to join. Nevertheless, while the Rock River Winnebago chiefs followed a policy of peace, many of their young warriors actively supported their brethren.[17]

A Winnebago named Red Bird initiated the uprising; he and two accomplices, The Sun and Little Buffalo, headed to Prairie du Chien determined to kill Americans. When they failed to find any of the handful of Americans who resided there, they chose instead to

attack Registre Gagnier and his family. Although the choice of a
Métis family was unusual, the choice was driven more by opportunity
than ethnicity. The three Winnebagos killed Gagnier and his hired
man and severely wounded Gagnier's infant daughter. Gagnier's wife
and son managed to escape. Red Bird and his companions proceeded
to their villages in the vicinity of Prairie La Crosse to execute the next
phase of the uprising. Federal officials probably would have handled
the murders as simply another crime committed by a few renegade
Indians, but the next event revealed that something much larger was
afoot. On June 30, 1827, two keelboats were descending the Mississippi after having delivered supplies to Fort Snelling. The Prairie La
Crosse Winnebagos were encouraged by Red Bird's actions and
decided that the war against the United States had to be continued.
They received word of the keelboats passing their encampment near
the mouth of the Bad Axe River. The boats looked to be an easy target, and the warriors attacked. They hit the first boat the hardest
and killed two men and injured four others. The crew fought back
and killed at least four Winnebagos and wounded about seventeen,
three of whom died later. The second keelboat passed the mouth of
the river after darkness, and it arrived at Prairie du Chien relatively
unscathed.[18]

The number of Winnebagos involved in the attack on the keelboat was about 150, about a quarter of them warriors. The war party
was composed mostly of Mississippi River Winnebagos from Prairie
La Crosse, but a few Santee Sioux were also known to have participated. The attack, while relatively small, was significant because it
was the first act of war committed against the United States by Indians in the region since the War of 1812. Although criminal acts may
have been the most common modus operandi for expressing anti-
American sentiments after 1815, they were certainly not the most
effective. Indians who sought to end the political domination of the
United States had to initiate and successfully conclude an armed
revolt to achieve this goal. The 1827 Winnebago Uprising was such
an attempt, and the transition from the Gagnier murder to the keelboat attack revealed the nebulous boundary that existed between
criminal acts and open warfare. Indian societies tended to see little
or no distinction between the two; both were considered legitimate
acts of war. Nevertheless, the Winnebago Uprising differed from the
earlier criminal assaults because it was an open revolt that sought to

encourage other Indian communities to rise up against the United States and end its hegemony in the region. This fact was not lost upon Lewis Cass, who, upon hearing of the attack on the keelboats, stated, "Hostilities have actually commenced in that quarter."[19]

The events that followed foreshadowed those of the Black Hawk War in many respects and helped to determine its outcome. Frontier commanders adhered to the strategic principles they had developed after 1815, and in addition to massing regular troops from the regional posts, they quickly organized volunteer militia units, both Indian and white, to augment the army. In addition to the military response, Indian agents worked to isolate other Indian communities from those in rebellion. Indian communities that remained neutral did not necessarily harbor positive feelings toward the United States; they simply believed that fighting, particularly without British support, was a futile endeavor. In both the 1827 Winnebago Uprising and the Black Hawk War, young warriors from neutral communities entered the fray, but they did so on their own without their tribal leaders' approval. Moreover, they often did not fight with the groups that were in rebellion. Young warriors, encouraged by the advent of hostilities, engaged in individual acts of war against whites. Thus, their actions were identical to those of warriors from various tribes who had committed crimes as a means of expressing their anti-Americanism after 1815. The United States, on the other hand, managed to convince other warriors and chiefs to become American allies. The communities that fought with the United States generally had no interest in the federal government's policy objectives but instead joined in order to pursue their own interests.

Thomas McKenney, the head of the Indian Department, and Lewis Cass took the first steps to quell the Winnebago Uprising. When the revolt began, both men were holding a treaty council at Little Lake Butte des Morts to settle the outstanding boundary differences between the Menominees and three other tribes that had recently emigrated from New York: the Oneidas, Stockbridges, and Brothertons. The Fox River Winnebago bands were also present. Cass instructed Indian agents throughout the region to invite Indian communities not involved with the uprising to the treaty grounds where they would be given presents and food. This, Cass argued, would keep them at peace with the Americans and separated from the hostile Winnebagos. The strategy worked, for over two thousand

Indians attended the council, many of whom were not originally invited.[20]

Cass and McKenney also organized volunteer militia units to augment the scant regular forces. Indeed, the three nearest posts— Forts Howard, Snelling, Armstrong—were distant from the main theater of the uprising and possessed only 207, 220, and 91 soldiers, respectively. During the 1820s, the army compensated for such shortages by concentrating a large number of troops at Jefferson Barracks near St. Louis. Because it was centrally located, commanders believed troops from Jefferson Barracks could be quickly dispatched to any conflict in the Mississippi Valley. The plan may have looked good on paper, but the Winnebago Uprising revealed that the troops at Jefferson Barracks could not always respond quickly and thus local volunteer forces were also required. Cass hurried to Prairie du Chien, hastily organized a militia company to defend the village, and then proceeded to St. Louis, where, along with William Clark and Brigadier General Henry Atkinson, he formulated a plan for ending the uprising. Atkinson left Jefferson Barracks by steamboat on July 15, 1827 with about five hundred men. On July 29, he arrived at Prairie du Chien, where he found Colonel Josiah Snelling of Fort Snelling waiting with an additional two hundred men. A 130-man mounted militia force composed mostly of white miners from the lead mining region and commanded by Henry Dodge, a man who would play a significant role in the Black Hawk War, joined Atkinson's force a few days later. Meanwhile, McKenney conferred with Major William Whistler of Fort Howard and put together another expedition that would arrive from the east. Because he had so few regular troops, Whistler rounded out his small force of about one hundred regulars with a 51-man militia force composed mostly of Métis residents from Green Bay. He also had two Indian contingents. The New York tribes at the nearby treaty council formed a 62-man volunteer company under the command of two American traders, while a regular army officer from Fort Howard commanded a Menominee company composed of 121 warriors.[21]

The Winnebago bands of the upper Mississippi Valley executed a common Indian tactic and concentrated their small communities into a single, more defensible site at the portage of the Fox and Wisconsin Rivers. Whistler's force left Green Bay on August 23, 1827, and arrived at the portage on September 1st. Atkinson moved his force of over eight hundred men up the Wisconsin River on August 29th and prepared to squeeze the Winnebagos in a vise. This became unnecessary when, on September 3rd, the Winnebagos surrendered Red Bird and The Sun to Whistler. During the impromptu surrender ceremony, Red Bird maintained a dignified appearance and remained expressionless, with one side of his face painted red, and the other side painted green and white. Around his neck he wore a collar of white and blue wampum decorated with panther claws at each end. Adding to the spectacle was the colorful force that Whistler had assembled. On one side stood the two companies of federal troops and the company of Green Bay militia, while on other the side were the company of Menominee warriors and the company composed of the New York tribes. There was a small military band present that played *Pleyel's Hymn*. Over the course of the next three weeks, the Winnebagos turned over an additional six men to the United States.[22]

Red Bird's attempt to lead a general Indian uprising failed but nevertheless revealed a persistent discontent. Thomas McKenney noted that there were no more "Pontiacs or Tecumthes [*sic*] to form and lead on confederated bands."[23] Yet, he knew that the danger had been real and that more Indians would have joined the uprising if he, Cass, and Atkinson had not taken the actions they did. One aspect of the uprising that would be repeated during the Black Hawk War was that anti-American factions among other tribes were encouraged by the uprising and used it as an excuse to commit depredations in other areas. Winnebagos from several bands targeted Americans in the lead mining region and robbed cabins, killed livestock, and even threatened to kill any Americans who refused to leave. Despite the rejection of Winnebago and Santee Sioux war belts by their tribal leaders, anti-American Potawatomis threatened the residents of Chicago to the point that an American trader rushed to Danville, Illinois, to raise a 100-man militia company to protect Chicago. A few Potawatomis in the vicinity of Peoria used the uprising as an occasion to commit robberies against Americans. The anti-American factions of the Santee Sioux undoubtedly would have become even more hostile had not the influential chief Wabasha prevented his warriors from joining the rebellion.[24]

The United States ultimately held only Red Bird, The Sun, and Little Buffalo for trial. Red Bird died during the year-long confinement that he and his comrades were forced to endure, and The Sun and Little Buffalo were found guilty by a white and Métis jury in Prairie du Chien in 1828. Both men were sentenced to hang. The situation actually played into the hands of the federal government, for the United States had long cast covetous eyes upon the Indian mineral lands of the region. President John Quincy Adams promised the Winnebagos he would spare the men's lives if the tribe sold their mineral lands; the Winnebagos reluctantly agreed. In August 1829, the United States purchased the mineral lands of the Winnebagos in a treaty at Prairie du Chien.[25] The United States would use similar tactics to purchase Sauk and Fox lands in aftermath of the Black Hawk War.

There was some talk after the Winnebago Uprising of the Santee Sioux renewing their alliance with the Winnebagos and sending war belts to the Potawatomis. These efforts came to naught, for the Winnebagos and Santee Sioux remained at peace with the United States, which indicates that the lessons of 1827 made a deep impression upon them. Moreover, after the uprising ended, the United States took several measures to insure that the Winnebagos remained quiescent. In August 1827, the War Department ordered that Fort Crawford at Prairie du Chien be reoccupied and that Fort Dearborn at Chicago be regarrisoned temporarily; the next year, permanently. The most significant change came when the War Department ordered a new post to be built at the Fox-Wisconsin portage in the heart of the Winnebago country. It was named, quite fittingly, Fort Winnebago, and it became the principal symbol of the federal government's power against the Winnebagos. The War Department ordered the construction and occupation of the post in August 1828. By October 1828, the new post had 110 soldiers.[26] The establishment of Fort Winnebago and the regarrisoning of Forts Crawford and Dearborn made any future revolts risky ventures that had little chance of success.

The Sauks and Foxes were conspicuous by their lack of participation in the Winnebago Uprising. The Prairie La Crosse Winnebagos had sent them a war pipe, but both tribes flatly refused despite the fact that one-sixth of the Sauks were staunchly anti-American. This act was not enough to overcome the Sauk-Fox enmity toward the Mississippi River Winnebagos, who were loyal allies of their enemies, the Santee Sioux. The Sauks and Foxes had pushed west into the hunting grounds of the Santee Sioux in the early nineteenth century, and this resulted in frequent fighting between them. The refusal of the Sauks and Foxes to join the uprising was indicative of the alliances and rivalries that existed. The rivalries and the altercations that resulted from them began to spiral out of control in the 1820s, and the enmity among the tribes rapidly began to overshadow the anti-Americanism. The longest running feud was between the Ojibwas and Santee Sioux, who began fighting in the 1730s. After about 1805, the Sauks and Foxes began to expand north and west into the territories of the Osages, Santee Sioux, and other Siouan-speaking tribes of the plains region.[27]

The expansion of the Ojibwas and the Sauks and Foxes created two alliance systems that, while loosely constructed, became more entrenched during the 1820s and 1830s. The anchors of the first alliance system were the Ojibwas and the Sauks and Foxes, who became allies because they shared a common enemy, the Santee Sioux. The Kickapoos in Illinois and the Iowas often joined the Sauks and Foxes in their forays, as did the confederated bands of the Potawatomis, Ojibwas, and Ottawas of the Illinois River and along the western shore of Lake Michigan. The Santee Sioux were the largest tribe in the second alliance system. Murders of Menominees by the Ojibwas forced the Menominees to join the Santee Sioux, and murders of Menominees by the Sauks and Foxes reinforced this alliance. The Winnebagos, particularly the Mississippi River bands and the Wisconsin River bands, were allies of the Santee Sioux, and murders of Winnebagos committed by the Sauks and Foxes increased the enmity between them.[28]

Indian agents and superintendents believed that the best way to prevent intertribal warfare was to establish boundaries between the tribes. This was done at a treaty council at Prairie du Chien in the summer of 1825. The council included representatives from the Santee Sioux, Ojibwas, Sauks and Foxes, Iowas, Ottawas, Menominees, Winnebagos, and the confederated bands of Potawatomis, Ojibwas, and Ottawas. Lewis Cass and William Clark were the federal commissioners who negotiated the treaty and optimistically proclaimed that it would result in a peace that would be "most favorable and permanent."[29] While Cass and Clark believed that the treaty would end the fighting, they were astute enough to know that small battles would undoubtedly occur in the future due to the young men in every tribe who were inclined to war and beyond the restraint of their chiefs. They were generally correct, for the peace between the tribes lasted for three years. During this period there were isolated incidents of violence, but tribal leaders and federal officials managed to defuse tensions. This became increasing difficult after August 1828, when the killing of six Ojibwas by the Santee Sioux led to a resumption of fighting in the upper Mississippi Valley. The fighting spread south by 1829, and Sauk and Fox war parties began to raid the Santee Sioux. By 1830, the Menominees and Winnebagos were involved once again on the side of their allies, the Santee Sioux.[30]

Federal officials feared this new round of fighting would escalate into full-scale war, for within Indian societies there were distinct differences in the kinds of war that they waged. "National" wars were large-scale ventures that involved entire tribes and confederations and required the participation of hundreds and even thousands of men. Individual warriors also led smaller war parties of between ten and fifty men in "private" wars to avenge personal wrongs. Young men in particular organized these parties because success, bravery, and notoriety in war were the principal means of gaining social prestige within their societies. Black Hawk became a warrior at the age of fifteen when he killed and scalped an Osage. This not only allowed him to wear war paint and eagle feathers but also to raise and lead his own war parties. Tribal leaders could attempt to stop private wars if they believed they were contrary to the interests of the community, but the loose nature of tribal government often made this difficult. Among the Sauks and Foxes, many young warriors routinely sneaked out of their villages at night and formed war parties without the knowledge or consent of tribal leaders.[31]

As the number of private war parties increased, the War Department sought to convene another peace council in the summer of 1830 led by William Clark and Colonel Willoughby Morgan of Fort Crawford. However, the council was plagued with problems even before it started. The year before, Sauks and Foxes had murdered a Winnebago woman. This crime was compounded by another disaster when the subagent to the Foxes at Dubuque Mines invited a delegation of Foxes to the Fever River area for an impromptu meeting with their enemies in early May 1830. Rather than talk peacefully, a party of Santee Sioux and Menominees killed fifteen of the sixteen Fox delegates (three of whom were prominent chiefs) in retaliation for the murder of the Winnebago woman the previous year. Clark met with the Sauk and Fox chiefs and managed to convince them to attend the treaty council later that summer by giving them enough presents to cover their dead. The council opened on July 7, 1830, and delegations of Sauks and Foxes, Iowas, Menominees, Santee Sioux, and Winnebagos were present. The speeches given in council indicated that each tribe wanted peace, but tensions were never far from the surface. Chiefs from both sides spoke angrily of past outrages committed against their people; one Santee Sioux speaker stated that the Sauks "talk of nothing but war—they don't talk of Peace."[32] In the final treaty, both the Santee Sioux and the Sauks and Foxes ceded strips of land twenty miles wide and about two hundred miles long between the Mississippi and Des Moines Rivers called the Neutral Ground that was to serve as a buffer zone between them. Clark was exuberant over the results and stated that the treaty "has terminated far more favourable than I had reason to expect."[33]

Yet, despite these efforts, peace proved to be elusive. The fighting resumed a few months after the treaty council when Ojibwas murdered three Menominees on the Chippewa River. Regional Indian agents maintained only the most tenuous peace, for the Menominees conspired with the Santee Sioux to renew hostilities against the Ojibwas if federal Indian agents failed to resolve the dispute to their satisfaction. To the south, the situation began to deteriorate the next summer. The worst incident occurred on July 31, 1831, when a party of about one hundred Foxes and a few Sauks killed twenty-six Menominees encamped at Prairie du Chien in retaliation for the murder of the Fox delegation the previous year. The Menominees were shocked by the killings. Indian agents implored them to remain at peace, and though the Menominee tribal leaders were willing to do so, they also demanded swift justice from the United States. News of the massacre reached the highest levels of the federal government. President Andrew Jackson was particularly disappointed that it had occurred only a few hundred yards from Fort Crawford and that the post commander had failed to prevent the massacre and block the retreat of the perpetrators. Lewis Cass, now serving as the secretary of war, told William Clark that the president himself ordered the apprehension of the perpetrators who violated the "solemn treaty stipulations" agreed upon the previous year. Cass asserted that a failure to apprehend the guilty parties would rightly result in the Menominees placing "as little confidence in our friendship, as in our justice." Cass also noted that it was equally important to punish the Indians responsible for the massacre since a failure to do so would inevitably result in "a border warfare, from which our own citizens would not be exempted."[34]

Thus, on the eve of the Black Hawk War, intertribal tensions ran high. It is ironic that in 1831, federal Indian agents, military commanders, and the Sauk and Fox tribal leaders were far more concerned with the very real likelihood of a general Indian war than with the remote possibility of a military confrontation between the United States and Black Hawk's followers. While the events that led to the Black Hawk War were developing at this time, intertribal warfare took center stage.[35] These deep rivalries between the tribes had a significant effect upon the course and outcome of the Black Hawk War, for the Winnebagos, the Santee Sioux, and particularly the Menominees were ready to take up arms against the Sauks and Foxes, and military commanders deftly used this fact to their advantage the next year. The Sauks and Foxes had their own allies, but they were reluctant to support Black Hawk's band, which they saw as a renegade faction that consisted of a minority of the two tribes. The other major factor working against Black Hawk was the stronger military presence in the region that the United States had established after the Winnebago Uprising. Both of these developments left Black Hawk extremely isolated and vulnerable in 1832.

3

RUMORS OF WAR

In the year 'twenty-eight Sacs and Foxes were told
That according to the treaty their lands would be sold,
And they must remove to the Iowa ground
Where good village sites could be readily found. . . .
But Black Hawk protested, his love was so strong
For his village, moreover he thought it was wrong
For white men to take land, and he would not admit,
That the treaty was valid by which they claimed it.
—AMER MILLS STOCKING

While intertribal warfare was the most pressing concern of both the federal government and the tribes, there were new problems in the 1820s that led directly to the Black Hawk War. The principal issue was the settlement of the 1804 land cession; once white settlers began to settle in the tract, they had immediate conflicts with the Sauks that put government officials in an awkward position. It would be tempting to simply assume that the federal government sided unequivocally with the settlers against the Indians, but this would ignore the complexity of the situation. Between 1827 and 1831, federal Indian agents and superintendents hoped to defuse tensions, but they were frequently stymied in their efforts by the state of Illinois. Moreover, the Sauks and Foxes were bitterly divided over what course to pursue. Even by the end of 1831, war was not inevitable, but it became increasingly more difficult for the various parties to find common ground for compromise.

The dust of the Winnebago Uprising had scarcely settled when, in the autumn of 1827, Illinois Governor Ninian Edwards called upon the federal government to remove all Indians—Potawatomis,

Kickapoos, and the Sauks and Foxes—from the ceded lands in his state in order to prevent any further Indian troubles. Edwards's admonitions soon bore fruit. Thomas Forysth, the Indian agent to the Sauks and Foxes, broached the topic with the two tribes in the spring of 1828. When Forsyth told them they should move off their ceded lands by the next spring, he was met by a chorus of protests. The Sauks and Foxes revealed that they were well aware of the stipulations of the 1804 treaty by this time and collectively believed that the treaty was illegitimate. According to Forsyth, they asserted that "they had never sold the land higher up the Mississippi than the mouth of the Rocky River [and] that they would not move from the land where the bones of their ancestors lay."[1] Despite these seemingly unanimous sentiments, by 1828 there was, in fact, a definite split within the two tribes (particularly the Sauks) between those who were willing to abide by the 1804 treaty, despite how odious it was, and those who would not. It was, in fact, a continuation of the divisions that the two tribes had experienced since the War of 1812. Black Hawk had not yet emerged as the leader of the anti-removal faction, and the Winnebago Prophet, who would later be one of his chief lieutenants, was far more concerned in 1828 with the trespass of white miners on the Winnebagos' mineral lands than with the controversy surrounding the 1804 treaty. Indeed, in 1828 the principal leaders of the anti-removal faction among the Sauks were Red Head, Bad Thunder, and Ioway.[2]

White settlers did much to aggravate the situation and bolster the position of the anti-removal faction. In the winter of 1827 and 1828, Black Hawk and members of his hunting band had had frequent and ugly contacts with white settlers in their winter hunting grounds in Missouri. A group of whites took all the pelts of one Sauk warrior in retaliation for cutting down a tree filled with honey that the settlers claimed was theirs. Another group accused Black Hawk of killing three hogs and beat him so severely and left him so bruised that he was unable to sleep for several nights. The federal government further aggravated the situation when it made the southern half of the Sauks' and Foxes' 1804 cession below the Rock River a tract for military bounty lands for veterans of the War of 1812. By the 1820s these lands also began to attract settlers. Saukenuk did not lie within this tract, but the northern boundary of the tract was situated less than twenty miles to the south.[3] Thus, while white settlers began to press rapidly upon the Sauks' tribal lands, the Sauks still held out hope that they would retain their lands around Saukenuk. The situation changed dramatically when, in 1828, the federal government ordered that the land around Saukenuk be surveyed and opened up for settlement. Although the first land sales did not occur until October 1829, the first squatters moved into Saukenuk in the autumn of 1828 after the Sauks had left for their winter hunts. That winter, Black Hawk heard that squatters had moved into his lodge, and he traveled ten days to discover that it was true. He had the interpreter at Rock Island write a letter that he presented to the settlers demanding that they leave, but to no effect. He discussed the matter with George Davenport, the principal fur trader at Rock Island. Davenport explained the terms of the 1804 treaty to Black Hawk and the necessity of leaving Saukenuk. Not satisfied, Black Hawk traveled to Prairie du Chien and talked to the subagent for the Winnebagos, John Marsh, who related the same advice. The Sauks returned from their winter hunts in the spring of 1829 to find that the squatters had torn down their lodges and fenced off their cornfields. Forsyth met with the Sauks in order to ease tensions. Quashquame was present, and he again asserted that he had never sold any land north of Rock River when he signed the 1804 treaty. Black Hawk was also at this meeting. Although he had not been a prominent member of the anti-removal faction prior to 1829, the occupation of his own home by the squatters most likely spurred him to assume a more significant leadership role. When Forsyth reminded Black Hawk that he had signed the 1816 treaty restating the terms of the 1804 treaty, Black Hawk told Forsyth that "the whites were in the habit of saying one thing to the Indians and putting another thing down on paper." Forsyth remained firm and demanded that the Sauks move to the west side of the Mississippi. Keokuk took Forsyth aside after the meeting and told him that most of the Sauks and all of the Foxes had moved across the Mississippi. He asked only that he and a few other families be allowed to remain in Saukenuk long enough to harvest the corn they had planted.[4]

Five days later, Forsyth met again with the members of the anti-removal faction, and they reiterated their intention to stay in Saukenuk. Keokuk was conspicuously absent. According to Black Hawk, the members of the anti-removal faction had asked him during this time to act as their leader. Anti-removal factions from other tribes farther to the south were also present, including members of the confederated bands of the Potawatomis, Ojibwas, and Ottawas as well as the Kickapoos, and they all vowed to support the Sauks. Black Hawk also related to Forsyth other incidents that he and his followers had had with the white settlers. A white settler had beaten a Sauk woman whom he had caught pulling up corn that he had planted, and a young Sauk man had died after being beaten by set- tlers for dismantling a fence. Keokuk visited with Forsyth after the meeting and stated again that most of the influential Sauk chiefs had removed to the west side of the Mississippi. Only the few who had planted corn in Saukenuk planned to stay, and they would leave after the harvest season.[5] However, the members of the anti-removal faction under Black Hawk had no such intentions.

From 1829 onward, the split between the Black Hawk and Keokuk became more pronounced. Although it would be tempting to label Keokuk as an American lackey, such a characterization would be inaccurate. Keokuk also harbored a deep distrust of the Americans; this was evident during the summer of 1829, when fed- eral commissioners attempted to arrange the purchase the Sauks' and Foxes' rich mineral lands on the west side of the Mississippi. Both tribes flatly refused. Keokuk, acting as the Sauks' spokesman, noted that during the 1804 treaty the Americans "cheated my Grand Father. . . and we are not going to be taken in . . . that way again."[6] Moreover, Keokuk was not a stranger to the British posts in Canada and had frequently visited Fort Malden to hear speeches by British Indian agents and receive presents. Thus, Keokuk distrusted Ameri- cans as much as Black Hawk, but he believed that nothing would be gained by resisting the United States and chose instead to abide by the 1804 treaty. A significant reason for Keokuk's acquiescence stemmed from his tour to Washington, D.C., in 1824, when he was accompanied by a group of Sauk and Fox chiefs, but not Black Hawk. The purpose of the trip was to settle the differences between the Sauks and Foxes and Santee Sioux, but federal officials used the trip as an opportunity to show the Sauk and Fox delegates the immense size of the United States. This was a common tactic in the nine- teenth century. The War Department reasoned that such tours impressed the Indians with the numerical strength of the Americans and the futility and foolhardiness of armed revolt against the United States. It was a remarkably effective policy. In addition to Washington, Keokuk toured Baltimore, New York, and Philadelphia.[7] Black Hawk would make a similar tour nine years later.

Neither Black Hawk nor Keokuk came from clans that provided civil chiefs, yet both achieved positions of leadership. Because civil chiefs had little real authority, other avenues existed by which leaders could emerge. Those whom whites labeled "war chiefs" usually attained their positions through brave deeds in battle rather than through clan affiliations. It is more accurate to call them "war leaders" since the nature of their office and the power that it wielded was much different from that of a civil chief. Because of his many exploits against the Osages and the Americans during the War of 1812, Black Hawk attained the status of war leader, and after the war he often accompanied one of the principal Sauk civil chiefs, Namoett, in council and served as his speaker. Prior to the War of 1812, Keokuk was a man of little note. During the war, he organized the defense of Saukenuk against a possible American attack. His organizational skills were exemplary, and by decree of the tribal council, he became a war leader. Afterward, his star was on the rise. By the 1820s, he led one of the two tribal moieties. Like other Algonquian tribes, the Sauks divided their young men into two major groups, or moieties. Members of the Oskû'sh (or Brave) moiety painted themselves black, while members of Keokuk's moiety, Ki'shko (or Long Hairs), painted themselves white. This division was purely ceremonial and insured an equal division of the tribe during games such as lacrosse, but the positions of leadership over the moieties were highly esteemed. Civil chiefs also chose men who possessed superior oratorical abilities to speak for them in council, and Keokuk's speaking abilities were so exceptional that many federal officials consulted with Keokuk more than with the civil chiefs for whom he spoke.[8]

Another avenue to leadership was the position of band leader. Bands among the Sauks and other tribes were loosely organized, not based on clan or moiety affiliation, and usually were formed as winter hunting groups. Bands spread out over a large area during the winter hunts (often many miles from their home villages) and came together with other bands in the spring and summer to form a single large village such as Saukenuk. Members of any clan or moiety could join or leave a band at will. Despite the informal manner in which they were composed, bands were not without structure. They had both civil chiefs and war leaders, although the position of band leader did not require any formal political or military rank; band leaders attained their positions due to the strength and charismatic nature of their leadership. This was the dynamic that led to the creation of the two factions that coalesced around Black Hawk and Keokuk. Black Hawk's faction generally contained the most staunchly anti-American members of the Sauks and was named the British Band for that reason. There were other dynamics at work as well. The British Band was only one-sixth of the Sauk tribe, or about 800 members. Keokuk's faction of about 4,500, on the other hand, constituted the majority of the tribe. Keokuk had the backing of the majority of the civil chiefs and the clans from which they came, and this official backing served to legitimate Keokuk's policies in the eyes of the majority of the Sauks.[9]

To bolster his own leadership, Black Hawk began consulting with a half-Sauk, half-Winnebago seer named Wabokieshiek, or White Cloud. He was better known as the Winnebago Prophet among whites, who tended to see him as a latter-day equivalent of the Shawnee Prophet. The Winnebago Prophet actually played a less influential role than his predecessor, but he shared many things in common with other Indian prophets. Although little is known about his religious teachings, the Winnebago Prophet was said to have contact with the spirit world. He gained a personal following, but his teachings, unlike the Shawnee Prophet's, failed to spark a widespread interest in militant nativism. This was due in large part to the fact that he talked little of resistance and instead preached mostly a message of healing and salvation that mixed Indian religious ideas with elements of Christianity. At his village about fifty miles up the Rock River, he attracted about two hundred followers from various tribes. Although many of his adherents held anti-American attitudes, the Winnebago Prophet himself seems to have possessed relatively moderate views, at least at first. He had family ties to the Rock River Winnebago bands, and during the 1827 Winnebago Uprising he worked to keep them at peace and prevent them from joining their brethren at Prairie La Crosse. In a discussion with the Winnebago Prophet a few weeks after the uprising, Thomas Forsyth noted that he had called the Prairie La Crosse Winnebagos "a very bad people," and that if any Rock River Winnebagos should attempt a similar uprising he would turn them over to the United

Figure 1. A sketch of the Winnebago Prophet made in 1833 by George Catlin. Reprinted from Catlin, *Letters and Notes on the Manners, Customs, and Condition of the North American Indians*, vol. 2.

States.[10] He continued to offer counsel to Forsyth and kept him abreast of potential revolts. However, the next summer hordes of white miners began to mine illegally on the lands of the Rock River Winnebagos. While he still professed peace, throughout the summer of 1828 the Winnebago Prophet increasingly began to voice his displeasure over the federal government's inaction in removing them.[11]

Black Hawk paid his first visit to the Winnebago Prophet during the winter of 1828–29. According to Black Hawk, the Prophet's message was one of persistence rather than resistance. He advised Black Hawk to stay at Saukenuk, and if he remained there the whites would not trouble him. This simply seems to have reinforced what Black Hawk already believed, and over the course of the next three years Black Hawk continued to preach this message to the Sauk leadership, particularly Keokuk, and to federal officials and anyone else who would listen. During the winter of 1829–30, Black Hawk and his followers had learned, to their dismay, that their trader at Rock Island, George Davenport, had purchased more than 2,400 acres of land in the Sauks' ceded territory, and his tract included all of the lands that comprised Saukenuk. Black Hawk and his followers had several meetings concerning these developments, and it was during this time that a young Sauk civil chief named Napope, or The Broth, emerged as another of Black Hawk's advisors, although he would consistently prove to be the least reliable. Indeed, Napope's suggested course of action—to kill all the federal officials in the region, as well as Davenport and Keokuk—was indicative of his rash nature.[12]

When the members of Black Hawk's band returned to Saukenuk in the spring of 1830 after their winter hunts, several events occurred that strengthened Black Hawk's position. Neither Forsyth, Keokuk, nor Pashipaho (not the same Pashipaho who signed the 1804 treaty), the principal civil chief of the Sauks who sided with Keokuk, were able to persuade Black Hawk and his band to move from Saukenuk. Moreover, Black Hawk's followers were joined that spring by a group of Kickapoo warriors and their families who, like Black Hawk's band, protested earlier land cessions made by their tribe. A total of twelve lodges (each of which contained about twenty persons), or over two hundred Kickapoos, joined the British Band, and most (but not all) remained with it until its final demise in 1832. Black Hawk also had initiated discussions with the Rock River Winnebagos and felt them out for a possible alliance. During this time, the murder of the Fox chiefs occurred, and Forsyth, Clark, and other federal officials became momentarily diverted from the problem of the British Band. It was also during this time that the federal government hosted the 1830 treaty council at Prairie du Chien in an attempt to quell intertribal fighting, and Black Hawk was conspicuously absent.[13]

Another event occurred in 1830 that soured the attitude of many of the Foxes toward the Americans. Up to this time, the Foxes had been relatively quiescent, and while many of them disliked the 1804 treaty, the Foxes of the upper Mississippi were less directly affected because they lived predominantly on the unceded lands of the west side. In May 1830, the Foxes temporarily abandoned their village at Dubuque's Mines and fled to Rock Island as they feared attacks by the Menominees and Santee Sioux. When word of the Foxes' absence arrived in the scattered mining camps on the east bank of the Mississippi, hordes of whites rushed across the river and began to mine and smelt ore on the Foxes' rich mineral lands at Dubuque's Mines. By early June, an Indian subagent reported that about one hundred miners had occupied the site. William Clark intervened and sent General Henry Atkinson to Dubuque's Mines to remove the squatters before the Foxes returned. The Foxes had long guarded Dubuque's Mines and related little about them to whites for fear of having them seized. The short occupation by whites in the summer of 1830 made the mineral wealth of the site common knowledge and made them even more anxious to seize the Foxes' lands. When the Foxes abandoned Dubuque's Mines again in the summer of 1831 due to fear of Santee Sioux attacks, the army sent a permanent detachment of soldiers led by a young lieutenant named Jefferson Davis (who would later serve as the president of the Confederacy) to secure the mines and prevent future incursions. This was only a temporary expedient, however, and one trader openly admitted that as soon as the troops left, "the citizens of Illinois and of Michigan Territory will, without doubt, again cross over."[14]

In the wake of these events, Black Hawk maintained contact with the Winnebago Prophet throughout the winter of 1830–31. He also began to send messengers to other tribes, some as far away as Arkansas and Texas. In his 1833 autobiography, Black Hawk stated that these runners did not take messages concerning his dispute with the United States but had "a secret mission, which I am not, at present, permitted to explain."[15] The delegation included Black Hawk's son Nashaweskaka (Loud Thunder, or Whirling Thunder); Ioway, one of the most anti-American of the Sauk warriors; and Namoett, one of the civil chiefs who supported Black Hawk. Although Black Hawk refused to state its purpose, the diplomatic journey may have had as its goal the search for a new home among friendly tribes should Black Hawk's hope of remaining at Saukenuk falter. Moreover, it is possible that Black Hawk expected a pan-Indian uprising sometime within the next two years and did not want to divulge information concerning such an event (which never happened) to white audiences. Regardless of the purpose of the mission, Black Hawk had failed to attract any new support for his cause. Moreover, during the return from Texas, Namoett and Ioway died, and a few months later Bad Thunder, the other major leader of the anti-American faction, died as well. These deaths deprived Black Hawk's faction of some of its most experienced leadership.[16]

During the autumn of 1830, Black Hawk told the new Indian agent at Rock Island, Felix St. Vrain, that he would return to Saukenuk the next spring. He made good on his promise, and in the spring of 1831 Black Hawk's followers, along with their Kickapoo allies, returned. They were joined later by disaffected Potawatomis from the Illinois River who also had grievances against the United States, and the Winnebago Prophet and his followers joined Black Hawk as well. By midsummer between 1,200 to 1,600 Indians, all strongly anti-American, resided at or near Saukenuk. However, 1831 proved to be far different than previous years for the British Band. The local white citizens sent several urgent petitions to the new governor of Illinois, John Reynolds, who immediately took action. In late May 1831, he called up seven hundred mounted militia volunteers to remove the British Band. Reynolds's mobilization of the militia was of dubious legality since Indian affairs were a federal responsibility. He rationalized his actions by asserting that despite the repeated petitions of the settlers to federal authorities, Black Hawk and his followers still remained. He was a new governor of a western state populated by a frontier population that loathed Indians, and Reynolds, no lover of Indians himself, believed he would be "condemned from Dan to Bersheba" if he did not act.[17] William Clark informed Major General Edmund P. Gaines, the commander of the army's Western Department at St. Louis, of Reynolds's order. Gaines hoped to prevent untrained state militia volunteers from interfering in what he and Clark saw as a federal responsibility, and he proceeded to Rock Island along with six companies of federal troops and two light cannon from Jefferson Barracks. Four companies from Fort Crawford and two from Fort Winnebago joined Gaines at Rock Island but did not arrive in time to be of use. Gaines did not intend to make war but instead expressed his hope that the Indians, seeing his large contingent of soldiers, would be urged to "to cross the mississippi to their proper position."[18]

Upon hearing of Gaines's departure, Black Hawk met with the Winnebago Prophet to determine a course of action. The Winnebago Prophet requested that he be given some time to see into the matter. He announced to Black Hawk the next morning that he had received the answer the night before in a dream. The Winnebago Prophet asserted that the object of Gaines's mission was to frighten Black Hawk and his followers from Saukenuk so that the white people could take it away, but that Gaines would not dare use violence. Moreover, he stated, as he had in the past, that "the Americans were at peace with the British, and when they made peace, the British required (which the Americans agreed to,) that they should never interrupt any nation of Indians that was at peace." As long as Black Hawk refused any of Gaines's overtures or offers, he would be able to stay in Saukenuk.[19] Certainly, the Winnebago Prophet had correctly gauged Gaines's true purpose. More interestingly, there is little doubt that his advice to Black Hawk was based upon the ninth article of the Treaty of Ghent. It was this article that had required the United States, after the War of 1812, to recognize Indian titles to all lands and return the tribes to the status quo antebellum. The Winnebago Prophet probably came to understand the contents of this article from British Indian agents in Canada, and he believed that because of it, the United States absolutely could not force any tribe from its lands. Throughout the course of the next year, he repeated this argument to Black Hawk and other Indian leaders.[20]

Black Hawk adhered to the Winnebago Prophet's advice when he and several of his followers, including Quashquame, met with Gaines a few days later on June 4, 1831. Also present at the council was Keokuk, several of his followers, and Wapello, the principal civil chief of the Foxes, who, like Keokuk and Pashipaho, advocated abiding in the 1804 treaty. Black Hawk arrived at the council singing a war song along with several of his warriors in order to impress Gaines with their courage. Gaines repeated what numerous other federal officials had stated before: that the Sauks and Foxes had sold their land on the east side of the Mississippi and had signed two treaties that testified to that fact. Quashquame asserted that he had never sold any land north of the Rock River, while Black Hawk stated that he refused to leave the place where the bones of his fathers rested. The next day, Gaines met with Keokuk, who, he learned, had convinced about fifty families, or about two hundred persons, to abandon Saukenuk and Black Hawk's cause. Three days later, on June 7th, Black Hawk met again with Gaines. He brought along several Sauk women who asserted that if they were forced to move they would not be able to harvest the corn they had planted and their children would starve. Unmoved by the women's pleas, Gaines told Black Hawk that he and his followers had three days to leave or he would forcibly remove them.[21]

Gaines did not move against Black Hawk and followers within three days as he had promised, for his troops from Forts Crawford and Winnebago had not yet arrived, and thus his force was not adequate. He was loath to start a war and preferred that the Indians move of their own accord, but local settlers took no chances. Panic spread through the nearby settlements, and settlers began to build stockades and small forts for what they believed would be a general Indian uprising. Although there was no chance of this happening, it reflected the almost irrational fears that whites harbored against Indians, and such precautions would be repeated the next year. Black Hawk, for his part, also sought to avoid violence and urged his followers to offer no resistance if Gaines's troops approached. He ordered the town crier to announce to all present that "not a gun should be fired, nor any resistance offered. That if he [Gaines] determined to fight, for them to remain quietly in their lodges, and let him *kill them if he chose!*"[22]

The stalemate continued for three weeks, during which time Black Hawk's position slowly weakened while Gaines's strength increased. On June 5th, Gaines requested the battalion of mounted militia that Reynolds had earlier promised. Reynolds rejoiced at receiving this order since it legalized his order that created the volunteer force. The residents of Illinois enthusiastically responded to Reynolds's call, and over 1,400 men assembled at Beardstown. The little army swelled so quickly with volunteers that they had to move across the Illinois River to nearby Rushville. The troops were organized into a brigade of two regiments, each with seven companies composed of between thirty and seventy-two men. The brigade also had a spy (or scout) battalion, an independent or "odd" battalion, and four odd companies. On June 20th, the volunteers, variously armed and accoutered and without uniforms, began the 130-mile march to Rock Island. During this time, Keokuk and his civil chiefs persuaded many of Black Hawk's followers to abandon him, and others began to grow weary of the standoff. By late June 1831, almost one-third of the Indians had deserted Saukenuk for the west bank of the Mississippi. Gaines also hired the steamboat *Winnebago* and armed it with his artillery pieces and two regular infantry companies. From approximately June 18th until June 23rd, he took the vessel up the Rock River in order to reconnoiter the area and show Black Hawk his resolve. In addition to his six companies from Jefferson Barracks, he had two from Fort Armstrong. Moreover, he had the Illinois mounted volunteers, which he needed to pursue Black Hawk's followers in case they fled and attacked white settlements, for the U.S. Army did not possess cavalry at this time. On June 25th, the Illinois mounted volunteers arrived at their marshalling area on the eastern bank of the Mississippi about twelve miles southwest of Rock Island and spent the remainder of the day issuing ammunition and making preparations for the next day's assault.[23]

On the morning of June 26th, Gaines's plan went into effect. He hoped to squeeze Black Hawk's band into a vise with forces advancing from the north and the south. He had one regular infantry company on board the *Winnebago*. Also aboard was an artillery piece used for shooting canister shot into the thick vegetation of the island directly across the river from Saukenuk, covering the movement of the the Illinois volunteers. Led by the spy battalion, the volunteers forded the Rock River on the east end of this island (called Vandruff Island), which they believed would be occupied by the Indians due to the superior terrain it offered. Meanwhile, about 270 soldiers from seven companies of the Third and Sixth U.S. Infantry Regiments, under the command of Major John Bliss, commander of Fort Armstrong, crossed the Mississippi from Rock Island and moved south to take the high ground to the rear of Saukenuk. In addition to two artillery pieces, the regulars had with them a group of sixty-one white volunteers from the vicinity of Saukenuk known as the Rock River Rangers. The regulars, the volunteers, and the Rock River Rangers found, to their surprise, that the entire village was deserted. The day before, Black Hawk's own scouts had seen the advance of the volunteers as they moved toward their marshalling area. Black Hawk was confident that Gaines and the regular troops would not harm him or his followers, but he knew that militia troops were undisciplined and unpredictable. He stated that he "would have remained and been taken prisoner by the *regulars*, but was afraid of the multitude of *pale faces*, who were on horseback, as they were under no restraint of their chiefs." On the night of June 25th, under the cover of darkness, Black Hawk and his followers slipped across the Mississippi to the west bank.[24]

Black Hawk had judged the situation well, for while Gaines later reported to his superiors with relief that violence had been avoided, the mounted volunteers expressed bitterness at being denied the war they had been anxious to fight. Governor Reynolds admitted that one of his greatest fears in organizing the operation was that the Illinois volunteers would kill any and all Indians they encountered because "the headstrong Americans, being so many in the brigade that hated the Indians, wanted *fun*."[25] His assessment proved to be accurate, for after they arrived at Saukenuk, it began to rain, and this further aggravated the already infuriated Illinois volunteers. The heavy rains were not enough to stop them from burning all the Indian lodges. Several men even dug up the corpses in the nearby Sauk graveyard and scattered the remains on the ground and threw one corpse into a fire. Not satisfied to destroy what remained of the village, the volunteers then procured food from the fields of the nearby white settlers. One of the Rock River Rangers watched in horror as the volunteers took all of his corn and potatoes. He lamented: "By this operation I lost all my crop for one year . . . the soldiers doing me ten times as much damage as the Indians had ever done."[26]

On June 30th, Black Hawk, accompanied by Quashquame, arrived at Rock Island to meet with Gaines. Also present at the council were the principal chiefs and warriors of the Sauks and the Foxes who sided with Keokuk. Their presence conveyed a clear, unmistakable message: they wanted Black Hawk and his band to end their resistance and remain on the west side of the Mississippi. Gaines had his aide, Lieutenant George McCall, read an agreement of capitulation that outlined several important promises. Black Hawk was to submit to the leadership of the Sauk and Fox tribes and remain forever on the west side of the Mississippi. Moreover, he was not to have any contact with British agents or posts in Canada. According to McCall, Black Hawk "arose slowly, and with great dignity" to sign the agreement, "while in the expression of his fine face there was a deep–seated grief and humiliation that no one could witness unmoved." McCall noted that when Black Hawk took the pen to sign, he "made a large, bold cross with a force which rendered *that* pen forever unfit for further use."[27] During the proceedings, Black Hawk told Gaines that the members of his band needed food to replace the corn that they had planted at Saukenuk. Gaines agreed to provide corn to make up for the loss of their crops. The volunteers, camped on the prairie across from Rock Island, soon found out about Gaines's agreement and derisively labeled it the "Corn Treaty." When Black Hawk and his followers determined a few weeks later that this would not be enough, a party went back across the river to gather some of the crops they had planted. They were fired upon by white settlers and departed without accomplishing their objective. The only consolation that Black Hawk received was a promise by George Davenport that when he died he could be buried at the graveyard in Saukenuk and repose alongside his "old friends and warriors."[28]

Black Hawk's removal in late June 1831 was neither a sign of cowardice nor of duplicity. He left to save his followers from certain destruction at the hands of untrained, Indian-hating volunteers, and he intended to abide by the agreement that he had signed with Gaines. However, a series of events occurred afterward that altered the situation significantly. The first occurred four weeks later, when the massacre at Prairie du Chien occurred that left twenty-six Menominees dead. The United States demanded that the Foxes surrender those responsible. The Fox leaders of the massacre visited Black Hawk, who told them that they were right to seek revenge for the murders of their chiefs the year before, particularly since the United States had demanded they turn over the Fox perpetrators but had not made a similar demand of the Menominees for the murders of the Fox delegates in 1830. Fearing that the Fox chiefs under Keokuk's influence would surrender them to the United States, between fifty and sixty of the Fox perpetrators sought refuge with the British Band in order to escape American justice.[29] This bolstered Black Hawk's band with a fresh group of followers who had a strong incentive to resist the United States.

In the autumn of 1831, Black Hawk received news from Napope, who, although relatively young, became the ranking civil chief of the British Band following the death of Namoett. Napope visited Fort Malden during the summer of 1831 while Black Hawk was involved in the standoff with Gaines. When he returned, Napope brought news that the British supported the British Band in its efforts to remain at Saukenuk. Napope asserted that the British agents told him that if the Sauks had not sold their village, the Americans had no right to tell them to leave. On his way back from Fort Malden, Napope had stopped at the village of the Winnebago

Prophet, who had received promises from the British of guns, ammunition, and provisions that would be sent to Milwaukee in the event of a war between Black Hawk's band and the United States. The Prophet had also received wampum and tobacco from the confederated bands of the Potawatomis, Ojibwas, and Ottawas along the western shore of Lake Michigan as well as from the Winnebagos, and these tribes pledged their assistance to Black Hawk.[30]

This information concerning support from the British and other tribes came not from any dreams or prophesies of the Winnebago Prophet but from the fertile imagination of Napope. Indeed, Black Hawk later blamed Napope, not the Winnebago Prophet, for making these promises, and after the war Napope denied that the Winnebago Prophet had said anything of the sort. Nevertheless, Black Hawk enthusiastically welcomed this news upon receiving it, and it is not difficult to see why. Only a few weeks before, he had been humiliated and disgraced as he and his followers, who earlier that spring had triumphantly returned to Saukenuk, were forced to leave their ancestral village. He was resigned to this defeat and certainly had no plans to violate the agreement he made with Gaines. Now, however, he had received news that seemed too good to be true. Indeed, he stated, "I thought over every thing that Ne-a-pope had told me, and was pleased to think that, by a little exertion on my part, I could accomplish the object of all my wishes."[31]

Black Hawk would soon find out that the news and promises brought by Napope were, indeed, too good to be true, and alas, none of them ever came to fruition. It is not clear whether Napope simply confused the message from the British agents or whether he fabricated the entire story, but his duplicitous actions in 1832 suggest the latter. Nevertheless, Black Hawk should have been more objective in his analysis of the situation; he possessed an abundance of information concerning the general lack of support from other tribes in the region, and this should have illustrated to him the outlandish nature of Napope's promises. Throughout the standoff with Gaines in 1831, Black Hawk attracted only a scant amount of support outside of the British Band, and those Indians who joined him tended to be the most adamantly anti-American members of tribes that also were under pressure to remove from their ceded lands. Exact numbers are difficult to determine, but as many as six hundred Indians joined the British Band that spring and summer, and this included approximately two hundred Kickapoos (most of whom had lived with Black Hawk's band since 1829), one hundred Potawatomis from the Illinois River, and fifty of the Winnebago Prophet's followers. Many of these joined with Black Hawk again in 1832, particularly the followers of the Winnebago Prophet and the Kickapoos, but their numbers were still relatively small.[32]

The Winnebago Prophet attempted to woo the Rock River Winnebago Bands to join Black Hawk in 1831, but except for a handful of warriors who visited Saukenuk, they steadfastly refused, as did the Wisconsin and Mississippi River Bands. In speeches with Indian agents, the Winnebago chiefs strongly affirmed their determination to remain at peace. This was a dramatic switch from the policy of low-level warfare that had characterized the tribe's relationship with the United States after the War of 1812. The reason for the shift derived from the Winnebago Uprising four years earlier, for the Winnebagos had witnessed how quickly the United States could assemble a force against them. John Kinzie, the subagent at Fort Winnebago, stated: "I know the Winnebagoes in this vicinity are entirely averse [to supporting Black Hawk] since the lesson they received in 1827, to join in any affair of this kind."[33] Black Hawk sent ambassadors to the Illinois River Potawatomis in order to garner their support, but except for the one hundred members who visited Saukenuk, the Potawatomi leadership also withheld its support.[34] These results were replicated the next year during the Black Hawk War; Black Hawk attracted a small number of warriors from both the Potawatomis and Winnebagos in 1832, but the majority of both tribes rejected his overtures.

Of course, the Santee Sioux and Menominees remained hostile to the Sauks and Foxes and did not distinguish between those who sided with Keokuk and those who sided with Black Hawk. According to Thomas Burnett, the subagent at Prairie du Chien, the two tribes would have fought either faction. In the case of Black Hawk, Burnett believed that the Santee Sioux and Menominees "would willingly unite with the whites if permitted" in fighting against Black Hawk during the summer of 1831.[35] His assessment turned out to be prophetic in 1832.

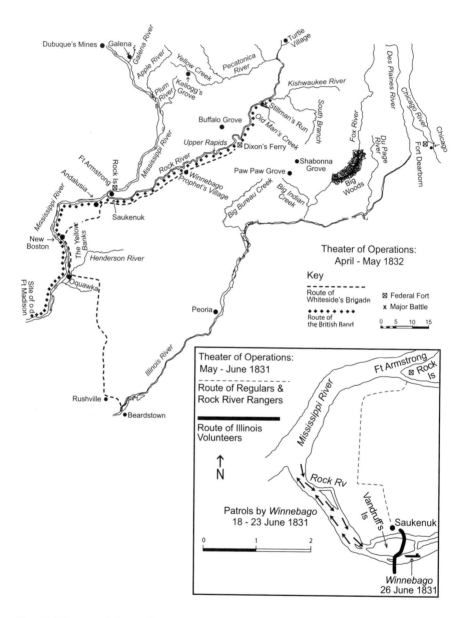

Map 3. Theater of Operations in Spring 1831 and Spring 1832

4

THE THUNDERBIRDS'
FIRST ROAR

The forces of Stillman and Bailey were keen
To move before Atkinson came on the scene
Not having been sworn as U.S. volunteers,
They were still state militia, as clearly appears;
And they pleaded with Reynolds to give them a chance
To go forth, and his fame with their own to enhance.
"The Old Ranger" consented, whate'er his belief,
And an order made out as Commander in Chief.
— AMER MILLS STOCKING

After Black Hawk received Napope's message concerning support from the British and other tribes, he spent the fall and the winter of 1831–32 working to keep his band together as well as sending delegations to recruit other tribes. Black Hawk and other members of the British Band attended a particularly large gathering at Keokuk's village in early 1832 and made one last attempt to win over Keokuk's followers. Members of the British Band made emotional pleas to Keokuk's band, but in the end Keokuk's impassioned oratory persuaded his followers of the futility of Black Hawk's plan. Keokuk's followers refused to join Black Hawk, and he issued a stern warning to Black Hawk that he should stay on the west side of the Mississippi. In the wake of this gathering, Keokuk and George Davenport both urged local Indian agents to allow Black Hawk to travel to Washington, D.C., so that he could see the power of the United States and have the president explain to him the importance of abiding in the past treaties, but Secretary of War Lewis Cass refused the request, citing a lack of funds.[1]

Cass also did not push for such a visit because he and other federal officials were far more concerned with the possibility of intertribal war exploding in the region, particularly after the 1831 massacre of the Menominees by the Foxes at Prairie du Chien. The Menominees asked nothing less than immediate satisfaction in the matter, and Indian agents did everything in their power to prevent the Menominees and their allies from seeking revenge. This became an all-consuming problem over the course of the next year, and little attention was paid to Black Hawk and his band. Indeed, the only action taken by the federal government in response to Black Hawk's 1831 standoff at Saukenuk was to regarrison Fort Dearborn at Chicago. The post had been abandoned in the spring of 1831 before the standoff began. Black Hawk's defiance illustrated the shortsightedness of this decision, and in response, the War Department in February 1832 ordered two companies from Fort Niagara, New York, to proceed to Chicago. However, the troops would not arrive until June 17, 1832, well after the Black Hawk War had started.[2]

Thus, the British Band was merely a distracting issue; the prevention of intertribal warfare remained the principal concern throughout 1831 and early 1832. Responsibility for both activities fell upon Brigadier General Henry Atkinson. The War Department ordered Atkinson to arrest the Foxes responsible for the Menominee massacre, and after consulting with William Clark, Atkinson decided that he would leave his troops at Rock Island to take custody of the guilty individuals and then proceed to Prairie du Chien to prevent the Menominees and Santee Sioux from moving against the Foxes. On April 8th, Atkinson departed from St. Louis with six companies of the Sixth Infantry Regiment totaling 220 men. By accident, Atkinson became responsible for the theater of operations during the Black Hawk War, for he was the immediate subordinate to Major General Edmund Gaines, who was in command of the Western Department throughout 1832. However, Gaines at the time was in Memphis, Tennessee, suffering from influenza and rheumatism. When word reached him concerning the events in the upper Mississippi, he attempted to make his way back to St. Louis and take command of the situation, but while enroute he learned that the president planned to replace Atkinson with Gaines's bitter rival,

Figure 2. Portrait of General Henry Atkinson.
Reprinted from Stevens, *The Black Hawk War.*

Major General Winfield Scott, commander of the Eastern Department. Gaines sat out the war in Tennessee, but Scott fared no better.
He arrived at Chicago in July 1832 with troops so infected with
cholera that he was virtually unable to employ them. Thus, command devolved upon Atkinson by double default.

Atkinson was the son of a wealthy North Carolina tobacco
planter, and he accepted an army commission with the rank of captain in 1808 at the age of twenty-six. He saw no fighting during the
War of 1812, yet he rose to the rank of colonel due to his adminis-
trative abilities. He also had an uncanny knack for not calling undue
attention to himself by avoiding the pitched political battles that

contemporaries like Winfield Scott and Andrew Jackson frequently fought in the halls of the War Department and Congress. The Indians called him "White Beaver," although it is not known why. Like most frontier officers, Atkinson believed that preventing Indian wars was preferable to fighting them. Prior to the Black Hawk War, Atkinson had never been in combat, and the only time that he commanded troops in combat was during the final battle of the Black Hawk War at the Bad Axe River in August 1832.[3]

The qualities that allowed Atkinson to prosper in peacetime were not enough to bring success on the battlefield. Indeed, Atkinson often exhibited sheer incompetence as a tactician. The first battle of the war, the Battle of Stillman's Run, was a fiasco that occurred in large part because Atkinson allowed untrained militiamen to make the initial contact with the British Band rather than more disciplined regular soldiers. Atkinson learned quickly from this mistake, and after Stillman's Run he became a more effective officer and paid attention to the many details required of a successful battlefield commander. However, he could not transform himself into a better tactician, and he succeeded in spite of this shortcoming. He was made to look competent by one of his subordinate commanders, Henry Dodge, who was far more imaginative, aggressive, and tactically competent. Atkinson's conduct of the war resulted in criticisms from various quarters in Washington, although after the war he returned to the routine tasks of the peacetime army with his reputation only slightly tarnished and his career progress not unduly hindered.[4]

While preparing for his mission to arrest the Fox perpetrators, Atkinson heard rumors that the British Band planned to reoccupy Saukenuk despite Black Hawk's promise the previous year. Black Hawk's band was fiercely determined to return to the east side of the Mississippi; the women were particularly resolute. Many of them believed that they had been unfairly removed and had been forced to give up their well-prepared corn fields at Saukenuk in exchange for the inadequate amount of grain that Gaines had promised. Moreover, there had been outlandish rumors that further enraged both the women and their men. Two Sauk warriors recounted one of these fables and noted that the Americans planned to capture all the Sauk men, castrate them, and then bring "a horde of negro men . . . from the South, to whom our wives, sisters, and daughters were to be given, for the purpose of raising a stock of *Slaves*."[5] These and other lurid rumors, coupled with the promises of Napope, insured enthusiastic support for Black Hawk's plans. Atkinson initially placed little credibility in these reports concerning the return of the British Band and continued to focus his efforts on preventing a wider war among the regional tribes.[6]

On April 5, 1832, the same day the British Band crossed the Mississippi, the Sauk and Fox agent, Felix St. Vrain, was visited at Rock Island by the Winnebago Prophet, who told St. Vrain that he had invited Black Hawk and his people to live at his village. He asserted that the agreement the year before stipulated that the British Band would not occupy Saukenuk, and thus having them reside at his village forty miles up the Rock River did not violate the agreement. He stated that because his village and the British Band were considered to be one, he did not think it would be improper to invite the British Band to live with his people at their village. The Winnebago Prophet later told Black Hawk that St. Vrain had urged him to abandon his plan, but the Winnebago Prophet continued to assert that "he would not listen to this *talk*, because no war chief [American military commander] dare molest us as long as we are at *peace*."[7] Thus, the Winnebago Prophet persisted in his belief that as long as the members of the British Band remained at peace, they would be allowed to remain on the eastern side of the Mississippi in accordance with the Treaty of Ghent. Nevertheless, he and Black Hawk wanted to pursue a prudent course of action. They knew the 1831 agreement with Gaines made the occupation of Saukenuk a risky move. The Winnebago Prophet's village had not been stipulated in the agreement, so the British Band's residence there would be an act of resistance but not an act of war. In his autobiography, Black Hawk does not clearly state what he and his lieutenants hoped to accomplish with this plan to cross the Mississippi in April 1832. The available evidence strongly suggests that Black Hawk and the Winnebago Prophet hoped that by attracting the support of the regional tribes and the British in Canada, they would be able to produce a strong show of force. Then the United States, wishing to avoid an Indian war, would be compelled to reconsider its policy and let the British Band remain on the east side of the Mississippi. Thus, despite the opinions of several federal officials in the region, Black Hawk did not intend to make war when he crossed the Mississippi; in fact, he hoped to avoid it.[8]

The most telling evidence for this assertion comes from the composition of the British Band itself, for it was structured not as a war party but as a tribal band with the requisite civil chiefs and war leaders. Of the nine civil chiefs, the Winnebago Prophet became the highest ranking one upon joining the British Band with his followers in the spring of 1832. Since his father was a Sauk and a member of a hereditary leadership clan, the Winnebago Prophet inherited the position of a Sauk chief, and this was enhanced by his status as a religious leader. Napope was the second highest ranking civil chief, and the remaining seven civil chiefs were Pamisseu (He That Flies), Weesheet (Sturgeon Head), Chakeepashipaho (The Little Stabbing Chief), Checokalako (Turtle Shell), Ioway (another chief with that name had died the year before), Pamaho (He That Goes On Water), and Towaunonne (The Trader). The British Band also recognized five war leaders. Black Hawk was the highest ranking, and, most importantly, he was the band leader. Black Hawk, the Winnebago Prophet, and Napope exercised the real authority, yet the British Band had the leadership structure required to lend an air of legitimacy to the band and its objectives. Equally important was the fact that the British Band had with it women, young children, and elderly members, none of whom ever accompanied war parties. Moreover, from April 5, 1832, to the Battle of Stillman's Run on May 14, 1832, the British Band's actions toward white settlers were generally peaceful. At one point, Black Hawk, the Winnebago Prophet, and Napope stopped at Dixon's Ferry (which would later serve as the command post for the army sent against the British Band), where John Dixon, the local proprietor, and his family treated the leaders of the British Band to dinner after Black Hawk had presented them with gifts.[9]

Black Hawk marshaled his band at the site where Fort Madison had once stood, marched north along the western bank of the Mississippi, and crossed over at a point along the Yellow Banks (near present-day New Boston, Illinois) on April 5, 1832. In addition to the Sauk members of the British Band, there were the Fox perpetrators, a small number of Illinois River Potawatomis, and the roughly two hundred Kickapoos who had joined Black Hawk in 1830. Upon reaching the Winnebago Prophet's village, they were joined by about one hundred of the Prophet's followers, making for a total of about eleven hundred persons, about five hundred of whom were warriors. The older persons and children traveled with the band's five hundred horses. The younger men and women traveled by water in over one hundred canoes packed with their belongings. Although Black Hawk and his lieutenants did not intend to initiate a conflict, they nevertheless took the precaution of putting out flank guards on horseback to guard against possible attack.[10]

Atkinson received his first definite news of the British Band's migration on April 10th while he and his troops were on their way to Rock Island. Although he believed the event was serious, he did not see it as an act of war. He immediately sent a letter to Washington, D.C., informing General Alexander Macomb, the commanding general of the army, and asking him for guidance. The six companies under Atkinson's command were not enough to compel so large a body of Indians to return across the Mississippi. Moreover, his information was sketchy, and he was not even sure of the British Band's route or location. He proceeded to Rock Island still under the impression that his most pressing duty was to arrest the Fox perpetrators and prevent a wider intertribal war from erupting. Ironically, as he steamed toward Rock Island, he passed the British Band during the night of April 12th near present-day Andalusia, Illinois. Black Hawk noted that seeing the troops alarmed his band, and he believed that Atkinson would post troops at the mouth of Rock River to prevent its passage up the river. However, Atkinson had no idea of the British Band's location at the time, and under cover of darkness Black Hawk's followers moved to the mouth of the Rock River. Relieved to find no soldiers there, the British Band proceeded up the Rock River.[11]

Atkinson arrived at Fort Armstrong on the night of April 12th, and there he learned the full scope of the situation. He continued with his original mission of securing the Fox perpetrators and met with the Sauk and Fox leaders on April 13th. He learned that most of the perpetrators were with Black Hawk; the rest were off hunting and far from their villages. The principal spokesmen were Keokuk and the Fox chief Wapello, both of whom noted that they had no power to bring the British Band back, nor could they do anything to secure the Fox perpetrators. Atkinson then sent a letter to Illinois Governor John Reynolds informing him of the situation. The letter did more harm than good, for in it Atkinson hinted, despite all evidence to the contrary, that the British Band would probably initiate hostilities at some point. He did not ask Reynolds to call out the militia, but he stated in his letter that his current force was too small to compel Black Hawk and his followers to return, and that Reynolds should "judge . . . the course proper to be pursued."[12] Atkinson may have intentionally exaggerated the danger posed by the British Band in order to provoke Reynolds into mustering the militia. Black Hawk had fled to the west side of the Mississippi the year before as the Illinois volunteers approached, and Atkinson may have believed that such a tactic would peacefully resolve the current situation. If this was Atkinson's intention, it worked, for Reynolds judged that the best course of action was to assemble another volunteer army at Beardstown, Illinois.[13] Nevertheless, Atkinson's rhetoric also lent credence to the unfounded rumors that were sweeping through the white settlements and creating irrational panic and fear.

Atkinson arrived two days later on April 15th at Prairie du Chien. On his way to Fort Crawford, Atkinson stopped at Galena, where he sent letters to the local Indian subagent and to Henry Dodge, who commanded a militia regiment in nearby Michigan Territory. Once again, Atkinson exaggerated the threat and told Dodge that the local citizens should be on guard against Indian attacks because there were rumors that the British Band would "strike upon the frontier inhabitants as soon as they secure their women and children in the fastness of the Rock river swamps."[14] Upon arriving at Fort Crawford, Atkinson proceeded with his original mission and issued orders to the post commanders of Forts Crawford and Winnebago and to the Indian agents at Prairie du Chien, Fort Winnebago, and Green Bay to prevent the Menominees and Santee Sioux from moving against the Sauks and Foxes.[15]

Back at Rock Island, Atkinson met with Keokuk and Wapello, who managed to secure three of the Fox perpetrators who had not gone with Black Hawk. With the problem of stemming the tide of intertribal war momentarily solved, Atkinson turned his attention to the British Band. Keokuk and Wapello had already taken the initiative to convince the British Band to return by sending a young Fox chief as an emissary to the British Band twice on April 12th and April 15th. The young chief attempted to persuade the band members to return; both times he was rebuffed. One of the Fox perpetrators even brandished a lance during the young chief's second visit and said that he had used it against the Menominees and now "hoped to brake [sic], or wear it out on the Americans."[16] Atkinson then sent two Sauk chiefs on April 24th to take an express message to Black Hawk, who, along with his band, was camped near the Winnebago Prophet's village. The two chiefs presented a message from Atkinson that ordered the British Band to return at once. Napope and Black Hawk sent back their answer, and it was not what Atkinson wanted to hear. Both men asserted that they had no "bad feelings," but neither did they intend to return. Napope said that the Rock River Winnebagos had invited the British Band to settle among them, and they intended to move farther up the Rock River to live with them. One of the Sauk chiefs sent by Atkinson noted that there were about twenty Rock River Winnebagos present who had urged the British Band to push farther north.[17]

Atkinson also instructed Henry Gratiot, the subagent for the Rock River Winnebago bands, to gather information. Gratiot first met with the chiefs of the Rock River Winnebago bands to ascertain what they knew of the motives of Black Hawk. The chiefs told Gratiot that Black Hawk had sent them red wampum, which, among the tribes of the region, was an invitation to join them in an alliance of war, but they had refused to accept the invitation. They told Gratiot they had resolved to remain at peace and sought to convince the Winnebago Prophet and his followers (many of whom, like the Winnebago Prophet, had relations among the Rock River Winnebagos) to break with Black Hawk. This was welcome news to Gratiot, and he decided to accompany the party that was to visit the Winnebago Prophet. On April 22nd, he departed with twenty-six Rock River Winnebagos from the Turtle Village (present-day Beloit, Wisconsin). The party included two of the most influential leaders of the Rock River Winnebagos: Whirling Thunder, a village chief, and White Crow, a war leader and orator.[18]

Gratiot had no interpreter and thus was forced to have the Winnebago delegates translate for him when he met with the leaders of the British Band. According to Gratiot, the Winnebago delegates advocated peace, which they signaled by flying a white flag. When a group of Sauk warriors arrived and replaced it with a British flag, Gratiot demanded that they take it down. Instead, they mocked him by flying their British flag alongside his white flag of peace. The Winnebago delegates assured Gratiot they were attempting to dissuade the British Band and their relations among the Winnebago Prophet's followers to end their defiance, but according to Black

Hawk, "they advised us to go on—assuring us, that the further we went up Rock river, the more friends we would meet."[19] The presence of Gratiot aroused many of the younger warriors of the British Band, and they clamored to make him a prisoner and kill him. Both Black Hawk and the Winnebago Prophet went to great lengths to protect Gratiot and even posted guards near his lodge. On the second day of their mission, Gratiot and the Winnebago delegates got into their canoes and slipped past the warriors, who gave chase but did not overtake them as they made their way downstream to Rock Island.[20]

The contradictory actions of the Winnebago delegates who accompanied Gratiot revealed the deep cleavages among the Winnebagos. The Rock River Winnebagos did not officially support the 1827 Winnebago Uprising, but there were several reasons why they supported the British Band during the Black Hawk War while other Winnebago bands generally did not. First, of the fifteen Winnebago tribal leaders who visited Washington in 1828, chiefs from the Wisconsin River, Mississippi River, and Fox River bands predominated. The trip had served its purpose, and the tribal leaders who went to the East saw how numerous the Americans were. The only Rock River tribal leader on the trip, surprisingly, was White Crow, and although he supported Black Hawk, he did so covertly rather than openly. The Wisconsin, Mississippi, and Fox River bands retained their anti-Americanism but became very unwilling to engage in any future insurrections against the United States. Second, the Rock River bands, unlike the other bands, were under pressure from white miners, were scheduled for removal from their lands ceded by the 1829 treaty, and were at greater risk of losing what remained of their lands. Familial bonds were a final factor that affected the loyalty of the various Winnebago bands. The Mississippi Winnebagos had intermarried heavily with the Santee Sioux, and therefore many were of mixed Winnebago-Santee Sioux parentage or had Santee Sioux relations. These family ties brought the Mississippi River Winnebagos into a tight relationship with the enemies of the Sauks and Foxes, and, by extension, the British Band. The Rock River bands, on the other hand, being in close proximity to the Sauks and Foxes, had many members who were of mixed Winnebago and Sauk and Fox parentage (the Winnebago Prophet was a prime example) or had relatives among the Sauks and Foxes. Thus, many Rock River

Winnebagos were drawn by family ties to support the British Band. White Crow publicly professed peace many times throughout the war when talking to Indian agents and army officers, but he and other Rock River Winnebagos secretly supported the British Band. However, they would be more interested in seeking revenge against white miners than lending support for a larger pan-Indian uprising in the region.[21]

As Atkinson, Gratiot, and Keokuk worked to dissuade Black Hawk from carrying out his plans, Reynolds began to assemble his volunteer army. He initially called for 1,600 volunteers to assemble by April 22nd but later increased the number to 3,250. He ordered his militia commanders to muster their units and first ask for volunteers; if necessary, they were to levy any remaining men from a draft of the enrolled militiamen. Reynolds also ordered Isaiah Stillman, an officer in the Illinois militia, to form a two-hundred-man battalion to range the northern portion of the state from the Mississippi River eastward toward the suspected location of the British Band. One of the men who assembled at Beardstown was a lanky twenty-three-year-old from New Salem named Abraham Lincoln. Like other men who volunteered for the campaign, Lincoln dreamed of quick military glory but instead witnessed only long days of tedium and hunger. Earlier that year, Lincoln had been elected captain of the local militia company, and when other volunteers from New Salem answered Reynolds's call, they decided to bestow the honor of command on Lincoln once again. Later in his career, Lincoln would say in his well-known tongue-in-cheek manner that he was "a military hero . . . in the days of the Black Hawk war" who "fought, bled, and came away." Although he never saw even one hostile Indian, he noted: "I had a good many bloody struggles with the musquetoes [sic]."[22]

At the time, however, Lincoln was sincerely honored at leading his company of sixty-nine mounted volunteers. While at Beardstown, Lincoln's company, like others in the volunteer army, drew equipment and provisions. Like many of the volunteers under his command, Lincoln did not own a weapon, and his company drew thirty muskets (all of them smoothbore flintlocks) as well as bayonets, belts, and scabbards. Each volunteer also drew rations that included twenty-nine pounds of pork, ten and a quarter pounds of beef, forty-eight pounds of flour, and about three and a half quarts of whiskey. The Beardstown rendezvous also was occupied by the usual diversions of white frontier society. When another company commander challenged Lincoln for a prime camping location, the members of both companies decided to settle the dispute with a wrestling match. Lincoln represented his company, and although he claimed to never have been "dusted" in a "wrastle," Lincoln's rival bested him in a match that "the whole army was out to see."[23]

While these events transpired at Beardstown, Reynolds began to put his army into service. He received an urgent message on April 20th from three prominent citizens of Galena who had heard rumors of impending violence from the British Band. They believed that the local Potawatomis and Winnebagos were sure to join Black Hawk, and they warned Reynolds: "We look upon War as inevitable & and without *immediate aid* the settlers in this section will be cut off."[24] Reynolds responded by ordering the creation of another two-hundred-man ranger battalion that was nearer to the encampment of the British Band and assigned command to a militia officer, Major David Bailey. Reynolds ordered Bailey to Dixon's Ferry (present-day Dixon, Illinois) on the Rock River about thirty miles to the northeast of the Winnebago Prophet's village. Reynolds's commanders at Beardstown noted that they had more difficulties raising troops than they had anticipated and even more trouble finding enough horses. All told, 1,750 men were mustered into service, and along with the two ranger battalions under Stillman and Bailey the total number of volunteers came to a little over 2,100. They were organized into a brigade under Brigadier General Samuel Whiteside that was composed of five regiments, although the fifth regiment was not created until later from Stillman's and Bailey's ranger battalions. In addition to the four mounted regiments organized at Beardstown, there was also a spy battalion and an odd mounted battalion. Reynolds preferred mounted troops, but since many men arrived without horses and others could not be procured, those without mounts were organized as an odd infantry battalion.[25]

Atkinson did not hear about Reynolds's call for troops until April 25th, well after the organization of the Illinois volunteers was underway. He welcomed the news, and the same day he ordered Henry Dodge to begin forming a military force from among the men in the lead mining region of Michigan Territory (present-day southwestern Wisconsin) that could move down from the north in conjunction with the Illinois volunteers, who would move up from the

Figure 3. A tintype of General Samuel Whiteside in his later years. Reprinted from Stevens, *The Black Hawk War.*

south. He organized a similar force in nearby Galena. He also began to assemble a stronger force of regulars at Fort Armstrong by ordering three companies down from Fort Crawford. On April 27th, Gratiot sent Atkinson a letter in which he stated that during his tense stay at the Winnebago Prophet's village, Black Hawk had received Atkinson's message urging the British Band to return. Although Black Hawk's response indicated that he had no "bad feelings," Gratiot's letter to Atkinson had a much harsher tone and stated that "[Black Hawk's] heart is bad—that he intends to go farther up Rock River—and that if you [Atkinson] send your officers to him he will fight them."[26] Black Hawk's autobiography, not surprisingly, tells a slightly different version of this event. He stated that he would fight if Atkinson wished to initiate hostilities, but he vowed "*not to make the first attack.*"[27] Gratiot may or may not have misinterpreted Black Hawk's words, but he correctly gauged Black Hawk's next course of action. Black Hawk knew that Atkinson and his troops would arrive sooner or later, and on April 26th he decided to move the British Band farther up the Rock River to the mouth of the Kishwaukee River (the site of present-day Rockford, Illinois), where he expected to gain support from the Potawatomis and the Rock River Winnebagos.[28]

Atkinson heard of the move the next day, and in addition to promising more than three hundred regulars he asked Reynolds to march the brigade at Beardstown to Dixon's Ferry. In his letter, Atkinson once again fanned the flames by making the situation more serious than it was. He conveyed Gratiot's message and told Reynolds that Black Hawk promised that "he will fight, and that he can whip us."[29] Although he initially believed that the British Band did not pose a threat, Atkinson's attitude shifted as he heard an increasing number of reports concerning the panic of white settlers. Atkinson was not the only one guilty of stoking the fire and spreading fear among the whites. Indeed, despite the assertions of Black Hawk and the Winnebago Prophet that they would not initiate violence, their young warriors often boasted that they were determined to fight the Americans. One Sauk warrior even said to a white trader that he "would rather kill Genl. Gaines than any other being on earth."[30] Others openly boasted that they would "attack the [white] settlements in small parties & run off to Malden . . . they shall take peaceable possession of Prophets Village but if the Whites want War they shall have it."[31] The reoccupation of Saukenuk in 1831 was not accompanied by such provocative rhetoric on the part of the British Band. As these statements found their way into the settlements after the British Band crossed the Mississippi, whites abandoned their farms and headed for safer ground; many found refuge within the walls of Fort Armstrong. Governor Reynolds noted that while he was at Beardstown, he received "almost daily horrid accounts of the determined hostility of the Indians" despite the fact the British Band was still at peace and had not yet committed even one act of violence.[32]

Atkinson and the warriors of the British Band were not the only parties guilty of sowing the seeds that ultimately led to war. The Illinois volunteers who answered Reynolds's call were also culpable, for they possessed sentiments very similar to those of the warriors they would soon face. Abraham Lincoln, according to one of his men, "expressed a desire to get into an engagement" so that his men could "meet Powder & Lead."[33] Indeed, when Lincoln's men found an old Potawatomi during their march to Dixon's Ferry before the war even began, the volunteers accused him of being a "damned Spy" and wanted to kill him since "we have come out to fight the Indians and by God we intend to do so." Lincoln intervened and prevented the men of his command from committing such an act.[34] Lincoln's men were hardly alone, for once the British Band crossed the

Mississippi, many white settlers in Illinois believed, despite evidence to the contrary, that war was inevitable.[35] It was attitudes such as these on both sides that triggered the initial battle and shattered Black Hawk's plan to merely put forth a show of force.

As the British Band moved farther up the Rock River, Black Hawk began to see that the promises and predictions made by Napope would not come to pass. Black Hawk met with the chiefs of the Rock River Winnebagos, who only a few days earlier had urged him to move farther north. They now told him that they wished the British Band to move no farther up the Rock River. In admonishment, Black Hawk asked if they "had not sent [his people] *wampum* during the winter, and requested [them] to come and join their people and enjoy all the rights and privileges of their country?" The Winnebago chiefs did not deny this but added the qualification that the offer stood only "if the white people did not interfere," but the current situation made such a proposition untenable. The lukewarm support of the Rock River Winnebagos came as a stinging blow to Black Hawk. When Black Hawk saw that the Rock River Winnebago bands could not be counted on as allies, he quickly surmised the true gravity of the situation. He assembled all of his chiefs one night in secret, and told them that they had been deceived and that "all the fair promises that had been held out to us, through Ne-a-pope, were *false!*"[36]

He and his chiefs kept this news from the members of the British Band so as not to lower morale. He repeated another of Napope's promises to bolster the spirits of his lieutenants when he told them that the British would send an officer to Milwaukee to meet them in a few days with supplies. Black Hawk's only hope for additional Indian allies lay with the Potawatomis of northern Illinois and present-day southeastern Wisconsin. He took his band to the Kishwaukee River and sent out runners to the nearby Potawatomi villages. The Potawatomis sent a delegation that met with Black Hawk. When he received a series of disturbing answers that signaled their lack of interest in his cause, Black Hawk asked them if they had heard anything about the British supplies that were to be delivered to Milwaukee. When they replied that they had not, he asked to meet with the Potawatomi chiefs. His last hope was to elicit their support, but even if they gave it, the lack of British supplies would make any resistance futile. He decided that he would tell the members of the British Band that they would heed Atkinson's order and return to the west side of the Mississippi. However, before doing so, he wanted to talk with the Potawatomi chiefs and see if there was any chance of making his original plan work.[37]

Meanwhile, Whiteside's brigade began its long march to the Mississippi through the cold, rainy April weather, and it reached the Yellow Banks near present-day Oquawka, Illinois, on May 3rd. Atkinson ordered Reynolds to march the brigade to the mouth of the Rock River, where it would receive additional provisions and where he and Reynolds could decide upon a plan of action. The volunteers arrived on May 8th, whereupon Atkinson mustered them into federal service. On May 10th, Whiteside's brigade began its march up the eastern bank of the Rock River. The 340 regular troops under the command of Colonel Zachary Taylor consisted of ten companies: six companies from Jefferson Barracks, three from Fort Crawford, and another from Fort Armstrong. Since the regulars had no horses, they moved by boat up the Rock River. Under Taylor's command were Captain William S. Harney and Lieutenant Albert S. Johnston, two officers who played significant roles in the Indian wars of the West and the Civil War. Along with the boat loads of supplies, the regular troops were accompanied by the dismounted battalion of Illinois infantry volunteers that numbered about 170 men.[38]

Atkinson believed that the British Band was encamped somewhere between the Winnebago Prophet's village and Dixon's Ferry, and he told Reynolds (who served as a major general on the expedition) and Whiteside to "move upon the Indians should they be within striking distance without waiting my arrival."[39] This was another serious lapse in judgment on Atkinson's part, for he literally encouraged a group of untrained, poorly disciplined volunteers and their commanders to take matters into their own hands. This mistake came back to haunt him. Moreover, he let Whiteside's brigade lead the movement while he stayed in the rear with his detachment of regular troops. This was wholly unnecessary considering that he had an experienced officer, Zachary Taylor, commanding the detachment. Atkinson's decision meant he was not up in the front where he could have better controlled the overall movement of his eclectic expeditionary force and, most importantly, any contacts that it made with the British Band. When the men of Whiteside's brigade arrived at the Winnebago Prophet's empty village, they concluded that the British Band had abandoned the site a week earlier. Whiteside's soldiers then proceeded to burn a few of the Indians'

Figure 4. An engraving of Colonel
Zachary Taylor. Reprinted from
Stevens, *The Black Hawk War.*

dwellings. An old Potawatomi man from the area and a local white
settler had informed Whiteside and Reynolds that Black Hawk and
his followers were farther up the river.[40]

Upon resuming the march, Reynolds sent three scouts ahead of
the main body to determine the movements and location of the
British Band. They spotted one of Black Hawk's scouting parties,
which managed to elude them, and they brought this information
back to Reynolds when he arrived along with Whiteside's brigade at
Dixon's Ferry on May 12th. Reynolds then tried to send a delegation
to meet with the Potawatomis and warn them not to ally with Black
Hawk, but this party was pursued by Black Hawk's scouts and forced
to return. The reports of his scouts and the party sent to meet with
the Potawatomis indicated that Black Hawk was only about twenty-
five miles away, and Reynolds was anxious to begin operations. At
the time, the two ranger battalions under Stillman and Bailey were
also at Dixon's Ferry. Since they had assembled there and not at the
Yellow Banks, they had not been mustered into federal service and
were not under Atkinson's command. Thus, Reynolds could order
them to move forward without consulting Atkinson. Reynolds
desired the two battalions to begin reconnoitering, but Whiteside,
now in federal service, told Reynolds he was subject only to Atkinson's orders. Whiteside believed that sending the 260 men against a
larger enemy force was reckless. Nor was this the only danger, for
Henry Dodge had sent a letter to Reynolds four days earlier stating

that even if such an attack should succeed, the retreating members
of the British Band would be forced into the mining district. There
they might gain the support of the local Winnebagos, and their combined forces would wreak havoc upon the region. Reynolds was not
deterred by these arguments. On May 12th, he gave Stillman overall
command and ordered him to take the two battalions to Old Man's
Creek (present-day Stillman's Creek) about twenty-five miles to the
northeast to scout for the enemy. It was a rash and unwise decision,
which earned Reynolds no small amount of criticism afterward.
Indeed, one regular army officer noted that Reynolds "would have
done for more service and less injury by remaining in his capital."[41]

It has been asserted that the Black Hawk War could have been
avoided at this stage because none of the leaders on either side
wanted the standoff to explode into violence. This had certainly
been the case with Black Hawk and the Winnebago Prophet, and
while Atkinson's actions had done more to aggravate the situation
than to defuse it, temperamentally, at least, he had always sought to
avoid Indian wars rather than initiate them. Had he been in a position to accept peacefully Black Hawk's surrender, he undoubtedly
would have done so. Moreover, as Black Hawk began to sense that
the Winnebagos and Potawatomis were not as supportive as Napope
had promised, his resolve weakened considerably.[42] However, the
idea that the war could have been avoided because of the cool heads
that prevailed among the leadership on both sides ignores a crucial
facet of the situation. The warriors of the British Band and the Illinois volunteers had different ideas, and rash members of both groups
were determined to fight the enemy. This fact is the key to understanding why the first shots were fired during the Black Hawk War,
and why once hostilities began, it was virtually impossible to stop
the fighting or prevent a wider conflict.

Stillman marched his command north, and the next day, May 14th,
the volunteers encamped near Old Man's Creek, where they found a
large, fresh trail made by the British Band. Black Hawk at that time was
about eight miles farther north meeting with the Potawatomis. The
first meeting took place on May 13th and involved the two most prominent chiefs among the northern Illinois Potawatomis: Shabonna and
Wabaunsee. Wabaunsee was decidedly more sympathetic toward Black
Hawk's cause, but Shabonna categorically refused to take part in any
conflict with the Americans. Black Hawk, Napope, the Winnebago

Figure 5. A photograph of Shabonna taken in 1859 shortly before
his death. Reprinted from Stevens,
The Black Hawk War.

Prophet, and other leaders of the British Band had visited with Shabonna and other Potawatomi leaders in February 1832 when Black Hawk was actively working to draw the tribes of the region to the standard of the British Band. At that time, Shabonna had taken over the leadership of the Potawatomis in northern Illinois, and he staunchly rejected an alliance with the British Band. Now, four months later, he again refused to yield to Black Hawk's admonitions. Shabonna asserted that he remained committed to peace with the Americans and therefore "could not think of raising the tomahawk against their people."[43]

Black Hawk also learned that the Potawatomis had heard nothing about the British bringing arms and provisions to Milwaukee. The next day, he had a second meeting with other Potawatomi chiefs in the hope that he could persuade them. He knew that this would be his last chance to make his original plan work by winning over the remaining Potawatomi leadership, and he pulled out all the stops. He treated the chiefs (including Wabaunsee) to a feast of boiled dog, a common ceremonial meal among Great Lakes Indians. He also spread the contents of his war bundles in front of them while they ate. A Sauk war bundle (like the war bundles of other regional tribes) was usually made of deerskin and contained animal parts such as buffalo tails, eagle feathers, and hawk skins, as well as various herbs, medicines, and paints to be used in combat; some even had human scalps taken in past battles. The Indians believed that supernatural powers abounded throughout the physical world and that the owner of a war bundle, by possessing objects with certain powers, could harness them for the purpose of war. Black Hawk's most prized war bundle was the one that he had received from his father and that had belonged to his great grandfather; he considered it to represent the very soul of the Sauk nation. The contents of a war bundle were taken out only during special occasions or times of peril. Black Hawk, desperate to win the Potawatomis as allies, believed that he faced such a perilous moment. However, the arrival of Stillman's men put an end to the feast and to Black Hawk's hope to create a regional pan-Indian alliance.[44]

Toward the end of the feast, Black Hawk heard that his scouts had seen several hundred mounted white men a few miles away. He sent three of his warriors with a white flag to tell the volunteers that he wished to meet with them and announce that the British Band would return across the Mississippi. He sent a second body of five warriors to observe the proceedings and, presumably, to cover the first party in case of hostilities. The sequence of events becomes sketchy and the details vary in the extant accounts, but according to Black Hawk, the first party was taken prisoner by several of Stillman's men, and the second party ran into about twenty others who fired upon them and killed two of the Sauks. Those who escaped alerted Black Hawk, who took about forty of his warriors present with him (the bulk of the British Band was about ten miles farther north). When Black Hawk and his party saw the whole of Stillman's force coming at them at full gallop, they opened fire from behind a row of bushes in a well-drilled manner. The entire body of poorly disciplined Illinois rangers broke ranks and retreated back to Dixon's Ferry in an unorganized, panic-stricken rout. Two of the Sauks who had been taken prisoner managed to escape in the melee; the other had been shot to death by one of Stillman's men.[45]

According to white accounts, the first party sent by Black Hawk approached the Illinois rangers' camp, but because no one there spoke the Sauk and Fox language, the purpose of the Indians could not be ascertained. Some sources say that the Indians unfurled a white flag, although one less reliable source states they showed a red flag, which was a sign of war. Whether the flag was white or red, the rangers believed it a ruse for buying time so that other Indians could surround them. They took the three Sauks prisoner. Shortly thereafter, several of the rangers sighted the second party on a hill one mile to the north, and about twenty rangers pursued them. The rangers were the first to fire and killed two Sauks in the second party. Thus, it can be concluded with certainty that it was the Illinois rangers who fired the first lethal shots of the Black Hawk War. The rangers pursued the Sauks for about five miles and were soon joined by the main body of Stillman's command. As Stillman's men formed a line in a swampy area, the Sauks with Black Hawk formed a skirmish line on a piece of high ground to the north near the Kishwaukee River. An Indian (most likely Napope) once again attempted to show a white flag of peace. Stillman believed it was a trick, and he ordered his men to advance, whereupon the Sauks, believing that Stillman's men would attack, let out a loud war cry and commenced firing. The forty Sauks under Black Hawk moved forward in a disciplined manner in alternating ranks, and despite the best efforts of Stillman and his subordinate commanders to maintain order, the Illinois rangers broke ranks and fled. They did not even attempt to rally at their encampment on Old Man's Creek but instead made their way back to Dixon's Ferry. Throughout the morning on May 15th, the dazed members of Stillman's command trickled in; some did not arrive until three days later. Many of them believed they had been attacked by as many as two thousand Indians, but Black Hawk's estimate of forty is more reliable. In the end, twelve Illinois rangers had been killed. Black Hawk's men were virtually unscathed. The only Sauks killed were the three members of the two parties sent by Black Hawk to make peace. It was an embarrassing defeat for the Illinois rangers, particularly since they were defeated by a force about one-fourth their size. Alcohol definitely played a part in the defeat, for the volunteers had consumed a considerable quantity of whiskey that evening. When Black Hawk's warriors pillaged Stillman's camp the next day, they found a number of whiskey barrels; all of them were empty.[46]

While the prospects for peace were slim before the Battle of Stillman's Run, they were nonexistent afterward. Blood had been spilled, and both sides clamored to avenge their dead. Black Hawk expressed his shock not only at the fact that the Illinois rangers had attacked his warriors who had attempted to make peace, but that his small force had routed a numerically superior foe. However, he knew also

Figure 6. A daguerreotype of Major Isaiah Stillman in his later years. Reprinted from Stevens, *The Black Hawk War.*

that more whites would be sent against him, and he stated that "instead of this *honorable course* . . . I was *forced* into WAR, with about *five hundred* warriors, to contend against *three* or *four thousand!*"[47] The cry for war also rose up among the citizens of Illinois, who began to leave their farms in large numbers and either sought safety at the nearby army posts such as Fort Armstrong or began to erect stockades and blockhouses. In Washington, President Andrew Jackson, a man with much experience in Indian wars, believed that Black Hawk could not be trusted and ordered Atkinson to demand Black Hawk's surrender. Barring this unlikely scenario, Jackson ordered Atkinson to "attack and disperse them."[48]

Atkinson would rather have used a force composed entirely of regulars and dispensed with the Illinois volunteers, but the U.S. Army had no mounted troops in 1832. During the American Revolution and the War of 1812, the army had had mounted infantry, or dragoons, who fought mounted and on foot and who also served as light cavalry. However, after the war, Congress, concerned with economy, disbanded all mounted units despite objections from army commanders. For this reason, Atkinson had been forced to call up mounted volunteers during the 1827 Winnebago Uprising, Gaines had been forced to do the same to remove the British Band in 1831, and Atkinson needed mounted volunteers once again in 1832. A second problem was the small number of regular soldiers available to Atkinson. The three nearest posts—Fort Armstrong, Fort Crawford, and Jefferson Barracks—had a combined strength of only 536 men, and even the more distant posts such as Forts Snelling, Winnebago, and Howard could provide only about 400 more. When word of the disaster at Stillman's Run reached Washington in late May 1832, Congress immediately acted and appropriated $300,000 to cover the costs of the war and also authorized the establishment of a six-hundred-man mounted battalion of regulars. Several legislators noted that the conflict would most likely be over by the time this battalion was organized, but it was agreed that it would provide a well-trained mounted force for any future Indian uprisings. The war would, indeed, be over by the time the first companies of this new battalion were ready to fight, and thus, despite his reluctance, Atkinson had little choice but to employ mounted volunteers.[49]

In the immediate aftermath of Stillman's Run, the initiative belonged to the British Band. Over the course of the next five weeks, Black Hawk's warriors conducted a series of small raids and battles in Illinois and present-day Wisconsin while the Illinois volunteers were in a state of disarray. Although many of these actions were successful, none of them were decisive, and in the end the British Band would be unable, after the month of July 1832, to press what few advantages it had retained. The war dragged on for another two and a half months after the Battle of Stillman's Run. During the course of the conflict, the deep cleavages that characterized the intertribal relations of the region revealed themselves. The persistent anti-Americanism that had manifested itself in the region for over a quarter-century brought other Indians to Black Hawk's standard, but it was a limited and qualified support that made virtually no difference in the end. Of far greater consequence were the Indian tribes who counted the Sauks and Foxes among their enemies and who attacked at the first opportunity, even if it was only a small renegade faction. In addition to the mounted volunteers and regular soldiers at his disposal, Atkinson was able to take advantage of intertribal rivalries and recruit several hundred Indians to fight on the side of the United States. As the British Band learned in the months ahead, the Americans would exploit the enmity that existed among the tribes with terrifying success.

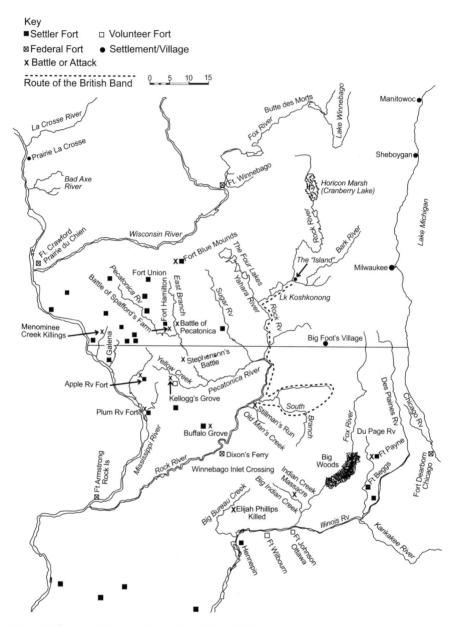

Key
■ Settler Fort   □ Volunteer Fort
⊠ Federal Fort   ● Settlement/Village
x Battle or Attack

- - - - - - - - - - - - - - - - - - -
Route of the British Band   0 5 10 15

Manitowoc ●

La Crosse River

Butte des Morts

Fox River

Lake Winnebago

Sheboygan ●

● Prairie La Crosse

Bad Axe
River

⊠ Ft. Winnebago

Horicon Marsh
(Cranberry Lake)

Lake Michigan

Ft. Crawford
Prairie du Chien

Wisconsin River

Fort Blue Mounds
x

The Four Lakes

Rock River

Bark River

The "Island"

Milwaukee ●

Fort Union

Pecatonica Rv

Battle of Spafford's Farm

Fort Hamilton

East Branch

Sugar Rv

Yahara River

Rock Rv

Lk Koshkonong

Menominee
Creek Killings

Galena

x
x Battle of
Pecatonica

Big Foot's Village ●

x Stephenson's
Battle

Yellow Creek

Pecatonica River

Apple Rv Fort

Des Plaines Rv

Chicago Rv

x
x □
Kellogg's Grove

South
Branch

Stillman's Run

Fox River

Du Page Rv

Plum Rv Fort
x

Ft Payne
x ■

Fort Dearborn
Chicago

x
Buffalo Grove

Old Man's Creek

⊠

Ft Armstrong
Rock Is

Mississippi River

Rock River

⊠ Dixon's Ferry

Big
Woods

Winnebago Inlet Crossing

Indian Creek
Massacre

Ft Beggs
■

Big Indian Creek

x

Kankakee River

Big Bureau Creek

x Elijah Phillips
Killed

Illinois Rv

□ Ft Johnson
Ottawa

Hennepin

□ Ft Wilbourn

Map 4. Theater of Operations: May–July 1832

5

THE EYE OF THE STORM

The old Chieftain small bodies of warriors sent out
To prey on the settlers scattered about.
Before in their sev'ral directions they sped,
He called them around him and solemnly said:
"This is the time to win renown
And gain the great bag handed down.
Go, show yourselves true braves to be;
Go, avenge our murdered three."
—AMER MILLS STOCKING

In the immediate aftermath of Stillman's Run, Black Hawk and his followers went back to the battleground and buried their dead and plundered the large quantity of arms, ammunition, and food left at the Illinois rangers' encampment. The British Band then moved farther north up the Rock River to find a location that provided greater security, particularly for the women and children. Black Hawk held Napope responsible for the situation of the British Band and asserted that his "British father . . . *sent word in lieu of the lies that were brought to me*, FOR US TO REMAIN AT PEACE" and that the British Band would only accomplish its own "RUIN, BY GOING TO WAR!"[1] While Black Hawk may have blamed Napope for the predicament of his band, he knew that he and his warriors now had to fight, and he did not shirk from leading them in this endeavor.

He accepted the offer of the Rock River Winnebagos to take the British Band to a secure location near Lake Koshkonong (which Black Hawk, who was unfamiliar with the area, mistakenly believed was part of the Four Lakes chain to the northwest). The main encampment of the British Band was at a point about five miles northeast of the lake at the confluence of the Rock and Bark Rivers on a piece of high ground surrounded by impenetrable swamps. The only way into this area was from the northeast, and thus the Rock River Winnebagos referred to the area as "the Island." The country was virtually unknown to whites, and it made an ideal location from which to conduct a war against nearby settlements. Two days after arriving at his camp, he called together his warriors. Presenting his war bundles, he reminded of them of their three fallen comrades who had died at Stillman's Run and addressed them saying, "Now is the time to show your courage and bravery, and avenge the murder of our three braves!"[2]

Over the course of the next month, the warriors of the British Band and their Potawatomi and Winnebago allies launched a series of raids in northern Illinois and present-day southwestern Wisconsin that spread a tremendous amount of panic among white settlers in the region. These raids reinforced whites' ideas concerning what they believed were the treachery and barbarism of Indian warfare, which depended upon ambushes, raids, and hit-and-run guerrilla tactics. However, these assessments failed to take into account the cultural practices that influenced Indian fighting methods. Indians generally avoided pitched battles that were costly in lives and fought only when they believed they could inflict damage against an enemy with a minimum number of casualties, particularly since every warrior lost meant one less man for future battles. Indian warriors preferred to utilize raids and ambushes that depended upon the element of surprise, and this reinforced in the minds of whites the "savage" nature of Indian warfare. Warriors avoided fighting an enemy with superior numbers, and they saw no shame in withdrawing from a battle when the tide had turned against them. Euro-Americans fought as units, which were essential to the maneuver of large numbers of men and which required group discipline. The Indian way of war, on the other hand, stressed individual initiative in battle. And, while Euro-Americans generally avoided aggressive actions against noncombatants such as women and children, Indians generally made no such distinctions. Finally, Euro-American warfare had as its principal strategic objective the neutralization of an enemy's ability to make war. Among the tribes of the upper Great Lakes and upper Mississippi valley, warfare served to avenge wrongs. Rather than being "massacres" as defined by whites, Indian military operations served to punish those who had committed unjust acts and to force enemies to practice what was perceived as proper behavior.[3] The raids conducted by the British Band and its allies during the spring and summer of 1832 provided textbook examples of these fighting techniques and their underlying motivations. Black Hawk did not undertake these operations in order to achieve his original goal of making a stand against removal by the federal government. As Black Hawk's speech to his warriors revealed, that objective evaporated after Stillman's Run. Instead, Black Hawk sought revenge for the deaths that his band had suffered.

For the first three weeks after Stillman's Run, the Winnebagos and Potawatomis committed all of the principal Indian attacks, but they generally used the advent of the war as an excuse to settle old scores with local whites or to achieve objectives other than those of the British Band. A group of about seven Rock River Winnebagos attacked five Illinois volunteers accompanying a mail contractor twelve miles northwest of Dixon's Ferry five days after Stillman's Run. They killed one man, William J. Durley. A war party of Potawatomis executed an even bloodier attack two days later despite the fact that Shabonna and Wabaunsee continued to advocate peace. When Shabonna received word of the British Band's victory at Stillman's Run, he and his son and nephew rode among the settlements and warned whites of the impending danger. When they arrived at Big Indian Creek, one man, William Davis, refused to leave, and he convinced several other families to stay as well. Davis had built a dam along the creek, and this prevented the fish from swimming toward the Potawatomi village six miles upstream. In the spring of 1832, he caught a Potawatomi tearing down his dam and flogged him viciously. This incident created no small amount of ill will among the Potawatomis. All told, twenty-three persons remained at the settlement when the retaliatory attack occurred. They included Davis and his family, the Hall and Pettigrew families, and three other adult men. The Potawatomi whom Davis had assaulted led the war party, which was composed of about fifty Potawatomis as well as three Sauk warriors of the British Band. At about half past four o'clock on the afternoon of May 21st, they descended upon the settlers. In a period of about ten minutes, the war party killed and dismembered fifteen men, women, and children. Several of the younger boys and men escaped, while two teenage girls, Sylvia and

Rachel Hall, were taken prisoner and moved to the camp of the British Band.[4] Davis and his mistreatment of the local Potawatomis was principal cause of the attack; Stillman's Run merely provided the spark. Moreover, Davis was the principal target; the others simply had the misfortune of being present at the time of the raid.

The Sauks who accompanied the Potawatomis spirited Sylvia and Rachel Hall northward to the camp of the British Band. At one point, the two girls watched the Sauk warriors stretch the scalps taken at Big Indian Creek onto hoops and were utterly horrified when they recognized several that belonged to their slain family members. The morning after they arrived at the camp, the girls saw the warriors erect a pole on which were hung the scalps taken during the attack. The Sauk women who attended to Rachel and Sylvia painted the sisters' faces red and black. The two girls first marched around the wigwams and then were forced to lie face down on a blanket near the pole while the warriors with their spears danced around it. The girls feared that at any moment, the warriors would thrust spears through them, but, unbeknownst to the sisters, they were in no danger. Like other Indian societies in the region, the Sauks and Foxes often spared captives so that tribal members who had recently lost family members could adopt them. The ceremony that the Hall sisters witnessed was a traditional scalp dance where the scalps taken during the raid were prominently displayed as war trophies. Concurrent with this was the adoption ceremony. Children, adolescents, and teens were seen as the ideal captives since they could replace younger tribal members lost to war or to natural causes. Thus, the Hall sisters, given their age, were spared. Sylvia and Rachel remained several more days with the British Band and received kind treatment. However, the Sauk women charged with their care watched them closely to prevent their escape.[5]

News of Stillman's Run, the Durley murder, and the attack at Big Indian Creek spread panic and prompted white settlers to organize volunteer military units for defense. By late May 1832, Galena alone counted six companies (which included a mounted company and an artillery battery), and the citizens of Galena also built a blockhouse for defense. Blockhouses and stockades went up in other settlements as well. During the course of the war, white settlers constructed upwards of thirty hastily built fortifications in this region, mostly small, cramped structures (see Appendix). Chicago became a major refuge for whites and Métis. After receiving word of Stillman's Run, Chicago Indian agent Thomas J. V. Owen sent runners to apprise settlers in the area of the danger. Within days, about 450 men, women, and children had arrived at Chicago, many bringing their cattle and horses. Most of the adult men formed a 196-man volunteer unit known as the Cook County Battalion, and along with their families, they occupied the abandoned post of Fort Dearborn. Areas farther to the east and those west of the Mississippi River were not immune from the panic, and as far away as Cincinnati men formed companies of volunteers that offered their services to the War Department. Indeed, a volunteer at Chicago noted that "one would think that Napoleon Bonaparte had risen from the grave and presented himself in the person of the Blackhawk."[6]

Although Chicago never suffered an attack during the war, the danger in northern Illinois and the lead mining region remained real, and the fortifications and blockhouses that had been erected soon became inviting targets. On May 21st, a seven-man war party, most likely composed of Rock River Winnebagos, attacked a blockhouse constructed by white settlers at the mouth of the Plum River along the Mississippi but were easily repulsed by the three men inside. The Rock River Winnebagos enjoyed greater success three days later on May 24th when a thirteen-man war party attacked a group of seven whites at nearby Kellogg's Grove (near present-day Kent, Illinois). The party killed four of the seven whites, including the Sauk and Fox Indian agent Felix St. Vrain, who was traveling with the group. About five Sauks of the British Band accompanied the war party, as did the Winnebago Prophet. In accordance with Indian custom, the warriors took the scalps of their victims.[7]

Even Indians who deserted Black Hawk used the onset of war to express anti-American sentiments. Some of the Kickapoos who had been traveling with the British Band abandoned Black Hawk shortly after Stillman's Run, but this did not stop them from holding a white trader and several friendly Potawatomis captive for a short while before letting them go. This same Kickapoo party was responsible from mid-May to late June for burning cabins abandoned by white settlers along the Fox and DuPage Rivers in northeastern Illinois, an area known as the Big Woods. Most of these Kickapoos ultimately fled to the Kickapoo villages along the Wabash River in Indiana or found refuge with the local Potawatomis. These local

Potawatomis, in all likelihood, also were responsible for many of the burning cabins along the Fox and DuPage Rivers. Moreover, all these depredations had the unintentional effect of assisting the British Band, for they led Atkinson to believe that the British Band had fled to this region after Stillman's Run. This faulty intelligence—which Black Hawk intentionally reinforced—influenced Atkinson's decisions for the next two weeks and caused him to commit his meager military resources to scouring this region in hopes of finding the British Band. Indeed, it was not until at least May 26th, when Whiteside's brigade was only days from disintegrating, that Atkinson discovered that the British Band had fled much farther to the north.[8]

The defeat at Stillman's Run on May 14th had such a negative impact upon the morale of Whiteside's brigade that Governor John Reynolds, on that same day, ordered that a new levy of two thousand troops assemble at Beardstown on June 3rd and at Hennepin on June 10th. Reynolds hoped these troops would join with those already in the field. However, further events continued to sap the morale of Whiteside's men, and they soon clamored for their discharges. A roll call taken of Stillman's two battalions the day after Stillman's Run revealed that fifty-two men were missing. It was later discovered that forty of the men simply fled in all directions after the battle and were lost for several days until they found their way back to Dixon's Ferry, but initially the news further dampened morale. The day after the battle, the troops of Whiteside's brigade moved north to survey the battlefield and bury the dead. There, the green Illinois volunteers were shocked by the sight of the bodies of their comrades, which, according to Reynolds, were scalped and "cut and mangled in a horrid manner."[9] The Illinois volunteers returned to Dixon's Ferry the next morning, and the next day, on May 17th, Atkinson arrived with his force of regulars. The Illinois volunteers expressed their dissatisfaction with the progress of the war and asked to be released from their terms of service. Reynolds and the officers of the brigade appealed to the men's sense of patriotism and convinced the volunteers to stay in service for another twelve to fifteen days.[10] They did so reluctantly.

In an effort to locate the British Band, Atkinson dispatched small scouting parties, one of which was commanded by William S. Hamilton, the son of Alexander Hamilton and a resident of the lead mining district. Hamilton was not a member of Whiteside's brigade, but he had built a small fort near his mining operation called Fort

Figure 7. A lithograph of Governor John Reynolds of Illinois. Reprinted from Reynolds, *The
Pioneer History of Illinois.*

Hamilton (present-day Wiota, Wisconsin), and organized his men in a
company for defense. He now offered Atkinson his services. Atkinson
also ordered the remaining elements of Whiteside's brigade to draw
ten days of provisions for what would be its final, inglorious mission,
and on the morning of May 19th, they marched from Dixon's Ferry.
Later that evening, Atkinson received word of the burning cabins
along the Fox and DuPage Rivers, and on May 21st Hamilton reported
that he and his scouting party had discovered a trail that led from the
area of Stillman's Run toward the Fox and DuPage Rivers. Convinced
he had located the British Band, Atkinson immediately ordered
Whiteside's brigade to scour the area between the Kishwaukee River
eastward toward the rivers. Isaiah Stillman's battered and humiliated
battalions (now mustered into federal service) remained at Dixon's
Ferry. There his men began to desert in droves, leaving the location
dangerously exposed. Atkinson returned to Dixon's Ferry on May

22nd with his regular troops so he could secure the area, particularly since he believed it was a vital communication link between Peoria and Galena.[11]

He ordered Colonel Zachary Taylor and Captain William S. Harney to stay with and supervise the volunteers, but Atkinson's absence had a further negative effect upon the army since he was not present to insure its discipline. Whiteside's men soon received word of the Big Indian Creek Massacre, which also sapped their morale, as did the fact that the volunteers' efforts at locating the British Band in the country between the Kishwaukee and Fox and Du Page Rivers proved to be fruitless. Indeed, Atkinson had fallen for one of Black Hawk's feints, for the wily Sauk did not go directly up the Rock River to Lake Koshkonong but decided instead to "go round the head of Kish-wá-co-kee, so that the Americans would have some difficulty, if they attempted to follow us."[12] Atkinson took the bait and had the volunteers follow the eastward trail. He instructed Whiteside that if his volunteers found the British Band, they were to give "pursuit of him [the enemy], persevering . . . until he is subdued or driven from the country." Reynolds would then be free to muster out his volunteers.[13]

The volunteers made no contact with the British Band, nor were they eager to do so. The later trails they discovered indicated that the British Band fled north along the Rock River after going around the headwaters of the Kishwaukee River, but the volunteers were reluctant to push north of the Kishwaukee headwaters. One member of Whiteside's brigade drew a dreary picture when he noted that over the course of several days "we changed our course very often, seemingly at a loss what direction to take."[14]

By May 23rd, the Illinois volunteers were refusing Atkinson's orders to pursue Black Hawk, and many began to desert. They had not been mustered into federal service for any stated length of time, but most assumed that the entire affair would be concluded in four weeks at the most, and they had now been in service that long. Reynolds and Taylor implored the officers to stay, but when put to a vote only half of them elected to continue. Whiteside made it clear that he no longer wanted to pursue the British Band, and since he exercised command authority in Atkinson's absence, he agreed to muster out the members of his brigade. In his autobiography, Reynolds placed the decision to dismiss the Illinois volunteers squarely upon Whiteside's shoulders, but Reynolds was actually quite willing to do so as well. The officers and men of Whiteside's brigade had buffeted him with constant calls to be mustered out of service, and he had little to promise the volunteers except additional, endless marches pursuing an enemy that seemingly could not be found. Reynolds also believed that Atkinson's orders of May 22nd gave him the authority to dismiss the troops whenever he deemed it prudent, although in reality Atkinson had stipulated that the British Band be subdued first. Nevertheless, on May 25th, Whiteside's brigade conducted its final march to Ottawa, Illinois, where on May 27th and May 28th it was mustered out of service.[15]

Atkinson was aware of the unrest that had permeated the ranks of Whiteside's brigade, and for this reason he hoped that the volunteers would find the British Band and put an end to the whole sordid affair. Barring such an optimistic outcome, he at least hoped that the brigade would stay in the field a bit longer. Reynolds's decision to dissolve the volunteer army dashed these hopes. Although Atkinson said little about the episode at the time, he was incensed by Reynolds's actions, and after the war he complained bitterly about "the embarrassment I was subjected to, by the premature discharge of Whiteside's Brigade."[16] Atkinson left Dixon's Ferry on May 28th and went to Ottawa to assist Reynolds in raising an interim body of troops from those who had been discharged; he also asked Reynolds to increase the number of men in the new levy from two thousand to three thousand. In the end, 305 Illinois volunteers from Whiteside's old brigade reenlisted in an interim regiment of six mounted companies under the command of Colonel Jacob Fry that was to serve for twenty days until a new levy could be organized. Abraham Lincoln reenlisted for this new unit, although he suffered a demotion from captain to private. Nor was he alone, for Samuel Whiteside also served as a private. Ironically, Lincoln was mustered into service by a regular officer named Lieutenant Robert Anderson, who almost thirty years later defended Fort Sumter under Lincoln's orders during the opening days of the Civil War. When asked later why he decided to reenlist, Lincoln merely stated: "I was out of work . . . I could do nothing better than enlist again."[17]

Volunteers in the lead mining region were organized by Henry Dodge with Atkinson's encouragement. Dodge was a product of America's frontier society. He was born in 1782 in Vincennes, Indi-

Figure 8. A sketch of Henry Dodge in 1833 as the commander of the United States Mounted Rangers. Reprinted from *Annals of Iowa*.

ana, and moved as a teenager with his father and uncle to the Ste. Genevieve District in what is today Missouri and which was then the Spanish province of Upper Louisiana. In addition to mining salt and lead, Dodge held numerous civil and military posts. During the War of 1812, he rose to the rank of major general in the Missouri territorial militia. In 1827, he moved to the lead mines of Michigan Territory and established what is today Dodgeville, Wisconsin. During the Winnebago Uprising that same year, Dodge offered his services to Atkinson for the campaign, and he raised a force of 130 mounted volunteers from among the local miners. In April 1832, shortly after the British Band had crossed the Mississippi, Atkinson wrote to Dodge, who held a commission as a colonel in the Michigan territorial militia, and encouraged him to begin organizing local defenses. Later, on April 25th, Atkinson once again turned to his old comrade and asked him to raise a body of mounted troops. Dodge was a wise choice, for he would be one of the most talented and able commanders that Atkinson would have during the Black Hawk War.[18]

Atkinson also directed the movements of regular troops and brought more of them under his command. Brigadier General Hugh Brady, the commander of the garrisons in the upper Great Lakes, had received orders to leave Detroit and assist Atkinson. He and his aide-de-camp left Detroit on April 16th and arrived at Fort Winnebago fourteen days later. At Atkinson's request, Brady led two companies, D and F, of the Fifth Infantry Regiment at Fort Winnebago on a march to Dixon's Ferry, where they provided Atkinson with an additional seventy-nine regulars. To compensate for the loss of men at the post, Brady ordered forty-five men of A and I Companies of the Fifth Infantry at Fort Howard to Fort Winnebago. Atkinson also ordered A and B Companies of the Sixth Infantry Regiment from Fort Leavenworth (in present-day Kansas) to join him, and this added an additional ninety-five men to Atkinson's force of regulars. All told, Atkinson had about 620 regular troops at his disposal by the month of May.[19]

Atkinson also recruited Menominee, Santee Sioux, Winnebago, and Potawatomi auxiliaries; the Menominees were particularly eager to assist. In the wake of Stillman's Run, the Menominees decided that they would be satisfied to join with the Americans and make war against the British Band (particularly since most of the Fox perpetrators of the Menominee massacre were with Black

Hawk) rather than fight the whole of the Sauk and Fox nations and incur the wrath of the federal government. Atkinson's original intent in calling for Indian auxiliaries was to organize a second force that would move from Prairie du Chien while the Illinois volunteers marched from their location in northern Illinois. At the time Atkinson made this request, the Illinois volunteers had not been mustered out of service, but he correctly observed that he would not have their services for much longer and would probably be forced to wait until the second Illinois volunteer army could be created. Thus, desperate for military manpower, Atkinson on May 26th had William S. Hamilton take a letter to the Prairie du Chien Indian agent, Joseph Street, that ordered him to collect as many Menominee and Santee Sioux warriors as possible.[20]

Street sent two of his subagents, Thomas Burnett and John Marsh, to meet with the Santee Sioux chief Wabasha at his village at Prairie Aux Ailes (present-day Winona, Minnesota). Like the Menominees, the Santee Sioux were eager to fight the British Band. On the way, Burnett and Marsh also stopped at Prairie La Crosse and talked with one of the principal chiefs of the Mississippi River bands, Winneshiek, and another Winnebago, One-Eyed Decorah. Both said that the Mississippi bands had twice received red wampum from the British Band and had rejected it. In contrast to their eagerness 1827, the Mississippi River Winnebagos, particularly those at Prairie La Crosse, were now loath to make war against the United States. Burnett and Marsh had admirably succeeded in their mission and returned to Prairie du Chien on June 5th with eighty Santee Sioux warriors and about twenty Prairie La Crosse Winnebagos. They were assisted in their recruiting by Waukon Decorah, who managed to recruit his brothers, Washington Decorah and One-Eyed Decorah. By June 7th, an additional eighty Winnebago warriors of the Mississippi River bands arrived at Prairie du Chien. To these were added forty-one Menominees at Prairie du Chien, who, according to Street, "greatly rejoiced that they would be permitted to go to war." The arrival of the Menominees raised the number of warriors in Hamilton's Indian force to 225.[21]

Hamilton planned to use this force to cut off small war parties of the British Band operating in and near the lead mining region. His force arrived in Galena on June 8th, and four days later they arrived at Buffalo Grove about ten miles northwest of Dixon's Ferry. They

encountered no enemy war parties, and the lack of any fighting dis-
couraged many of the warriors, for by the time they arrived at Buffalo Grove only 170 men remained. More warriors began to desert,
including twenty-three who made their way back through Galena.
By June 16th, Hamilton had moved his dwindling Indian force to
Fort Hamilton. He and his warriors attempted to assist Henry Dodge
at the Battle of Pecatonica, but they arrived too late to be of assistance. By July 24th, Hamilton reported to Atkinson that the lack of
activity had so disheartened the Indian force that only twenty-five
Menominees remained as a local defense force around his fort.
Joseph Street intercepted some of the returning warriors and
demanded to know the reasons they had abandoned Hamilton. One
warrior, a half-Winnebago, half-Santee Sioux named the Larc,
replied, "Our feet are sore, and our mocasins wore out; we want to
see our families."[22] Although this first attempt to recruit the Indian
auxiliaries ended in disappointment, more successful efforts came
about during the later phases of the war.

Atkinson also asked the Chicago Indian agent Thomas J. V.
Owen to provide information concerning the willingness of the
Potawatomis to serve against the British Band, and the news was
overwhelmingly positive. Atkinson was particularly eager to gain
their assistance since they possessed an intimate knowledge of the
country where the British Band had fled. Owen's task was made easier because by late May 1832 many of the Potawatomis who lived in
northeastern Illinois had congregated at Chicago in order to prevent
being killed by the ill-disciplined Illinois volunteers. About fifty
Potawatomis joined twenty whites and Métis in a scouting party,
and while they did not find any hostile Indians in the region of
northeastern Illinois, they confirmed for Atkinson that the British
Band had not fled to this area after Stillman's Run. Owen also shared
with Atkinson that he had met with Big Foot, the principal Potawatomi chief whose village stood at the western end of Lake Geneva
(present-day Fontana, Wisconsin). During the 1827 Winnebago
Uprising, Big Foot worked with the anti-American faction of the
Rock River Winnebagos under White Crow and attempted to recruit
support among the Potawatomis. For this reason, several federal
officials doubted his fidelity, and although Big Foot had hardly been
converted to the American cause, he, like many Indians in the
region with anti-American sympathies, saw little to be gained from

attempting another failed uprising. Big Foot assured Owen that he would not assist the British Band. Owen also met with Solomon Juneau, a full-blooded French Canadian trader at Milwaukee, who informed him that the confederated bands of the Potawatomi, Ojibwa, and Ottawa along the western shore of Lake Michigan—traditional allies of the Sauks and Foxes—had no intention of supporting Black Hawk. Juneau also related that the Indians at Milwaukee had received a message from Black Hawk in which he stated that because he had failed to secure any additional support, British Band would head west, skirt north of the lead mines, and attempt to cross the Mississippi.[23] Indeed, Black Hawk became painfully aware of the fact that the Sauks' and Foxes' allies would not support what they perceived to be a renegade band.

On the other hand, the Rock River Winnebagos (particularly those in the lower Rock River Valley) continued to support the British Band covertly and did just enough to assist the Americans to avert suspicion. However, Henry Dodge continued to harbor doubts, and he did much to further antagonize the Rock River Winnebagos. The main villages of these bands were at Lake Koshkonong, the Turtle Village (present-day Beloit, Wisconsin), the Four Lakes (present-day Madison, Wisconsin), the Sugar River (present-day Brodhead, Wisconsin), and the Pecatonica River (near present-day Freeport, Illinois). Whirling Thunder and White Crow were the principal leaders of these Winnebagos. Dodge held two councils with the Rock River Winnebagos in late May 1832, and in both instances, the chiefs and warriors present expressed their friendship to the United States. This goodwill seemed to be confirmed on June 1st when a party of Rock River Winnebagos under White Crow and Whirling Thunder ransomed Sylvia and Rachel Hall from the British Band and delivered the two sisters to the settler fort at the Blue Mounds. Dodge arrived at the fort about an hour later and took possession of the Hall girls. At the urging of the whites in the fort and the men under his command, he also took the entire Winnebago party hostage. Henry Gratiot caught up with Dodge, found the Winnebagos in an understandably outraged state, and in an effort to assuage their anger gave them horses and other presents. On June 3rd and 4th, Gratiot and Dodge held a council with the party, and White Crow and Whirling Thunder again voiced unequivocal friendship. However, they were not completely honest with Dodge. White Crow had, of course, urged the British Band to continue in its resistance a month earlier, and Rock River Winnebagos had committed the murders of Durley and St. Vrain's party. Moreover, the British Band was camped near Lake Koshkonong at the invitation of the Rock River Winnebagos and was receiving food and other goods from them. Dodge was rightly suspicious and demanded that the Winnebagos admit that they had sold horses and provided food to the British Band. Dodge was not fully convinced of their loyalty when the council ended, but at Gratiot's urging he released all members of the party except five: Whirling Thunder, White Crow, and three others. They were to serve as hostages to insure the good behavior of the Rock River bands. However, the damage had been done. Gratiot noted that the Winnebago party, after being taken hostage by Dodge and his men, could "scarcely brook the indignity with which they consider themselves treated."[24]

White Crow, Whirling Thunder, and the other hostages remained under the watchful eye of Dodge and Gratiot, but some of the others decided to exact revenge. On June 6th, a group of about five of the Rock River Winnebagos who had been held hostage attacked two men outside of the fort at the Blue Mounds and killed one of the men, William G. Aubrey. A few weeks earlier, a local Winnebago, Thick Lip, apparently attempting to goad Aubrey's wife, bragged that he and other Winnebagos would kill her husband and thus precipitated a minor altercation. Although the actions of Dodge were the principal cause of Aubrey's murder, and although Winnebago leaders did not name Thick Lip as one of the perpetrators, the incident between him and Aubrey's wife appears to have influenced the choice of the target.[25]

Because they were Dodge's hostages, White Crow and Whirling Thunder were forced against their will to serve against Black Hawk for the next month as spies. On June 14th, Gratiot, at Dodge's request, sent the five hostages and a French Canadian named Oliver Emmell (who was married to a half-blood Winnebago woman) on a spy mission to ascertain the strength and position of the British Band. They stopped first at the Winnebago village at Lake Koshkonong, where one warrior threatened to kill Emmell because the "French, English, and Americans all smell alike . . . for we have determined that all who wear hats shall be treated as enemies."[26] White Crow managed to keep the warrior from killing Emmell, and he and

the other Winnebago spies dressed him as an Indian in order to protect him before they proceeded to the nearby camp of the British
Band. The party returned almost two weeks later and provided valuable intelligence and confirmed what the Potawatomis had told
Owen earlier: that the British Band planned to move west and cross
the Mississippi. White Crow had not completely succumbed to
American blandishments, however, and he told Gratiot upon his
return that the Indians under Keokuk were "hypocrites pretending
to be friends" who should be destroyed by the United States.[27]

While White Crow and Whirling Thunder were at the camp of the
British Band, Black Hawk and his warriors were absent conducting
attacks. The narrative of Rachel Hall indicates that the British Band
arrived at its Camp near Lake Koshkonong on May 28th, two weeks
after Stillman's Run. Once settled in, Black Hawk immediately had
his warriors secure provisions. Only after this was done, roughly three
weeks after Stillman's Run, did Black Hawk consider beginning large-
scale attacks against the Americans. Indeed, the only warriors of the
British Band who partook in attacks during this period were those
who accompanied some of the Potawatomi and Winnebago war parties. Black Hawk delayed, in part, because, after hearing that Whiteside's brigade had disbanded, he believed that time was on his side.
His decision to begin launching attacks was most likely based upon
his discovery that Atkinson was forming another volunteer army. He
also decided to conduct his operations farther to the west, most likely
to draw Atkinson and his new army away from the main camp of the
British Band near Lake Koshkonong. The first known attack committed by the British Band occurred on June 8th when a group of warriors
stole twelve horses from the fort erected along the Apple River (near
present-day Elizabeth, Illinois) and shot at two men, both of whom
made it safely into the fort.[28]

It is ironic that at this time Abraham Lincoln, who later professed to have never seen a hostile Indian during the war, passed
through the region where Black Hawk and his two hundred warriors
lay in wait. Atkinson had not heard anything from Galena in many
days, and he ordered Elijah Iles's company, which belonged to the
interim regiment, to march there and reopen communications. Lincoln was a member of Iles's company, which departed from Ottawa
on June 6th. The mission proceeded without so much as a shot being
fired, although Iles's men did mistake Henry Dodge's command

(which was on the way to Dixon's Ferry) for a party of the enemy; luckily, no gunshots were exchanged. They also passed by Hamilton's Indian force at Buffalo Grove. On their way to Galena, Iles's men had only seen the abandoned homes of white settlers. They reached the Apple River Fort on June 8th, the same day that Black Hawk's warriors committed their attack there. Iles and his men found all of the settlers inside the stockade and genuinely terrified. Iles's company reached Galena on June 10th, and one member later admitted that he and several other men visited the whorehouses while there; he did not say if Lincoln joined them. After Iles and his men departed Galena the next day and began their march back to Ottawa, they noticed that the same homes they had passed only days earlier were abandoned and now burning.[29]

Obviously, Black Hawk's warriors had been active in the area. Those who went west to commit raids and attacks in northwestern Illinois and present-day southwestern Wisconsin created two large war parties, each with about two hundred warriors, and they probably worked as smaller units when circumstances necessitated it. On June 9th, a number of Black Hawk's warriors plundered a farmhouse roughly six miles from the Apple River Fort. Five days later, on June 14th, thirty miles to the north, members of another war party conducted the first major attack by the British Band when they targeted the farm of Omri Spafford about five miles southeast of William Hamilton's fort in Michigan Territory. About thirty of Black Hawk's warriors surrounded six men as they worked in a field and killed and scalped four of them; the other two escaped, and one of the fleeing survivors managed to kill a warrior.[30] Commonly called the Battle of Spafford's Farm, the attack was of little importance, but it led to the next major battle in the region, and the first real loss for Black Hawk's men.

A few members of the war party that attacked Spafford's farm found themselves in much less comfortable circumstances two days later. Upon hearing of the battle, Henry Dodge led his company from Fort Union at Dodgeville to nearby Fort Hamilton to find and engage the war party. Upon their arrival, Dodge's men learned that the war party that attacked Spafford's farm had just killed a German named Henry Apple about half a mile away. Dodge took twenty-nine men, sighted the war party, pursued it for about two and half miles, and finally cornered eleven warriors in a horseshoe-shaped bend of the

Pecatonica River. Dodge posted four men on a nearby piece of high ground to prevent any escape by the Indian warriors, left another four with the horses, and advanced on foot with twenty-one men (see Figure 9). The warriors of the British Band opened fire and severely wounded four of Dodge's men, two of them fatally. Not to be outdone, Dodge's men opened fire and in less than a minute killed all eleven warriors (although some of Dodge's men later claimed the number was seventeen). Dodge's men even scalped them in the Indian manner. Within an hour, William Hamilton arrived with his force of friendly Menominees and a few Winnebagos who, as mentioned, were too late to join the battle. Dodge let the friendly Indians have the scalps and noted that they "appeared delighted with the scalps [and] they went to the ground where the Indians were killed and cut them literally to pieces."[31] Commonly called both the Battle of Pecatonica and the Battle of Horseshoe Bend, the first real victory for the United States in the Black Hawk War had been produced by Henry Dodge. While it was not a significant tactically or strategically, it was an important psychological victory. Citizens of the lead mining region greatly rejoiced and applauded Dodge for his triumph. The citizens of Prairie du Chien officially expressed their appreciation for Dodge by presenting him with the gift of a double-barreled shotgun, and they praised "the bold and energetic course which you have pursued in behalf of our suffering country."[32]

That same day, about twenty-five miles to the south, another war party had somewhat better luck. Adam Snyder, who commanded one of the companies of the interim regiment, was ordered by Zachary Taylor to proceed to Kellogg's Grove along with three companies of regulars under Major Bennett Riley. By this time, Atkinson knew that the main camp of the British Band was near Lake Koshkonong, and Taylor believed that Snyder's men and the regulars could, by occupying Kellogg's Grove, cut the lines of communication between the main camp and Black Hawk's war parties operating farther to the west. On the night of June 15th, one of Snyder's sentinels came under fire, and the next morning Snyder left camp with forty-three men in pursuit of the enemy. About thirty miles to the west, Snyder's men found an abandoned camp and a trail that led back to the east. They went back the way they had come, and during the pursuit overtook and killed four warriors while losing one Illi-

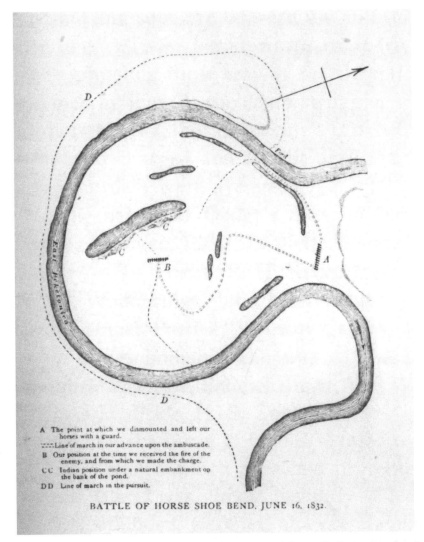

A   The point at which we dismounted and left our
      horses with a guard.
:::: Line of march in our advance upon the ambuscade.
B   Our position at the time we received the fire of the
      enemy, and from which we made the charge.
C C Indian position under a natural embankment on
      the bank of the pond.
D D Line of march in the pursuit.

BATTLE OF HORSE SHOE BEND, JUNE 16, 1832.

Figure 9. Diagram of the Battle of Pecatonica (also called the Battle of Horseshoe Bend). Reprinted from *Iowa Historical Record.*

nois volunteer. Snyder's company made contact with the war party's main body of about thirty warriors near Kellogg's Grove. The Indians laid in ambush and killed two volunteers. The Indians held a piece of high ground while Snyder's men formed a line about one hundred yards away. Firing commenced on both sides, although the war party stopped firing when one of Snyder's men (ironically, it was former Brigadier General Samuel Whiteside) killed the war party's leader. The Indians withdrew to some thick brush, and the volunteers, paralyzed by the excitement and fear that came from participating in their first real action, consulted for the next half-hour over whether to pursue the war party. By that time, nightfall was coming and pursuit was deemed impossible. The Illinois volunteers had lost a total of three men while the British Band had lost five in what is known as the First Battle of Kellogg's Grove.[33]

It was most likely this same war party or part of it that returned to the Apple River. On the morning of June 18th a group of eighteen mounted volunteers from Galena and the Apple River Fort under the command of James Stephenson followed the trail of a ten- or eleven-man war party and made contact with it along Yellow Creek roughly twelve miles east of Kellogg's Grove. The volunteers pursued the warriors of the British Band into a dense thicket where a pitched battle ensued that involved close-quarter fighting. Three volunteers and five, or possibly six, members of the Indian war party were killed (Black Hawk later asserted that only one of his men died, but he was not present at the battle). The two parties were a mere thirty feet apart, but about half of the war party managed to escape into the thicket. The Rock River Winnebagos also made attacks in this region, and on June 20th, a war party of at least forty (including some from the Winnebago Prophet's village) launched a second attack against the settler fort at the Blue Mounds and killed two white men. One of the men was particularly mutilated after he was killed, and in addition to being scalped, his arms, legs, and head had been severed and his heart torn out of his chest.[34]

As these attacks occurred to the west, the area of northeastern Illinois remained relatively quiet for three weeks after the attack on Big Indian Creek. The only white person killed during this period was an itinerant preacher named Adam Payne, who was shot to death on May 24th about fifteen miles northeast of Ottawa. Payne's killing was almost certainly the work of local Potawatomis. On June 16th, a war party of between fifteen to twenty-eight Indians killed an Illinois volunteer about a mile and half from a settler fort known as Fort Payne (present-day Naperville, Illinois). On June 24th, a party of between ten to fourteen warriors killed three white settlers near Big Indian Creek. Thomas J. V. Owen reported that the Potawatomis had seen a twenty-eight man Sauk war party in the area, but there remains some doubt whether this was true. All three sets of killings occurred in an area inhabited by the Potawatomis, and Black Hawk's main war parties at the time were working much farther to the west. Moreover, no sources mention any war parties of the British Band working in this area. Of course, the Potawatomis who related the information to Owen may have intentionally lied in order to protect their anti-American kinsmen. Indeed, Potawatomis most likely committed these attacks, although the stray Kickapoo band that was known to be in the area since crossing the Mississippi with Black Hawk may also have committed them. It was definitely Potawatomis who carried out the attack on June 18th along Bureau Creek. There, a war party killed a settler, Elijah Phillips, as he left the house of another settler, John Ament. As with the Big Indian Creek Massacre, local disputes, rather than Black Hawk's call to arms, had been the cause. Ament had claimed land upon which local Potawatomis harvested maple sugar for many years. The Potawatomis would have preferred to kill Ament (who had also shot some of the Potawatomis' dogs). However, Phillips was the first to leave Ament's cabin while the war party waited in ambush, and he caught a bullet in the chest.[35]

Black Hawk at the time continued to operate farther to the west. On the afternoon of June 24th, he led his two-hundred-man war party against the Apple River Fort, which possessed a garrison of roughly thirty-six Illinois volunteers. A party of four Illinois volunteers acting as couriers had stopped at the fort, and after eating and resting, they resumed their journey toward Dixon's Ferry. They had traveled five hundred yards when Black Hawk's warriors opened fire. The four volunteers immediately yelled as though they were summoning a larger force to their rear. Although no such force existed, it had the desired effect, for Black Hawk's warriors fell back, took cover, and awaited the approach of reinforcements that never arrived. The ploy gave the four men the opportunity to run to the safety of the fort and warn the volunteers and local settlers. This proved fortuitous for them, for Indian warfare depended to a large extent upon surprise, and now this element was lost to Black Hawk. Instead, he and his warriors commenced a forty-five-minute siege against the fort. Inside, women and young girls molded bullets and loaded muskets while the volunteers returned the warriors' fire. One man raised his head above the pickets to take aim, whereupon one of Black Hawk's men took a well-directed shot and killed him. Surprisingly, he was the only white person killed during what was a very pitched battle, which afterward became known as the Battle of Apple River. Black Hawk, on the other hand, lost several men (the exact number is unknown), and he concluded that it would be futile to press the attack any further. Black Hawk was again following Indian martial conventions, for warriors generally avoided prolonged sieges. Black Hawk's men settled instead for pillaging the local homes and took all the horses, about thirty cattle (a few of which were slaughtered and butchered on the spot), and a number of hogs.[36] Black Hawk and his war party moved to the northeast afterward, little knowing that they would engage in another major battle the next day at Kellogg's Grove.

Reynolds and Atkinson had not been idle, and during this time they began to create a new army of volunteers to replace Whiteside's brigade. They established a small installation known as Fort Wilbourn (opposite present-day LaSalle, Illinois) ten miles downstream from Ottawa on the south bank of the Illinois River. This was the highest point on the river to which steamboats could navigate, an ideal location because it could serve as both a supply depot and assembly point for the new levy of volunteers. The area around Fort Wilbourn soon teemed with men and horses, and one regular army officer described the volunteers as "a swarming hive; catching horses, electioneering, drawing rations, asking questions, shooting at marks, electing officers, mustering in, issuing orders, disobeying orders, galloping about, 'cussing and discussing' the war, and the rumors thereof."[37]

By June 16th, the First Brigade had been organized under the command of Brigadier General Alexander Posey and had a total of 962 men and officers. The next day, the Second Brigade with 959 men under the command of Brigadier General Milton K. Alexander came into existence; and, finally, on June 18th, the Third Brigade was formed with 1,275 men under the command of James D. Henry. Henry, who fought as a teenager in the War of 1812, proved to be the most valuable of the three brigade commanders. The First and Second Brigades were composed of three regiments while the Third Brigade had four. Regiments generally had five companies (the average size of which was fifty men), although the Second and Third Brigades had regiments with six and even seven companies. Each

Figure 10. A lithograph of General Milton K. Alexander, based on a daguerreotype and reprinted from Armstrong, *The Sauks and the Black Hawk War.*

brigade also had a spy battalion composed of three companies. In addition to these 3,196 mounted volunteers, Atkinson also had fourteen companies of regular infantry composed of 629 men at Dixon's Ferry. However, Atkinson was forced to detach many volunteers and regulars to guard logistics depots and to serve as local security forces. Thus, he had only about 450 regulars and 2,100 volunteers at his disposal when he began his campaign in late June. He dubbed this eclectic force of volunteers and regulars the "Army of the Frontier." A New York journalist traveling through Illinois in the summer of 1832 passed by Dixon's Ferry and saw the raw volunteers who composed the bulk of the Army of the Frontier. He described

them as "a hard-looking set of men, unkempt and unshaved, wearing shirts of dark calico, and sometimes calico capotes [hoods]"; he
also noted that the local settlers complained that the volunteers
were more apt to make "war upon the pigs and chickens" than the
British Band.[38]

In addition to the three brigades of the Army of the Frontier,
Reynolds and Atkinson also authorized the creation of odd battalions
and companies, and other independent units. Most, but by no means
all, served as local defense forces, and many were not taken into federal service. It is difficult to know how many of these units there were
and how many men actually served during the war, but in Illinois
alone it has been estimated that between six and seven thousand men
served in some capacity. Abraham Lincoln joined one of the independent units after mustering out of the interim regiment. Lincoln joined
the odd company of Jacob Early, which Atkinson had ordered into federal service as an "independent spy company" that was to operate sep-
arately of the three brigades of the new army. Another important unit
that was separate of the Army of the Frontier (although ultimately
under Atkinson's command) was the battalion of mounted volunteers
commanded by Henry Dodge. By late May, Dodge had fifty mounted
volunteers organized into two companies. In early June, Atkinson,
knowing that Dodge was an asset that could not be squandered,
ordered units of Illinois volunteers from Galena to join Dodge's command; this gave Dodge an additional 213 men. At its strongest,
Dodge's command had a total of 250 men, but, as with most volunteer
units during the Black Hawk War, his battalion suffered the usual
problems of having to discharge men for a variety of reasons such as
attending to affairs back home or having horses that were unfit for
service. By mid-July, Dodge commanded 150 men organized into a
battalion of five companies.[39]

Atkinson also continued to recruit and employ Indian auxiliaries for a variety of purposes. He recruited a large contingent of
Potawatomis from the Chicago area and from the western shore of
Lake Michigan to accompany his new army and act as scouts and
guides since they were familiar with the region around Lake Koshkonong. He would ultimately have a total of ninety-four Potawatomi guides and scouts. There were fourteen prominent civil chiefs
and war leaders among the assembled Potawatomis, led by Billy
Caldwell. Caldwell, of Anglo-Irish and Mohawk ancestry, had had a

colorful career as a British army officer in Canada and a trader at Chicago. In his later years, he attained a position of influence among the Potawatomis in northern Illinois. Shabonna, Wabaunsee, and Big Foot also served along with Caldwell.[40]

The Indians had already been extremely valuable to Atkinson up to this point, even more so than to Black Hawk, particularly because they provided Atkinson with crucial intelligence concerning the location of the British Band and its planned movements. Prior to disbanding, Whiteside's brigade had at least confirmed for Atkinson that the British Band had fled north and not eastward toward the Fox and DuPage Rivers as he had initially believed. Several Winnebagos ultimately provided Atkinson with the exact location of the British Band. The Rock River Winnebagos told Dodge on June 4th that the British Band was at the confluence of the Bark and Rock Rivers about five miles northeast of Lake Koshkonong. Waukon Decorah of the Mississippi bands and his brothers gave this same information to Indian agent Joseph Street at Prairie du Chien on June 6th, as did Wabaunsee when he met with Owen at Chicago on June 11th. By June 11th, Atkinson was in possession of this valuable intelligence, although knowledge of the region was poor (as were his maps) and he erroneously believed that Lake Koshkonong was part of the Four Lakes chain. Equally valuable was the information provided by Big Foot and other Potawatomis that the British Band planned to flee west and cross the Mississippi River. Thus, he was able with confidence to report to General Alexander Macomb in Washington that he had "a reasonable prospect" of defeating the British Band before it began moving west, stating, "I cannot fail to put an end in a short time to the perplexed state of Indian hostility."[41]

Not everyone in Washington shared his optimism, for both the secretary of war and the president began to grow impatient with Atkinson's apparent lack of progress. The acting secretary of war wrote a rather petulant letter to Atkinson on June 12th stating that he and the secretary of war had received numerous letters regarding the war from persons at Dixon's Ferry, St. Louis, Rock Island, Chicago, Detroit, Galena, and Prairie du Chien, but they had not received any correspondence from Atkinson since early May. The acting secretary asserted that President Andrew Jackson "views with utter astonishment and deep regret this state of things." He went on to say that Atkinson's last communication of May 10th indicated that he had an adequate force, and thus the president had "a right to anticipate promptness and . . . a speedy and effectual termination of Indian hostilities." The letter concluded with the rather ominous warning that "some one is to blame in this matter, but upon whom it is to fall is at present unknown to the Department."[42]

Atkinson responded by saying that he had written numerous letters to the commanding general of the army, Alexander Macomb. Atkinson's judgment in doing so was sound but he had failed to take into consideration the nebulous political situation that existed. The office of commanding general had been ill defined since its creation after the War of 1812, and although Macomb considered himself to be the principal commander of all armies in the field, Secretary of War Lewis Cass and President Jackson believed that Macomb's role was largely advisory and that they were responsible for the conduct of military operations. Thus, Cass and Jackson believed that they, not Macomb, should have been the recipients of Atkinson's reports. Moreover, 1832 was an election year, and Jackson was locked in a difficult battle with the National Republicans under his rival, Henry Clay. While Jackson's war against the Bank of the United States took center stage in Washington that summer, the Black Hawk War was becoming another thorn in his side, and anti-Jackson newspapers like the *National Intelligencer* took much delight in criticizing the slow pace of the conflict. Jackson could ill afford for the war to drag on and affect his reelection prospects. Therefore, three days after the acting secretary of war wrote his scathing letter to Atkinson, Jackson ordered General Winfield Scott, commander of the Eastern Department, to take troops from eastern garrisons and repair to Chicago to take command of the theater of war. However, Atkinson would not receive this news until the early part of July.[43]

President Jackson had added a postscript to the letter sent by the acting secretary of war and instructed Atkinson that "the black Hawk & his party must be chastised and a speedy & honorable termination put to this war, which will hereafter deter others from the like unprovoked hostilities by Indians on our frontier."[44] Jackson's postscript is instructive because it illustrates why the federal government felt it necessary to prosecute a war against the British Band in the summer of 1832. Black Hawk, of course, felt compelled to fight in order to avenge his warriors' deaths at Stillman's Run. Federal officials and their white constituents, on the other hand,

GEN. ANDREW JACKSON.

Figure 11. An engraving of President Andrew Jackson. Reprinted from Stevens, *The Black Hawk War.*

believed that if Black Hawk and his followers were not thoroughly defeated, their disaffection might spread to the Potawatomis, Winnebagos, Santee Sioux, and other tribes. This explains why, in the wake of Stillman's Run, neither Atkinson nor any other white Americans made any attempt to end the situation diplomatically. Such a solution would have been possible had Atkinson or some other American official decided to use the Winnebagos or Potawatomis as envoys to the British Band, but in the minds of virtually all white Americans, Stillman's Run and the subsequent attacks committed by the British Band negated any peaceful solution. Moreover, the fact that the anti-American Rock River Winnebagos and Potawatomis were using the war as an excuse to commit their own attacks only hardened these attitudes. Thus, Black Hawk would not be allowed to surrender or escape unharmed to the west side of the Mississippi; his people would have to be brutally punished, if for no other reason than to serve as a chilling example for other tribes. Lewis Cass summed up these sentiments perfectly when he described what a failure to punish the British Band would mean. "Year after year, our frontier may be exposed, the settlers driven in with the loss of their crops . . . the people harrassed by continued militia calls, heavy expenses entailed upon the government, and our standing and influence with the Indians destroyed, unless an example is now made, the effect of which will be lasting." Thus, Henry Atkinson, even before he received instructions from Washington concerning how to prosecute the war, essentially knew what was expected of him.[45]

Although he was anxious to prosecute his next campaign, Atkinson had no desire to see a replay of the mistakes that had led to Stillman's Run. He became a more attentive commander, as illustrated by his initial orders for the campaign, which mirrored almost exactly the standard practices laid out in the *General Regulations of the Army* for the period. He ordered that all movements be in columns that had flank, rear, and advanced guards to prevent surprise attacks. All encampments had to be square and troops were to remain mounted while occupying an encampment until guards were posted. If attacked while in camp, troops were to form a line immediately in front of the tents. From June 20th to the 23rd, Atkinson also had each of the three brigades conduct independent marches to Dixon's Ferry, which served as the marshalling area for the new army. Thus, if Black Hawk's warriors attacked, he would suffer, at most, the loss of only one-third of his army rather than all of it. He also ordered Jacob Early's independent spy company to Dixon's Ferry, and Atkinson ordered Colonel Zachary Taylor (who remained in command of the regular forces there) to begin employing Early's company as he saw fit.[46]

Upon hearing of the murder of Elijah Phillips, Atkinson decided to use part of his new army to scour the area along Bureau Creek, and he ordered the First Brigade's spy battalion (which was considered one of the better units) to perform detached service. The spy battalion departed Fort Wilbourn on June 19th under the command of Major John Dement and spent several fruitless days looking for the war party that had killed Elijah Phillips. After performing this duty, Dement was ordered to report to Taylor at Dixon's Ferry. Dement and his men arrived there sometime between June 21st and the 23rd, about the same time as the volunteers of Captain Adam Snyder and the regulars under Major Bennet Riley had arrived after departing Kellogg's Grove. Riley's and Snyder's troops had remained there after the First Battle of Kellogg's Grove, and they used that time to fortify the house that stood there. However, Snyder and his men were on twenty-day enlistments, and they departed once their enlistments ended. The regulars left as well, most likely because Riley did not think his three companies of dismounted infantry would be of much use without mounted troops. Taylor, whose original impetus for sending Snyder's and Riley's men to Kellogg's Grove was to intercept war parties operating in the region, did not want to see the area abandoned, so he immediately ordered Dement's men to occupy Kellogg's Grove. Taylor had to implore the tired volunteers to assume this new mission, and, according to one source, he argued: "You are citizen soldiers, and some of you may fill high offices, or even be President some day, but never unless you do your duty."[47] An interesting footnote is that Taylor later became the president of the United States, and Abraham Lincoln (who arrived at Dixon's Ferry a few days later) also served as president.

Dement's battalion arrived at Kellogg's Grove on June 23rd. At about 4:00 a.m. on June 25th, a local miner brought word that a large trail had been found eighteen miles to the west. At daybreak, Dement took about thirty men and headed out to see the trail, which he conjectured had been made by the main body of the British Band moving west to cross the Mississippi. In reality, the trail had been made by Black Hawk's two-hundred-man war party as it made its way to attack the Apple River Fort the day before. Having finished the attack, Black Hawk decided to head back to Lake Koshkonong. While traveling east, Black Hawk sighted Dement's scouting party about a mile and half from Kellogg's Grove. He ordered his warriors to hide in a nearby thicket. A small advanced guard of between six to eight volunteers, riding half a mile ahead of Dement's scouting party, saw several of Black Hawk's men in the distance, and in their excitement they pursued the warriors. It was a foolish move, for they rushed headlong into an ambush; Black Hawk's men began firing and killed two of them. Dement rushed forward with the remainder of his party; he later stated that he was "bravely animating his little party, to stand and relieve their brother soldiers" and that the men with him "bravely met the charge of upwards of two hundred Select Warriors."[48] He conveniently forgot to mention that most of the men with him retreated back toward their camp when

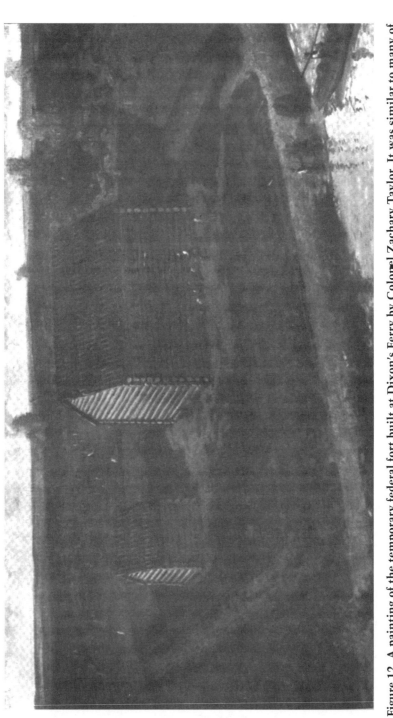

Figure 12. A painting of the temporary federal fort built at Dixon's Ferry by Colonel Zachary Taylor. It was similar to many of the temporary fortifications built during the Black Hawk War. Reprinted from Stevens, *The Black Hawk War.*

the firing commenced. However, Black Hawk was impressed with Dement's leadership and noted that he and several of his men stood their ground and "acted like *braves*."[49]

After the surviving members of the advanced guard rejoined Dement, he wisely retreated back to Kellogg's Grove. Black Hawk's warriors pursued and took cover in a small ravine along the edge of the prairie surrounding the fort. Several of the volunteers who had fled from the initial melee went back and warned their comrades, whom Dement, before leaving, had ordered to be ready to fight. Dement managed to rally at least some of his men upon arriving at his camp, and soon a pitched battle ensued as Black Hawk's war party swept out of the ravine. The surrounding prairie became a scene of considerable confusion. Dement continued his attempts to rally his panic-stricken men, but they instinctively headed toward the relative safety of the fort, which had no stockade around it and was little more than a three-room log house with reinforced walls and a sturdy door. Soon, the entire battalion of roughly 140 men was crowded into the tiny structure. Three volunteers failed to make it into the fort and were killed by Black Hawk's men. The other volunteers continued to fire from inside and killed nine of Black Hawk's men. Unable to engage the volunteers, Black Hawk's warriors began to shoot their horses; they killed at least thirty-two, wounded another fifteen (many of which subsequently died), and fourteen more were either taken by the war party or wandered off during the battle. Black Hawk's warriors continued their siege for two hours. Dement believed that the bravery of his men caused the warriors to end their attack, but, as Black Hawk made clear, his men were only too eager to continue their assault and burn the fort. Black Hawk did not think this a wise use of their available gunpowder, and, like all Indian war leaders, he disliked sieges. He believed his warriors had accomplished their objective and noted: "as we had run the bear into his hole, we would there leave him."[50] Thus ended what is known as the Second Battle of Kellogg's Grove.

The five dead volunteers brought the death toll of whites up to sixty-two, while the nine dead warriors pushed Black Hawk's losses up to between thirty-five and forty men. The number of whites included two settlers who were killed on June 29th along the Menominee Creek near Sinsinawa Mound (in present-day Grant County, Wisconsin), although this attack was most likely committed by either

Foxes or Iowas who sympathized with the British Band. The casualties on both sides had been rather light but steady, and this caused
Governor John Reynolds to write, "Blood flows here on a small scale
tolerably fast."[51] The blood continued to flow, but increasingly it was
that of the British Band. The supply of available white volunteers was
relatively inexhaustible; Black Hawk, on the other hand, had lost
roughly ten percent of his available warriors, and he lacked the ability
to replace those who died. The Second Battle of Kellogg's Grove was
Black Hawk's last victory and ended a string of successes that he
enjoyed in the five weeks after Stillman's Run. However, none of
these battles had been decisive. Indeed, Atkinson described them as
"annoying" and "distressing"; he knew Black Hawk's attacks had not
gained the British Band any real advantage.[52] Black Hawk understood
this as well, and he returned with his war parties to the main camp of
the British Band at Lake Koshkonong. He learned that Atkinson had
started to move with his new army, and this influenced his decision
to begin moving the British Band and, hopefully, escape to the safety
of the west side of the Mississippi. He was also influenced by the fact
that the British Band was desperately short of food. The unexpected
flight to Lake Koshkonong disrupted Black Hawk's original plans to
grow corn at the Winnebago Prophet's village, and although the Rock
River Winnebagos supplied the British Band with some food while at
Lake Koshkonong, they did not have enough of a surplus to feed an
additional one thousand mouths. By late June, Black Hawk's people
were forced to dig for roots and eat tree bark. The day after Black
Hawk arrived back at Lake Koshkonong, the British Band commenced
its movement toward the Mississippi.[53] First, however, it had to evade
Atkinson by moving farther to the north.

Atkinson knew that Black Hawk was going to attempt to cross
the Mississippi, but he hoped to catch the British Band before it
began its movement. He had become far more judicious and refused
to react impulsively to every small-scale assault or depredation.
This is well illustrated by his actions in the aftermath of the Second
Battle of Kellogg's Grove. At about 8:00 a.m., as the fighting began to
wane at Kellogg's Grove and Black Hawk's war party started its
withdrawal, Dement sent a five-man detachment to Dixon's Ferry
to inform his superior, General Posey, of the battle. Posey assumed
that the war party conducting the attack had been the main body of
the British Band, and when he and his men arrived at Kellogg's

Grove by 6:00 p.m. that day, Dement implored him to begin a pursuit. Posey believed it was too late in the evening and refused. As it turned out, he did exactly what Atkinson wanted him to do, for the next day, on June 26th, Atkinson ordered Posey to remain at Kellogg's Grove and gather whatever intelligence he could about the subsequent movements of the war party. Atkinson disregarded Posey's assertion that the battle had been the work of the entire British Band and noted correctly that the attack had been carried out by only "a detachment of the enemy . . . in order to draw my attention from a pursuit of the main body up Rock river."[54]

Nevertheless, on June 26th, Atkinson ordered Milton Alexander to take his brigade west toward the Plum River in the unlikely event that Posey was correct and the British Band was making its way toward the Mississippi. Indeed, Atkinson took no chances and sought to insure that even the most remote possibilities did not become humiliating fiascos. Posey remained at Kellogg's Grove, and Atkinson berated him on June 28th for failing to provide the intelligence he had asked for two days earlier. Atkinson had also ordered Jacob Early's company to move to Kellogg's Grove and gather additional intelligence. Early's company departed Dixon's Ferry on the night of the battle and arrived at Kellogg's Grove at sunrise the next day. There, Abraham Lincoln and his comrades had the melancholy duty of burying the dead Illinois volunteers, using only hatchets. Early also developed a low opinion of Posey's abilities and believed that his "tardy movements" had prevented him from gathering the information Atkinson desired.[55] Of course, Black Hawk left the area after the battle and headed back to Lake Koshkonong, but had Posey been more prompt and aggressive, he probably could have alerted Atkinson to this fact. Even then, the information probably would have done little or nothing to change Atkinson's battle plan; on June 28th, he began moving his army forward from Dixon's Ferry toward Lake Koshkonong in order to finish the war that Isaiah Stillman's ill-disciplined volunteers had started six weeks earlier.[56]

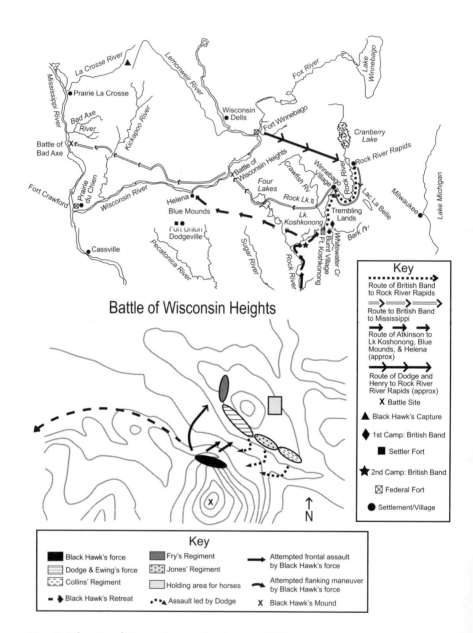

Battle of Wisconsin Heights

Key

Route of British Band to Rock River Rapids

Route to British Band to Mississippi

Route of Atkinson to Lk Koshonong, Blue Mounds, & Helena (approx)

Route of Dodge and Henry to Rock River River Rapids (approx)

X Battle Site

▲ Black Hawk's Capture

◆ 1st Camp: British Band

■ Settler Fort

★ 2nd Camp: British Band

⊠ Federal Fort

● Settlement/Village

Key

Black Hawk's force

Dodge & Ewing's force

Collins' Regiment

Black Hawk's Retreat

Fry's Regiment

Jones' Regiment

Holding area for horses

Assault led by Dodge

Attempted frontal assault by Black Hawk's force

Attempted flanking maneuver by Black Hawk's force

X Black Hawk's Mound

Map 5. Theater of Operations: July–August 1832

6

THE SILENCE AND THE FURY

It was June the eighth and twentieth day
When Atkinson's forces started away
From Dixon's, their course up the river to take,—
On the third of July they reached Koshkonong Lake.
On the fourth, Alexander, no foe having found,
As ordered, came on to his chief's camping ground.
Its course to Burnt Village the army now made:
Dodge's troop there joined them, and Posey's brigade.
    —AMER MILLS STOCKING

When the various elements of the Army of the Frontier arrived at Dixon's Ferry, Atkinson followed standard military procedure for the period and divided the force into two divisions. Posey's and Alexander's brigades composed the first division, and Posey, as the ranking brigadier general, exercised overall command of the division as well as his brigade. Henry's brigade and Zachary Taylor's 450 regulars (who also had a six-pound artillery piece) constituted the second division under General Hugh Brady. Like most regular army officers, Brady had a low opinion of the volunteers and complained of the "difficulties & disappointments which have been thrown in the way of General Atkinson, by the ridiculous conduct of the Militia."[1] He did not exaggerate, for despite Atkinson's attempts to introduce tighter discipline, the volunteers continued to act more like a loosely structured mob than an army. This, of course, should not have been surprising, for once mustered, the volunteers received no military training of any kind, and few had any real military experience. Moreover, they did, indeed, impede Atkinson's progress. On the night of June 25th at Dixon's Ferry, James Henry decided to have his men test their guns by platoon. Despite Henry's rather specific orders, the men discharged their guns with no sense of order, and many reloaded and discharged again. The continuous roar of fire-arms caused a stampede of the brigade's one thousand horses. The next day was spent rounding up the stray horses rather than preparing for the campaign.[2]

Atkinson also doubted the abilities of his volunteer commanders, particularly Posey. Because he had sent Alexander to scout along the Plum River on June 26th, Atkinson decided to revise his original plan and ordered Posey to move without Alexander to Fort Hamilton. There, he was to join Dodge and place himself under Dodge's command. Thus, Atkinson essentially dissolved his first division and placed his weakest commander, Posey, under Dodge, in whom he had much more confidence. His army was now in four locations: Alexander was at the Plum River, Posey was at Kellogg's Grove, Dodge was at Fort Hamilton, and he was with the second division (composed of Henry's brigade and the regulars) at Dixon's Ferry. He ordered Dodge, Posey, and Alexander to rendezvous with him at the mouth of the Pecatonica River. However, his geographical information continued to be rather distorted and he incorrectly concluded that his intelligence had pinpointed the British Band near this location; the British Band was actually about twenty-five miles farther to the north. Luckily, his Potawatomi guides had a better knowledge of the area. Atkinson departed from Dixon's Ferry with his second division on June 28th at about noon and managed to march twelve miles up the Rock River the first day.[3]

However, Atkinson's problems with his subordinates persisted. When Posey's brigade arrived at Fort Hamilton on June 29th, a debate ensued over who should assume command. Although Atkinson's orders explicitly stated that Dodge was to do so, Posey was reluctant to give up command. Dodge's and Posey's men settled the debate in a decidedly nonmilitary manner: they took a vote. Posey won the election; his men outnumbered Dodge's, but many voted against him and he won only by a narrow margin. Thus, Posey remained in command. William Hamilton and his Menominee scouts joined Dodge and Posey in their march to Lake Koshkonong. Dodge also clashed with Hamilton, for, according to one of Dodge's men, Dodge had been upset that Hamilton and his Indian force had not arrived in enough time to be of use to him at the Battle of Pecatonica two weeks earlier. Dodge challenged Hamilton to a duel to settle the matter of honor between them, but Hamilton declined (his own father had been killed in a duel with Vice President Aaron Burr many years earlier). Dodge then reportedly told Hamilton, "Damn you, obey my orders hereafter."[4] Thus, Dodge, Posey, and Hamilton marched with their men—accompanied by their personal animosities toward one another—as a single column toward Lake Koshkonong.

On the second day of its march up the east bank of the Rock River, the second division camped on the ground of Stillman's Run; dead horses, scraps of clothing, and wagons still littered the area. Atkinson had ordered seventy-five of the Potawatomi guides under Billy Caldwell to meet him at the mouth of the Kishwaukee River. Atkinson did not stop to meet his other two columns at the mouth of the Pecatonica River as he had originally ordered. He undoubtedly figured out with the aid of his Potawatomi guides that his previous conclusions were mistaken and that the intelligence he had received concerning the location of the British Band referred to a point farther north on the Rock River. Alexander's men lingered at the mouth of the Pecatonica momentarily before they realized Atkinson had gone farther to the north. The volunteers in Henry's Third Brigade became more edgy as they approached Lake Koshkonong, and on the night of July 2nd, as they camped near the mouth of the Yahara River, one of the sentinels mistakenly shot another volunteer, although not fatally. The next day, the Third Brigade's spy battalion, along with Jacob Early's spy company and several Potawatomi scouts, picked up a trail that led to what had been the second main camp of the British Band on the southwest end of Lake Koshkonong. Atkinson arrived with the remainder of the second division on the morning of July 3rd. Much to his chagrin, he found that the camp had been deserted for at least three days. The next day, Alexander's brigade arrived, and along the way he picked a party of eleven Rock River Winnebago guides under Oliver Emmell. By July 5th Posey, Dodge, and Hamilton arrived on the west side of the lake, and Dodge had with him a party of thirty-one Winnebago scouts under White Crow.[5]

The absence of the British Band was hardly the July 4th celebration for which Atkinson had hoped. It was evidence that he had not planned for every contingency. He had convinced himself that Black Hawk would remain at his camp and make a stand, despite the fact that his intelligence made it clear that the British Band planned to cross the Mississippi. Thus, he would waste several more precious days reconnoitering the area in the hope of finding Black Hawk. Worse yet, he was running low on food; the volunteers in particular were notorious for wasting provisions, and given the fact that he had over three thousand men, his food stores were just about exhausted. The British Band, short on food as it was, left not a single morsel behind. The only Indian in the camp was an old, blind, half-starved Sauk named Kakekamak (Always Fish) who, due to sickness, had been left behind. Upon questioning him, Atkinson learned that the British Band had marched north along the east bank of the Rock River, but the old Sauk knew little more since the chiefs had not told him their destination. Posey's men, eager to engage any enemy combatant, later took the helpless Sauk elder captive and shot him. Atkinson's glum mood was made even more so when, on July 6th, he received the scathing letter from the acting secretary of war as well as the news that Major General Winfield Scott was on his way to Chicago to take command of the war.[6]

After receiving this news from Washington, Atkinson initiated a frenzy of activity and sent out small parties to locate the British Band before Scott arrived. What he found instead were the various places the British Band had occupied during its five-week stay in the area. The main Sauk camp for the first two weeks or so of June was at the high ground known as the Island. It was at the confluence of the Rock River and the Bark River, which Atkinson and his subordinates consistently mislabeled Whitewater Creek (Whitewater Creek was actually a branch of the Bark River farther to the east). The members of the British Band moved to a new camp along the south shore of the lake in mid-June and stayed there until they fled. The lack of food was almost certainly the reason for the move, for the Island, while safe, lacked game and gatherable food resources such as berries and nuts. The second camp offered better possibilities. A white settler who, in 1836, purchased the land where this camp stood found many piles of clam shells three to four feet across and a foot deep. In addition to this camp, the British band also had several smaller camps spread out along the south shore of Lake Koshkonong and on the Rock River below the lake.[7]

Atkinson and the second division followed the course of the Rock River and approached Lake Koshkonong from the west (rather than from the south, as some sources claim) when they found the deserted second main camp of the British Band at the west end of the lake on July 3rd. Atkinson then established his camp about five miles farther east. He had parties from Henry's Third Brigade scout both sides of the lake on July 3rd and 4th. Once Alexander arrived, Atkinson sent him across the Rock River at the southern end of the lake on July 6th so that he could scour the west side of the lake with Dodge, who had just arrived with Posey. Atkinson ordered Posey, on the other hand, to cross with his men to the east side and attached Posey to the second division. Dodge had asked Atkinson to do this because of the problems between the two men, and Atkinson, who probably wanted to have tighter control over Posey, obliged him. Thus, on the morning of July 6th, Atkinson again had two divisions scouting the east and west sides of Lake Koshkonong. Both sides of the lake had numerous trails that headed north, and these led Atkinson to believe that the British Band was still at the confluence of the Rock and Bark Rivers. By the end of the day on July 6th, the second division had gone up as far north as the Bark River. About three miles to the east, near the confluence of the Bark River and Whitewater Creek, stood an abandoned Winnebago hamlet known as the Burnt Village (near present-day Cold Spring, Wisconsin), and it was in this vicinity that the second division established its camp. Dodge and Alexander made camp that evening somewhere on the west side of the Rock River north of Lake Koshkonong.[8]

The trails had indeed been made by the British Band, but Atkinson had not yet figured out that Black Hawk and his people were no longer on the Island but were actually much farther north. His Winnebago guides insured that he did not figure this out immediately and successfully convinced Atkinson that the British Band was still right across the Bark River on the Island. On the morning of July 7th, Atkinson planned to have his army cross the Bark River over to the Island and attack the enemy. The morning started off poorly, for three of the Winnebago guides, probably in an effort to fool Atkinson and his men into believing that the British Band was still on the Island, crossed to the other side of the Bark River and shot and mortally wounded one of the regulars fishing along the south bank. Thus, Private David W. Dobbs was the first regular soldier killed in the war, and Atkinson did not learn until later that his army's own guides committed this act. The Winnebago guides assured Atkinson that it was folly to attack by crossing over from the west bank of the Rock River because Black Hawk had impregnable defenses on that side. Atkinson obviously took this seriously, for, in his two attempts to storm the Island (July 7th and 19th), he attempted to do so by crossing the Bark River both times.[9]

Atkinson ordered Dodge and Alexander, both of whom had White Crow as their chief guide, to cross from the east side of the Rock River at a point near the mouth of the Bark River on July 7th. White Crow urged Dodge and Alexander to disobey the order and follow him farther up the west bank of the Rock River. Several volunteers later interpreted this as proof that he planned to lead Dodge and Alexander into an ambush; however, this was unlikely. First, as Atkinson's scouts soon learned, the British Band was already several days ahead of Atkinson's army. Second, White Crow definitely knew this; he was most likely trying to lead Dodge and Alexander on more fruitless marches. Finally, Black Hawk's autobiography makes no mention of such a plan, and he needed his warriors far more to assist in finding food for his hungry band than to perform harassing operations. White Crow's sympathies were still with Black Hawk, and his actions at Lake Koshkonong undoubtedly were designed to throw the army off his trail. Dodge and Alexander obeyed Atkinson's order, although Dodge was upset because he believed it had diverted him from closing in on Black Hawk. Once across the Rock River with Dodge and Posey, White Crow found additional opportunities to mislead the army.[10]

Atkinson did not wait for Dodge and Posey. On the morning of July 7th, he marched the second division nine miles eastward and probed along the south bank of the Bark River for a fordable spot. Unlike the Rock River, which could be crossed at many points, the Bark River was deeper and surrounded on both banks by thick swamps. As the second division marched east, Whitewater Creek, which was also surrounded by swamps, flowed across its path and slowed the movement considerably. Indeed, Atkinson left his camp at 9:00 a.m., but the swamps of Whitewater Creek prevented him from resuming his search for a fording spot until noon. The men of the second division slogged through the bogs and swamps along the banks of the Bark River, and what often looked to be solid ground was nothing more than mud in which horses sank up to their stomachs and threw their riders into the murky waters as they struggled to free themselves. That evening, Alexander and Dodge caught up with Atkinson. To add to Atkinson's problems, Dodge's and Alexander's men had depleted their rations. That night, the exhausted army camped along the south bank of the Bark River about fifteen miles east of its mouth. Just before daybreak, one of the sentinels, thinking the enemy was nearby, shot the Officer of the Day as he made his rounds. Unlike his less fortunate regular counterpart who had been killed the day before by the Winnebagos, the volunteer officer eventually recovered.[11]

The next morning, Atkinson convened a council of all his officers and White Crow, who told Atkinson that the Bark River was impossible to ford. White Crow continued to insist that the British Band was right across the river on the Island. Atkinson and his officers unanimously decided to return to the camp that the second division had occupied the night of July 6th near the Burnt Village. The decision was made in large part because a white messenger from Chicago acquainted with the area had just arrived and suggested that the point near the mouth of Whitewater Creek was the best place to throw a makeshift bridge across the Bark River. Thus, the entire army marched back over the ground it had covered the previous day. One volunteer noted that the march required him to "go back cross [sic] the worst bogs I ever crossed with a horse."[12] The next morning, on July 9th, Atkinson had his men construct a makeshift bridge over the Bark River using grass, sticks, logs, and whatever else could be procured. Using the portion of the bridge that had been completed as well as makeshift rafts, Jacob Early's company managed to get across the Bark River, as did William Hamilton and his Menominee scouts.[13]

The news they brought back was not what Atkinson wanted to hear. Early's and Hamilton's scouts examined the entire area and pushed nine or ten miles to the north and northwest; they found ample evidence that the area had been occupied, but the trails indicated that the British Band had vanished farther to the north. This area contained the extensive swamps and bogs of the Trembling Lands (as the Winnebagos had named this area) that stretched for miles. Early believed that the British Band was only a little farther to the north and could be overtaken by the army, but, as one scholar of the Black Hawk War has noted, "Capt. Early seemed always a little too *early* in finding Indian trails."[14] Atkinson no longer believed that the British Band was within his reach, and he immediately stopped construction of the bridge across the Bark River. He figured that his volunteers had only three days of food left, and without the British Band anywhere to be found, he did not need their soldiering for the moment. He decided to halt all operations and send the volunteers away to secure more provisions. Atkinson was, no doubt, bitterly disappointed, and he blamed the profligacy of the volunteers as much as he did the swamps for slowing down the campaign. Atkinson's complaints were not without merit, for the volunteers had wasted much of the twenty days of rations issued to them. Now, thirteen days later, their provisions were exhausted. One officer noted that, on the other hand, the regular soldiers, "due to the care they took of the rations, and to their experience," still had enough food to last another seven days.[15]

Atkinson ordered Henry, Alexander, and Dodge to march to Fort Winnebago to secure provisions, and he ordered Posey to move to Fort Hamilton for the same purpose. In his journal, Atkinson's aide-de-camp noted that when Atkinson sent Henry, Alexander, and Dodge to Fort Winnebago, he also instructed them to "pursue the trail of the enemy if it was met going or returning."[16] In his final report written in November 1832, Atkinson reiterated once again that he gave these instructions, but such an assertion is spurious. His original orders contained no such instructions, and the portions of his aide-de-camp's journal that contain these instructions were added at a later date. Moreover, after the war, Dodge and Henry both asserted that they never received any such instructions from Atkinson.[17] The volunteers sent to Fort Winnebago did, indeed, make contact with the British Band, but this was not due to any instructions issued by Atkinson.

Once the volunteers departed on the morning of July 10th, Atkinson abandoned his camp near Whitewater Creek and moved the regulars to a new camp at the confluence of the Bark and Rock Rivers. Several other significant events transpired over the next few days. First, all but three of Hamilton's Menominees departed, most likely because of their disappointment at not finding the British Band. Seventy Potawatomis departed as well, but since an additional nineteen had arrived a few days earlier, Atkinson still had twenty-four Potawatomi scouts. Due to the lack of provisions, he also dismissed all of the Winnebago scouts except for White Crow and his son, both of whom continued to work as guides for Atkinson and Doge. Atkinson was probably elated when Reynolds and his entourage decided to head back to southern Illinois. He now could command his army without Reynolds breathing down his neck. Atkinson also decided that he had more men than he needed, so he mustered out Jacob Early's spy company. Abraham Lincoln finally ended his service after almost two months. His horse had been stolen the night before he mustered out, and he and two of his comrades, having only one horse between them, took turns riding and walking as they made their way home. Upon reaching Peoria, Lincoln and another discharged volunteer purchased a canoe and later procured a raft. They made their way down to Havana, Illinois, and walked the final twenty-three miles to New Salem. Later that month, Atkinson probably suffered his most serious loss when his most experienced subordinate, Brigadier General Hugh Brady, contracted dysentery, which put him out service for the remainder of the war.[18]

Brady spent the remainder of the war in the small stockaded fort with two blockhouses that Atkinson had his regulars build at the mouth of the Bark River. By July 17th they had completed the fort and bestowed upon it the appellation Fort Koshkonong. Atkinson did not know it at the time, but this little fort, which stood for another four years, would be the most enduring and, indeed, only monument to his leadership during the Black Hawk War. It became the nucleus of the town that today bears his name: Fort Atkinson, Wisconsin. In addition to constructing the fort, Atkinson on July 11th also sent some of his regulars as well as his Potawatomi scouts on another scouting mission into the Trembling Lands. Captain William S. Harney commanded the two-day mission. He and his men went twenty miles north and discovered that the British Band had gone sixty to eighty miles farther north, but they could not determine the exact location. It was Atkinson's hope to resume the campaign once the volunteers returned, but he believed that at its current pace, with the British Band nowhere to be found and probably hiding somewhere deep in the impenetrable swamps to the north, the war could conceivably drag on until winter. When he first arrived at Lake Koshkonong, he thought that the British Band might have fled toward Lake Michigan; now, with Harney's intelligence, he believed that Black Hawk and his people were somewhere in the extensive swamplands between Lake Winnebago and the headwaters of the Rock River.[19] Nevertheless, he faced the same situation he had faced a month earlier: he had no idea where the British Band was.

Atkinson and other officers pinned the blame for this failure on the duplicity of their Rock River Winnebago guides. Indeed, the Rock River Winnebagos, particularly those under White Crow, assisted the British Band even as they served as guides, spies, and scouts for Atkinson's forces. It was during this lull that Atkinson and his subordinates began to question the trustworthiness of their Winnebago allies. White Crow had insisted that the British Band was on the north side of the Bark River on the Island when, in fact, it was not. At the July 8th council, White Crow even tried to convince Atkinson that Black Hawk had fled east toward Milwaukee, which would have sent Atkinson in the opposite direction once Black Hawk began his trek toward the Mississippi. When one considers that the British Band was always working with and living among the Rock River Winnebagos while at Lake Koshkonong, it would have been impossible for White Crow not to know that the British Band had departed, especially since several Rock River Winnebagos fled the area with the British Band. Although Atkinson's men initially thought that it was Sauks who killed David W. Dobbs, the two scouting parties under Early and Harney confirmed that the British Band had abandoned the area north of the Bark River long before the army had arrived. Thus, it was apparent that the army's own Winnebago scouts had crossed to the north side of the river and shot Dobbs. Atkinson was incensed that this false intelligence had caused his needless delay at Lake Koshkonong while Black Hawk and his band made their way north. One regular officer stated that "the Winnebagos, our professed allies, were operating on both sides and in both camps. . . . They went out into a fog and shot a man [Dobbs] . . . and before the wounds of the soldier were dressed they were again in our camps, eating Uncle Sam's beef with an air of innocence."[20]

The behavior of the Potawatomi guides was definitely better in Atkinson's eyes, and this was primarily due to the Potawatomi leadership. Whereas the principal leaders of the Rock River Winnebagos—White Crow and Whirling Thunder—condoned and even participated in anti-American activities, Potawatomi leaders such as Shabonna and Wabaunsee were squarely within the American camp and forbade any such behavior. Thus, the anti-American faction of the Potawatomis that committed attacks in northeastern Illinois was forced to do so outside the sphere of the tribal leadership's authority. Atkinson was not completely sure of his Potawatomi guides; he noted that they seemed sincere, and that, unlike the Rock River Winnebagos, none of them appeared to be disaffected. Even so, Atkinson did not think they strongly supported the American cause, and he concluded that they seemed "more disposed to be neutral than taking part with us."[21]

One member of Jacob Early's spy company noted many years after the war that the Potawatomis were eager to serve as scouts only because Atkinson gave them generous rations of beef. Indeed, the Potawatomis brought live, government-issued cattle with them and slaughtered them as needed. They also loved the bread issued to the Illinois volunteers and stole it from them every chance they could. There was extensive fraternization between the Potawatomis and the volunteers, and the two groups frequently participated in running and wrestling competitions. The Potawatomis enjoyed a semi-autonomous status, and Atkinson, by his own admission, exercised little real control over them. The Potawatomis and Winnebagos, however, were also quite aware that the Illinois volunteers were not well controlled by Atkinson or any other officer, and they did not want to be mistaken for the enemy. All the Winnebago and Potawatomi guides wore white handkerchiefs on their heads so they could be readily identified, and when approached by a volunteer, the guides were quick to utter in broken English "good Winebago" or "good . . . Potawatamie."[22]

While the Rock River Winnebagos served both sides during the war and the Potawatomis served the United States in an indifferent manner, the Menominees exhibited an intense zeal to fight Black Hawk. The small number of Menominees who lived along the Mississippi eagerly volunteered their services to William Hamilton. Even after his Santee Sioux and Winnebago scouts had abandoned him, the Menominees remained with Hamilton until early July. However, the bulk of the Menominee nation resided at Green Bay, and the tribal leaders there had asked to fight in the war as early as May 19th. It would be two months before Atkinson formally requested their services, but the Menominees at Green Bay did not wait and began assisting in any way they could. The fur trade community at Green Bay was composed predominantly of Métis fur traders who were heavily intermarried among the Menominees. By mid-June, the Menominees provided 150 warriors to protect the Green Bay settlement. The residents were so buoyed by their arrival that the forty-four men of the volunteer company that had been put together returned to their homes and farms. However, this was far too passive a role for the tribe's warriors. Grizzly Bear, one of the chief orators of the Menominees, met with George Boyd and Samuel Stambaugh—the new and outgoing Indian agents at Green Bay respectively—on June 22nd. His message was short, clear, and direct: "Our Enemies have taken the heads of our men women & children—carried them to their lodges and danced the war dance over them. *We ask revenge.*"[23]

Boyd sent a copy of this speech to Atkinson and offered the services of two hundred Menominee warriors. Atkinson received Boyd's letter in July while he was at Lake Koshkonong. The timing, in Atkinson's mind, must have been perfect. Black Hawk's followers, he believed, were somewhere near the headwaters of the Rock River and Lake Winnebago and would possibly cross the Fox River. Indeed, they appeared to be fleeing toward the country of their enemies, the Menominees, who, Atkinson believed, could be of great service. On July 12th, he wrote to Boyd and told him that he accepted the offer of the Menominees. The Menominees demanded that their outgoing Indian agent, Stambaugh, serve as their commander. Boyd noted that the Menominees were very poorly armed and procured an additional 110 rifles and shotguns from local merchants, but even this was not adequate and the Menominees were forced to craft spears to make up for their shortage of firearms. By July 25th, the Menominee force was organized as a battalion of two companies, and its organization reflected the social hierarchy of the tribe and the composition of the Green Bay community. A total of 232 Menominee warriors volunteered to serve, as did another eight Métis and Anglo-American men, including Stambaugh. The warriors served as privates, the tribal war leaders functioned as sergeants, and the Métis and Anglo-American volunteers served as officers and interpreters. The Grignon family was well represented; Augustin Grignon served as the commander of one company, his son Charles was a first lieutenant and interpreter in his company, and his nephew Robert Grignon served as a second lieutenant in the other company.[24]

While the Menominee force was being organized at Green Bay, Secretary of War Lewis Cass worked with General Winfield Scott to put together a force of regulars from the army's garrisons in the East. Troops from Fort Columbus in New York City, Fort McHenry in Maryland, Fort Monroe in Virginia, and New Castle Arsenal in Delaware were ordered into service. Two companies of the Fourth Infantry Regiment were also ordered up from Baton Rouge Barracks in Louisiana. Also, on their way up the Hudson River, Scott's forces stopped at the United States Military Academy at West Point and picked up twenty-nine cadets of the class of 1832 (which had a total of forty-four members) who relished the chance to have their first taste of combat. Scott was also authorized to take selected companies from three of the principal frontier posts in Michigan Territory: Forts Gratiot, Brady, and Mackinac. The War Department's difficulties in putting together a force of one thousand men (out of an army of only a little over six thousand soldiers) was reflected in the fact that many of the units constituting Scott's force were artillery batteries that had been instantly converted to infantry. In all, Scott had twenty companies composed of about 950 men. This included the two companies that had arrived at Chicago on June 17th from Fort Niagara in western New York and that had been ordered to regarrison Fort Dearborn in February 1832. As his force made its way west in late June, Scott's aide-de-camp noted that there had been an outbreak of cholera in Canada, and advised precautions to prevent its spread. He suggested using chloride of lime to disinfect the troop transports.[25]

Such preventive measures were common in the early nineteenth century but were utterly useless to stop the spread of the disease. At the time, cholera was associated with immoral persons who lived in filth and poverty, and it was believed to spread among such populations through the air. The reality was that it traveled not through the respiratory system but the digestive tract, and a person became infected by contact with food or water that carried the cholera bacteria. Thus, simply cleaning away dirt and grime did little if food and water were not properly cooked and boiled. The disease made its first appearance in Europe in the fall of 1831 and by the spring of 1832 had made its way across the Atlantic. It first appeared in Montreal on June 6th, and within about a week it was in New York state. By June 24th, the first case occurred in New York City, just as many of Scott's troops were leaving the city to fight in the Black Hawk

Figure 13. A portrait of General Winfield Scott painted around the time of the Black Hawk War. Reprinted from Stevens, *The Black Hawk War.*

War. Indeed, his troops from Fort Columbus almost certainly had come into contact with the disease before they departed their post. The infection of Scott's force, more so than any other factor, was the principal reason the disease spread during the summer of 1832 into the far reaches of the Great Lakes.[26]

Scott's troops traveled on four steamboats that were due to arrive at Chicago between July 9th and the 16th. However, as his force approached Lake Huron, the first cases of cholera occurred. Scott had four sick men on his ship, the *Sheldon Thompson;* they were dropped off at Fort Mackinac, which only helped the disease to spread there. Nevertheless, men continued to get sick, and the *Sheldon Thompson* soon became a nightmarish spectacle for those aboard; sixteen men died, and their bodies were thrown overboard into Lake Michigan. The *Sheldon Thompson* made it to Chicago by July 10th, and another steamboat, the *William Penn*, arrived on July 21st. The residents of Chicago, who for over a month had shuttered themselves into the walls of Fort Dearborn fearing an Indian attack, now fled upon hearing that Scott's troops brought cholera. The other two vessels, the *Henry Clay* and the *Superior*, never made it to Chicago. They stopped at Fort Gratiot north of Detroit to drop off their infected soldiers, but the cholera was so prevalent on the *Henry Clay* that discipline broke down completely. Upon landing at Fort Gratiot, men dashed off the vessel and ran into the surrounding woods; many subsequently died. By late July, Scott had only 350 men available at Chicago, and by late August, despite his best efforts to control the spread of the disease, cholera had depleted this number to 330.[27]

When the troops aboard the *William Penn* arrived at Chicago, they were generally free of cholera. This allowed Scott to put together an improvised force of 350 regulars. Scott set out with his staff of three other officers in a horse-drawn wagon on July 29th for Fort Crawford. He ordered Colonel Abraham Eustis to command the regular troops and leave Chicago three days after Scott's departure. Scott's decision to leave before his regulars were ready was also due, in large part, to the fact that on July 21st the volunteers under Atkinson's command made contact with the enemy along the Wisconsin River. It was obvious to Scott that the British Band was fleeing toward the Mississippi, and he sought to link up with those troops in pursuit of Black Hawk and take charge of what he hoped would be the final battle of the war. By taking only his staff in a wagon, he was able to move faster than if he traveled with Eustis's dismounted infantry. By August 4th, Scott had reached Galena, but he was already too late; in addition to missing the battle of July 21st at a place called Wisconsin Heights, he also missed the final battle of August 2nd at the mouth of the Bad Axe River along the Mississippi. Thus, Henry Atkinson, not Winfield Scott, ended the conflict in the summer of 1832. Indeed, the cholera among Scott's troops proved to be a godsend for Atkinson, for it allowed him to continue prosecuting the war and rescue his professional reputation. Scott was still the ranking officer in the theater of operations, and Atkinson, never one to make waves with his superiors, made an effort to at least nominally come under Scott's command. Scott had called the forces he brought with him the North West Army, and Atkinson, as a sign of symbolic subordination, quit using the appellation Army of the Frontier when referring to his forces and instead called them the North West Army.[28]

Before he could resume his operations, Atkinson had to wait for his volunteers. Dodge, Henry, and Alexander arrived at Fort Winnebago by July 12th, and although they managed to obtain their provisions, their problems persisted. On the night of July 12th, the horses—which numbered well over one thousand and approached two thousand by one estimate—grazed in a nearby pasture. Something spooked them and caused them to stampede. The only horses that did not stampede were those that were too fatigued or that suffered from physical disabilities and injuries. While many horses simply ran in circles, at least three hundred dashed off on a trail for about thirty miles toward the Wisconsin River. The next two days were spent rounding up the stray animals; at least ninety-one were lost for good, and many of those that were retrieved were unfit for further service.[29] Despite these losses, the prospects of the volunteers were about to become much brighter.

Whereas Atkinson simply planned to resume the same ineffectual operations along the Bark River when his volunteers returned, Dodge had other ideas and aggressively sought out intelligence concerning the location of the British Band. His efforts soon bore fruit, for while at Fort Winnebago, he made contact with Pierre Paquette, who asserted that the British Band was in the vicinity of the Rock River Rapids (present-day Hustiford, Wisconsin) near the Winnebago village there. Paquette's intelligence was indeed sound, for he had received it from the Rock River Winnebagos, to whom he was related. Paquette was born to a French Canadian father and a Winnebago mother whose brother was White Crow. Nevertheless, Paquette's sympathies were not automatically granted to his Winnebago kin, for despite the fact that he spoke fluent Winnebago and had strong familial and economic ties to the Rock River bands, Paquette, like virtually all mixed-race persons in the Great Lakes region, did not necessarily equate race with identity. What mattered most to those of biracial descent was the community into which one was born and raised. Thus, persons of mixed descent who lived in Indian communities considered themselves fully Indian, while those like Paquette who engaged in the fur trade and lived in fur trade communities saw themselves as fully Euro-American. Paquette, like most Great Lakes Métis, saw himself as French Canadian, despite the fact he was half Winnebago. He certainly took advantage of his relations among the Rock River Winnebagos in order to advance himself economically, but he had cast his lot with the American order. Thus, while the sympathies of his Winnebago kinsmen were with Black Hawk, Paquette's were with the United States.[30]

Dodge had Paquette and seven or eight Winnebagos from both the Rock River and Wisconsin River bands lead him to the Rock River Rapids. While some sources state that White Crow was part of this group, more reliable sources indicate that he returned to Fort Koshkonong with those volunteers under Alexander's command. Among the Winnebagos under Paquette was a young man named White Pawnee. However, Paquette managed to attract only a handful of young men, and none were civil chiefs or men with any significant leadership roles. Indeed, there was generally little enthusiasm among the Wisconsin River bands for the American cause and quite a bit of sympathy for the British Band. A young warrior of the Wisconsin River bands who lived at the Portage noted that within the Wisconsin River Winnebago bands, there was "among us a strong feeling of friendliness toward the Sacs . . . [that] was of friendly pity, not a desire to help them fight."[31] Thus, like their Rock River kin, many of the Wisconsin River Winnebagos sided with Black Hawk, and while they may not have been as active in their support, the evidence suggests their role was more than simply passive. Those Rock and Wisconsin River Winnebagos willing to work with Paquette and act as guides for Dodge (that is, without being coerced), were definitely in the minority.

Participants and scholars of the Black Hawk War have long debated whether it was Dodge or Henry who formulated the plan to march to the Rock River Rapids, for it was this decision that ultimately led to the defeat of Black Hawk and the British Band. Not surprisingly, the issue has generated very partisan points of view; those who served under Dodge and hailed from Wisconsin have tended to support Dodge, while those who served under Henry and lived in Illinois have tended to support Henry. Nevertheless, the evidence clearly illustrates that it was Dodge who formulated the plan and provided the leadership necessary for it to succeed. After Dodge received the crucial intelligence from Paquette concerning the location of the British Band, he called a council of all the volunteer officers at Fort Winnebago, and he proposed heading back to Fort Koshkonong via the Rock River Rapids in the hope of intercepting Black Hawk. Henry agreed, but Alexander objected to the plan since the orders from Atkinson required them to return immediately and directly to Fort Koshkonong. Dodge and Henry therefore moved to the Rock River Rapids, while Alexander marched back to Fort Koshkonong with his brigade and those volunteers from all three commands who had lost their horses in the stampede.[32]

Alexander and his men arrived at Fort Koshkonong on July 17th in what he thought was strict obedience to Atkinson's orders. He soon learned that Atkinson did not condemn the course that Dodge and Henry pursued but wholeheartedly approved of it, for it fit perfectly into his plans. However, Atkinson's lack of tactical skills continued to be his greatest limitation. He knew that the British Band was somewhere to the north, probably at least thirty or forty miles away. His intelligence, based upon the work of his scouts from July 9th to the 12th, was generally correct, although, unlike Dodge, Atkinson did not know the precise location of the British Band. On July 19th, he had Alexander's brigade and the regulars under Taylor resume their push eastward along the south bank of the Bark River with White Crow and sixteen other Rock River Winnebagos serving as their scouts. In a letter to Scott, Atkinson stated that with Dodge and Henry at the Rock River Rapids, he could have the troops at Fort Koshkonong push up from the south and squeeze the British Band between the two forces. However, this movement made little sense. Atkinson was completely wedded to the idea that in order to ascend north on the east bank of the Rock River, he first had to cross the Bark River. It made more sense to move up the west bank of the Rock River and cross to the east side somewhere farther to the north. Obviously, White Crow's warnings about approaching the Island from the west had made a deep impression upon Atkinson, but his own scouts had already determined that there were no hostile Indians there.[33]

While, in a driving rain, Atkinson continued to slog eastward through the swamps that surrounded the south bank of the Bark River, Dodge and Henry departed Fort Winnebago on July 15th and arrived at the Rock River Rapids three days later. Both commands were seriously undermanned by this time; Henry had about 600 men while Dodge had about 150. Dodge began to discuss the location of the British Band with the Rock River Winnebagos who resided there. Not surprisingly, they also attempted to throw the volunteers off Black Hawk's course. They stated that the British

Band was twenty miles to the north in the vast swamp lands of Cranberry Lake (present-day Horicon Marsh). Several of the volunteers noted that the Winnebagos at the Rock River Rapids were heavily intermarried among the Sauks, although none of their Sauk relations were to be seen, most likely because they feared being captured or killed by the volunteers. One man even noticed a Winnebago woman wearing a white woman's dress with a bullet hole in it and believed it might have been taken during the attack at Big Indian Creek. Dodge initially believed the Winnebagos, and on the evening of July 18th, he sent several of his men along with one of Paquette's guides, a young Winnebago named Little Thunder, to relay his information to Atkinson. The small party had only traveled about ten or twelve miles when it found a large trail heading toward the southwest. It was indeed the trail of the British Band. Bark had been stripped from the trees for food along the way by Black Hawk's hungry followers. Little Thunder figured out that the trail had been made by the British Band, and he immediately turned around and headed back to relay the news to Paquette.[34]

The next day, on July 19th, Dodge ascertained that the intelligence he had received from the Winnebagos at the Rock River Rapids the day before had been a ruse. He sent another messenger to Atkinson, who learned on July 20th that the trail of the British Band had been found. Atkinson immediately suspended his operations along the Bark River and had his regulars and Alexander's brigade return to Fort Koshkonong. He was jubilant upon receiving the news, and he ordered Dodge and Henry to "press on with all haste and never lose sight of the object till the enemy is overtaken, defeated & if possible captured."[35] Atkinson moved his available men across to the west side of the Rock River and had Alexander's spy battalion, several Potawatomi guides, and two Winnebago guides (under the close supervision of one of his regular officers) move forward of his main body to find the trail of the British Band. He had to leave a significant number of men at Fort Koshkonong, for in addition to having one of Alexander's battalions provide a garrison for the post, he also left behind those men without horses and those who were sick and unfit for duty. The hard march was conducted in a driving rain as Atkinson raced to find Black Hawk. However, Atkinson was already too far behind, for on July 21st, as his troops crossed the Rock River on the first day of their march, Dodge and Henry had already caught up with Black Hawk and fought the first battle of the campaign twenty-five miles to the west.[36]

Dodge and Henry immediately mounted up their men and began moving toward the trail of the British Band on the morning of July 19th. Divested of their wagons and taking only a minimal amount of rations, they pushed their men mercilessly that morning so that they could catch up to Black Hawk and prevent his escape. It had been three weeks since the start of the campaign, and the location of the British Band had been a mystery up to that point. Indeed, historians have long struggled to ascertain where the British Band was during this period. Black Hawk's autobiography is of little use because he makes virtually no mention of this period, and what little he does say is so vague that it is difficult to determine whether he is discussing the earlier camp near Lake Koshkonong or a later camp. Some scholars have speculated that the British Band went to Lac La Belle (present-day Oconomowoc, Wisconsin). However, this conclusion is generally based upon a rather inaccurate map made by Lieutenant Meriwether Lewis Clark, one of the regular officers under Atkinson and the son of explorer William Clark (see Figure 14). The most reliable sources make it clear that the British Band left its camp near Lake Koshkonong as Atkinson's army approached in late June, and Black Hawk and his followers then fled north up the east bank of the Rock River and established a new camp at or near the Winnebago village at the Rock River Rapids. What prompted the British Band to flee this location, undoubtedly, was that Black Hawk and his people learned that Dodge and Henry were approaching from Fort Winnebago. The members of the British Band probably left only a day or two ahead of Dodge's and Henry's arrival at the Rock River Rapids, and they might have made it safely to the Mississippi had not Little Thunder stumbled across their trail.[37]

After leaving the Rock River Rapids, Black Hawk's starving followers were hard pressed to stay out of reach of Dodge's and Henry's men. The members of the British Band were unfamiliar with the area, so two of the sons of the Winnebago chief Winneshiek and three other Winnebagos served as guides on their journey to the Wisconsin and Mississippi Rivers. Winneshiek was a member of the Mississippi River bands, but he was originally from the Rock River region, and, in addition to having a Sauk wife, he was a brother-in-law of the

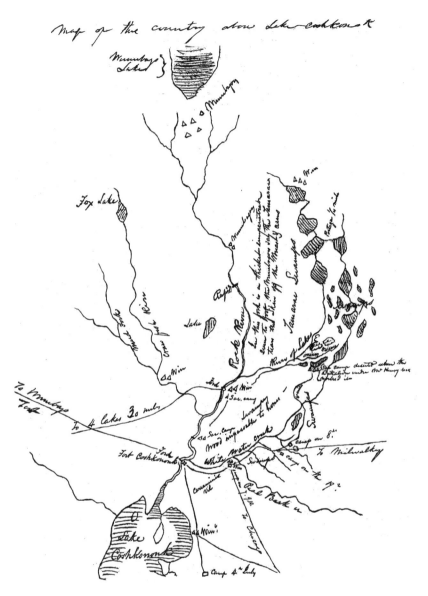

Figure 14. Sketch of the area around Lake Koshkonong by Lieutenant Meriwether Lewis Clark, 1832. From Meriwether Lewis Clark to William Clark, 25 July 1832, RG 107, Records of the Secretary of War, Letters Received, C-353(30), NA.

Winnebago Prophet. Black Hawk, like Atkinson, suffered from a continual bleeding of his available manpower, but unlike Atkinson's army, the British Band had not been resupplied with food and included women, children, and elders. Black Hawk lost close to fifty of his warriors in the five weeks after Stillman's Run. White Crow told Dodge in early June that while the British Band was at Lake Koshkonong, the Potawatomis and the Rock River Winnebagos had removed all their people who were married to members of the British Band. Assuming that White Crow was telling the truth, this would have been a further drain on the British Band. Some of Black Hawk's followers were known to have deserted him throughout June and July, and now starvation and fatigue were beginning to take their toll. At the most, the British Band had about six hundred members by late July as it marched toward the Mississippi.[38]

After leaving the Rock River Rapids, the volunteers under Dodge and Henry crossed the Crawfish River near present-day Aztalan and picked up the British Band's trail, which consisted of one main trail and two smaller trails made by parties of warriors providing flank security. At certain points, there were as many as seven smaller trails, all heading west toward the Four Lakes region. By July 20th, the volunteers reached the isthmus between the third and fourth lakes (Lakes Monona and Mendota, respectively). Upon reaching the northeast corner of the third lake, Henry saw a small stream that entered the lake creating a neck of land, and he had his spy battalion scout the area before moving forward. Although nothing was there, it was undoubtedly a wise move, for the volunteers saw a group of Indians about a mile and a half in the distance. They were definitely scouts of the British Band, and upon being seen, they scattered into the brush. That evening, a war party with as many as two hundred warriors set up an ambush position along the southern end of the fourth lake, from which it could attack the volunteers if they pursued the British Band that evening. Dodge and Henry decided that it was too late in the day and instead established a camp on the northeast shore of the third lake. Black Hawk's warriors abandoned their ambush position around midnight when they were certain the volunteers would not attack. Black Hawk's people made their camp that night about ten miles to the west on the northwestern shore of the fourth lake (at present-day Middleton, Wisconsin).[39]

The volunteers were ready to move at sunrise the next day on July 21st, and Dodge and Henry formed their units into an order of battle with two principal elements. The smaller lead element was commanded by Dodge, and the larger main one was under Henry. The lead element was composed of Dodge's five companies and Henry's spy battalion (which now had only two companies) under the command of Major William Ewing. Ewing's two companies formed the center column, and Dodge had two of his companies march in a column on the left flank and two others in a column on the right. His fifth company served as scouts and marched about 150 to 200 yards forward of the lead element. Behind Dodge and Ewing were the three regiments of Henry's brigade, with Colonel Gabriel Jones on the left, Colonel James Collins in the center, and Colonel Jacob Fry (who had earlier commanded the interim regiment) on the right. Each regiment moved in a column formation behind the respective companies of the lead element (see Figure 15). Keeping the movement orderly was no small task given the dense underbrush. Moreover, the rains that had soaked the volunteers for the better part of the previous two days began again later in the day.[40]

The volunteers headed southwest down the isthmus between the third and fourth lakes, and during the course of that day they ran across two stragglers from the British Band. After crossing the Yahara River that links the third and fourth lakes, Dodge's scouts killed the first straggler on the shore of the third lake. The available sources disagree about why the warrior had fallen behind; some say he was sick while others say he was mourning over the grave of a recently deceased family member. The sources all agree upon the location and assert that he was killed a quarter-mile due east of where the Wisconsin capitol building stands today. Several volunteers shot at the warrior, one of whom was Dr. Addisson Philleo, a physician and newspaper editor from Galena who served as a private and surgeon in one of the Illinois companies assigned to Dodge. Philleo was particularly bloodthirsty and cruel. He led a special party that morning consisting of ten men from Dodge's battalion with a mission to find, kill, and scalp straggling members of the British Band. Philleo took the dying warrior's own knife and scalped him. The pain apparently brought the warrior back to consciousness. He did little more than utter a few words to Philleo, who

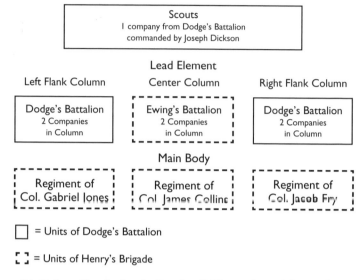

Figure 15. Order of battle for the Battle of Wisconsin Heights, July 21, 1832. By the author.

taunted him by saying, "If you don't like being scalped with a dull knife, why didn't you keep a better one?"[41]

The volunteers soon rounded the southern shore of the fourth lake and reached the encampment that the British Band had occupied the night before on the northwest side. The volunteers now found it easy to follow the desperate members of the British Band. The trail was littered with kettles, mats, and other items that had been discarded. Somewhere between five to ten miles from the fourth lake, Philleo's men came upon another Indian, who, as they were pursuing him, cried "Winnebago! Winnebago!" in a desperate attempt to fool the volunteers into thinking he was friendly. They were not deceived and answered with a volley of shots. The warrior was fatally wounded, but before he collapsed, he managed to brace himself against a tree and fire a shot that wounded one of Dodge's men in the thigh. Philleo scalped the second man as well and reportedly kept his scalps as trophies and displayed them at his residence in Galena for many years after the war.[42]

It is unknown what the first warrior said to Philleo as he was scalped. He did not, however, cry out or scream. This illustrated a significant facet of Indian warfare, for when a warrior suffered even excruciating pain due to scalping or other tortures, it was considered unmanly and cowardly to scream. Indeed, it would not have been unusual for a warrior being scalped while still alive to dare his tormentor to scalp him, or even to assert, as the knife cut and sawed into the flesh, that it did not hurt at all but actually felt pleasant. The warrior whom Philleo scalped probably uttered something similar. Whites never showed such incredible composure when they were scalped alive or otherwise tortured. Moreover, scalping on the part of Indians was a tradition that was deeply embedded in their cultural practice of warfare. The victors had the honor of taking the scalps of those whom they had defeated. The taking of a scalp also bestowed upon the victim a certain amount of honor. The scalp was, in a sense, a sign that the slain warrior's manhood had been transferred to his opponent. Indeed, warriors in many Great Lakes tribes wore scalplocks: a single lock of hair on an otherwise bald head that was often worn long and woven into a braid designed to make it easier for enemies to remove their scalp (see Figure 17). In a sense, the scalplock sat atop a warrior's head as a dare to an opponent—a symbol that he was not afraid to die and be scalped.[43]

Figure 16. A depiction of an Indian scalp dance. Reprinted from McKenney, *Memoirs Official and Personal.*

Figure 17. Sketch of an Indian with a scalplock. Reprinted from Catlin, *Letters and Notes on the Manners, Customs, and Condition of the North American Indians*, **vol. 2.**

Whites could not make these claims. When they committed acts such as scalping, they were generally just exacting cruelty upon their Indian enemies. Indian-hating by white frontiersmen had already had a long history by the time the Black Hawk War was fought. Most frontiersmen saw Indians as little more than vermin deserving of extermination. Yet, it would be a mistake to think that the atrocities committed by whites against Indians were devoid of any meaning in their own minds. Indeed, the atrocities committed by whites during the Black Hawk War (particularly scalping) were integral to the war's principal purpose. As stated earlier, politicians in Washington, military officers and Indian agents, and white settlers on the frontier believed Black Hawk and his followers had to be defeated for two distinct reasons. First, the members of the British Band had to be thoroughly punished for the violence they had wreaked upon the frontier. Second, their defeat would serve as a warning to other tribes. The cruelties and horrors that the volunteers exacted upon the British Band during the final weeks of the war were the means by which these two policies were implemented and given expression. Indeed, the volunteers showed little restraint once they actually began to fight Black Hawk's people, and, as one volunteer noted their motto was "*no quarter.*"[44]

As the volunteers moved closer to the Wisconsin River, the scouts out front increasingly encountered the warriors who composed the rear guard of the British Band. Virtually all of the Kickapoo warriors who joined the British Band in 1830 were part of this rear guard, as were about fifty Sauk warriors. As the battle commenced on July 21st, Black Hawk initially assumed that Napope commanded the rear guard, but this was not the case. Napope had been detailed by the Winnebago Prophet on the morning of July 21st to go out with one of several hunting parties that probably served as scouts as well. The movement of Dodge and Henry's force on the 21st cut off these parties from the main body of the British Band, and finding it impossible to effectively make his way back to Black Hawk, Napope and a companion fled to White Crow's village. Napope remained there for six days before he embarked on another journey of seven days toward the Mississippi. Black Hawk was far from pleased when he learned later of Napope's actions. He noted that several other warriors who had been sent out managed later to slip past the volunteers and rejoin the British Band whereas Napope chose instead to sit out the remainder of the war. As the volunteers approached, Black Hawk assumed command of his rear guard detachment of Kickapoo and Sauk warriors while the remainder of his warriors assisted the main body in crossing the river.[45]

Black Hawk commanded, at the very most, 120 men that morning. His detachment had at least fifty Sauk warriors and between about sixty to seventy Kickapoos. The Kickapoo warriors ended up bearing the brunt of the fighting, and all but one died that day. Black Hawk's small detachment had the unenviable task of holding back a force six times its size while the main body of the British Band attempted to cross the Wisconsin River. Black Hawk's followers had to use hastily constructed rafts and makeshift canoes made from elm bark. The place where the British Band crossed was a low sandy area with prominent high ground to the east. A ravine cut into this high ground, and the Sauk and Kickapoo warriors were deployed along the south ridge. Black Hawk was mounted on a horse and posted himself on a prominent mound to the rear and above his line of warriors. It was the perfect vantage point from which he could control his men, monitor the enemy, and see the progress of those crossing the river below. It was a strange coincidence that the place Black Hawk chose to cross the river was near a place called Prairie du Sac, or, in English, the Sauk Prairie. It was here that his people had a major village site from roughly the 1730s until about 1783, before they migrated to the Mississippi River Valley.[46]

Dodge pushed his companies relentlessly that morning so that he could catch up to the British Band before it could cross the Wisconsin River; Ewing drove his men hard just so they could keep up with Dodge's columns on the left and right. In early nineteenth-century warfare, the purpose of the lead element was to initiate and develop the battle so that the main element could move forward to finish the fight. Ewing and Dodge did an admirable job in this regard, but Dodge did not stop at merely initiating the battle; instead, he directed most phases of it. Although Henry was the senior officer and commanded the main element, he was also younger, less experienced, and thus generally acquiesced to Dodge. Dodge's and Ewing's companies were about a half an hour or so ahead of the main element for most of the day. Once the battle started, Dodge was in the best position to command not only his and Ewing's troops but also Henry's three regiments once they arrived. The rapid pace that Dodge set began to exhaust many of the horses, and about forty men were forced to abandon their mounts and proceed on foot. As the volunteers approached the Wisconsin River, Black Hawk's rear guard harassed the lead element with a heavy volume of fire from various hilltops along the route. Twice, they managed to force the volunteers to stop and dismount. By the third time, the companies of the lead element were not so easily deceived and did not deploy into a battle line but maintained their formation in three columns. Dodge's scout company arrived first at the ridgeline occupied by Black Hawk's warriors. The ridge was about a half-mile from the Wisconsin River. The scouts galloped over the crest of the ridge in pursuit, but they were pushed back by Black Hawk's numerically superior rear guard. This occurred at the same time that Dodge and Ewing arrived with the companies of the lead element. After detailing a few men to stay with the horses, Dodge had his and Ewing's men dismount, deploy into a battle line, and advance over the ridge.[47]

Dodge and Ewing arrived at about 5:00 p.m., and once he reached the crest of the ridge, Dodge began to direct the movements of his men and also Ewing's. On the other side of the ravine roughly two hundred yards away was the ridgeline held by Black Hawk's warriors, and on the small mound atop the ridgeline, Black Hawk sat on his white horse directing his men. Black Hawk made several futile attempts to have his warriors dislodge the volunteers from their ridgeline. Black Hawk's warriors made their first attempt by conducting a direct frontal assault. As in all Indian assaults, Black Hawk's warriors screamed a war cry as they charged. The war cry was a tactic to demoralize and frighten an enemy, and it often worked, especially with whites. However, whereas the loud Indian war cry was one of the reasons that Stillman's men had panicked two months earlier, Dodge kept his men steady. To their credit, the volunteers stood their ground. Indeed, Dodge let Black Hawk's warriors get within about thirty yards, had his own men answer with their own war cry, and began firing. In the process, at least one of Black Hawk's warriors was killed and several wounded. Faced with what looked to be a superior force in a secure position, the warriors followed the common Indian practice of breaking off the attack.[48]

Henry's three regiments arrived shortly after Dodge and Ewing. Henry also had his men dismount their horses, form a battle line, and move forward over the ridge. Paquette, one of White Crow's sons, and White Pawnee were with Henry and fought alongside his volunteers. Dodge's and Ewing's men occupied a ridgeline that came to a point as it fell off into the ravine and were almost directly opposite Black Hawk's warriors. Black Hawk saw another opportunity and sought to attack Dodge and Ewing on their exposed left flank. However, he was too late, for soon Henry had moved Collins's and

Jones's regiments into this area. Black Hawk then attempted to move his warriors toward Dodge and Ewing's right flank, but soon Fry's regiment arrived, occupied the extreme right of the ridgeline, and managed to repulse Black Hawk's thrust. Black Hawk, by his own admission, was boxed in and unable to maneuver his warriors effectively. The firing between the volunteers and the warriors went on for about an hour after Henry's regiments arrived. It was also obvious to Dodge that Black Hawk had no options, and he discussed with Henry the best course of action. Dodge suggested that they charge, and he wisely decided to take those troops on his left flank since they were in the best position to attack Black Hawk's right flank. Dodge took all of his companies along with those of Ewing, Jones's entire regiment, and part of Collins's regiment. He had his soldiers mount bayonets, but before the volunteers could reach the Indian positions, Black Hawk's warriors began a retreat toward the river.[49]

Black Hawk believed that he had accomplished his mission; he sought to fight the volunteers only long enough to give the remainder of his band time to cross the river. He had other sound reasons to retreat as well. First, he was greatly outnumbered, and his attempted frontal assault and outflanking maneuvers had been unsuccessful. Second, in the Indian way of warfare, it was not considered cowardly to withdraw from battle when the odds were stacked against a war leader. The odds were certainly against the British Band that day since Black Hawk's 120 warriors faced roughly 750 volunteers. Black Hawk's attacks against the volunteers' ridgeline and the retreat to the river also exposed his small detachment to a much greater volume of fire. Although only one volunteer died in the fighting that day and another seven were wounded, Black Hawk lost sixty-eight warriors—over half of his entire rear guard detachment. It was for this reason that Black Hawk could boast, "I would not have fought there, but to gain time for my women and children to cross. . . . A warrior will duly appreciate the embarrassments I labored under— and whatever may be the sentiments of the *white people*, in relation to this battle, my nation . . . will award to me the reputation of a great brave."[50]

Black Hawk did not have to wait very long for acclaim from his enemies. No members of the regular army were present at what became known as the Battle of Wisconsin Heights, although a few, particularly Lieutenant Jefferson Davis and Fort Winnebago sutler

Satterlee Clark, later made false claims to the contrary. After hearing details of the battle from their volunteer counterparts, several regular officers were more impressed with Black Hawk's military leadership than with Dodge's. One young regular army lieutenant stated it the most clearly: "Black Hawk, although encumbered with the women, children, and baggage of his whole band, covering himself by a small party, had accomplished that most difficult of military operations—to wit, the passage of a river,—in the presence of three regiments of American volunteers!"[51]

Black Hawk's followers did get a small respite after the battle, for the volunteers did not pursue the retreating warriors any further after they chased them off the high ground and down to the riverbank. It was about 7:00 p.m. as the battle ended, and by 8:00 p.m. the volunteers moved to set up camp for the night on the battle site. It was getting dark, it continued to rain, and the volunteers had marched over forty miles that day and fought a pitched battle at the end of it. Dodge and Henry decided to wait till morning to resume their attack. Before retiring, the volunteers cut off the scalps of thirteen dead warriors, and Paquette and his Winnebago guides took another eleven before they departed. The fact that the volunteers did not press their attack on the evening of July 21st confounded Black Hawk. He rarely had anything good to say about Americans and how they fought, and his attitude in the immediate aftermath of the Battle of Wisconsin Heights was no exception. The British Band was in such a precarious and vulnerable position that the entire war could have been finished at the river's bank that evening if the volunteers had pressed their attack. Black Hawk was relieved they did not, but he nevertheless expressed surprise.[52]

Upon crossing the Wisconsin, Black Hawk suffered additional losses as many of his followers left the British Band and decided instead to descend the Wisconsin River in their makeshift canoes and rafts. Black Hawk noted that he felt no bitterness toward those who did so because he fully understood the desperate and deplorable conditions his people faced. However, the majority of those who made it across decided to stay together and march toward the Mississippi. Unlike the area around the Rock River, which was low and filled with numerous wetlands, the unglaciated country west of the Wisconsin River (known as the Driftless Area) through which the British Band now traveled was higher and more rugged. As the remaining members of the British Band pushed west, Black Hawk assumed that Atkinson's army had given up its pursuit after the Battle of Wisconsin Heights. Thus, he posted no warriors as rear guards during the march. It was a rather foolish assumption on Black Hawk's part, for while Dodge and Henry were not able to maintain their pursuit, Atkinson would, in only a few days, pick up the trail of the British Band on the west side of the Wisconsin River.[53]

The day after the battle, Henry had his men scour the area near the river bank. All that the volunteers found were the many items abandoned by the British Band before crossing the river and the blood of the dead and wounded. They had not pursued the British Band because they lacked transportation across the river, and so they returned to their camp and attended to other duties. That night, the second night that the volunteers camped on the battle site, the horses were spooked and ran from the pasture up to the camp. Dodge and Henry feared that Black Hawk's warriors had startled the horses in preparation for an attack. The number of guards was doubled and all men were ordered to sleep on their rifles. A few hours before sunrise, the volunteers were startled to hear the voice of an Indian from a hillside about a half-mile away. Most of the men and officers believed it was the signal to begin an attack, and Henry delivered a spirited and motivational speech. He reminded the volunteers of the disgrace caused by Stillman's Run and how it was their duty to redeem the honor of Illinois in the upcoming battle as they had done the previous day. However, no attack came that night.

None of Black Hawk's followers left a record of who the speaker was, but captured members of the British Band later recounted that the speaker that evening was talking in Winnebago, and he was attempting to tell any Winnebagos in the volunteers' camp that the women and children of the British Band were starving and the warriors were unable to fight anymore; they wished only to cross the Mississippi in peace and promised to make no more mischief. The speaker's efforts were in vain, for there were no Winnebagos present in camp; Paquette and his guides had departed immediately after they had taken their scalps the day of the battle.[54] Even if Winnebagos had been in the camp, it almost certainly would not have mattered; the men of Atkinson's army were determined to utterly destroy what remained of the British Band.

The next day, on July 23rd, the volunteers left the battle site and marched toward the Blue Mounds to meet Atkinson. They arrived that day after dark; Atkinson and his force arrived there on July 24th after making a final march of twenty miles without water. That same day, messengers brought the letters of Dodge and Henry to Atkinson while he was still on the march, and from these he gained his first information concerning the Battle of Wisconsin Heights. The next day, Atkinson wrote to inform Scott of the situation and to explain how the lack of water transport had prevented Dodge and Henry from pressing the attack. He was undoubtedly pleased by what he considered to be a major victory after a frustrating month of long, ineffectual marches. Moreover, it was only the second victory of the war, and it was bigger and more decisive than Dodge's earlier win at the Battle of Pecatonica. Atkinson told Scott that he planned to move the entire army to a point on the Wisconsin River roughly twelve miles north of the Blue Mounds to a small lead mining hamlet known as Helena. There, he would build rafts so his army could cross the Wisconsin and continue the pursuit of Black Hawk. The volunteers and regulars were exhausted, and Atkinson knew it. However, he knew that the British Band was in an even worse condition, and therefore the army could not afford to rest for too long but had to catch up with Black Hawk while he and his people were in a vulnerable state. Indeed, Atkinson wrote to Scott that, "although we are worn down with fatigue and privation . . . [the enemy] must be much crippled, and is suffering for subsistanc[e]."[55]

Atkinson, of course, was correct, and Black Hawk's autobiography makes clear that after crossing the Wisconsin River, the British Band began to disintegrate rapidly. Many members deserted or fled down the river. The band was completely out of food and barely surviving on tree bark and roots. This was inadequate nourishment for the elders and young children, many of whom perished during the hellish march to the Mississippi. Black Hawk hoped to make it across the Mississippi and back into the country of the Sauks and Foxes, but he soon found out that the nightmare his people faced was about to get worse.[56]

7

THE THUNDERBIRDS' LAST FLIGHT

And captured or killed all the Sauks who were there,
Save a few, who midway between hope and despair,
Plunged into the Father of Waters so wide,
To battle for life with its onflowing tide;
But the steamboat, The Warrior, had come back and lay
In their course to take toll on that terrible day.
—AMER MILLS STOCKING

After the Battle of Wisconsin Heights, Henry Dodge became a whirlwind of activity. He assumed virtual control of the war while Atkinson was on the march, and his actions did much to insure that the fate of the British Band would be sealed. He instructed Captain Gustavus Loomis, the commanding officer at Fort Crawford, to place an artillery piece near the mouth of the Wisconsin River to shoot those members of the British Band who were making their escape down the river. Dodge believed that Black Hawk and the main body of the British Band would attempt to cross the Mississippi about twenty miles above Prairie du Chien. In anticipation, he asked Loomis to begin procuring water transport to move the army across the Mississippi. He also sent Posey augers and axes and instructed him to move his men from Fort Hamilton north to the Wisconsin River and begin constructing rafts so the army could cross.[1]

Atkinson's most pressing problem was the fact, that as every day passed, his army continued to dwindle due to sickness and a critical lack of horses. By the time he marched from the Blue Mounds to Helena, he had lost even more men and horses and had only 922 volunteers at his disposal. Posey had a mere 127 men; Alexander, 296; Henry, 367; and Dodge, 132. When added to the roughly 400 regulars, Atkinson had a force of a little over 1,300 men out of an army that once numbered almost 4,000. Despite the victory at Wisconsin Heights, there continued to be disaffection and low morale among the Illinois volunteers. Men from Henry's brigade begged for a few additional days of rest at the Blue Mounds, particularly for their worn-out horses. They argued that Posey's and Alexander's brigades had as yet seen no combat while their brigade (along with Dodge's battalion) had done all the fighting. It was, of course, out of the question; Atkinson needed every man he could get. Men under Alexander's command were frustrated with the endless marches that Atkinson seemed to demand of them. Alexander's aide-de-camp wrote that, "Had there been good management on the part of the Commanding Genl. [Atkinson] the war would have been ended some time since. Our men are generally . . . in good spirits but much displeased with Atkinson."[2]

By July 26th, Atkinson, the regulars, Henry's and Alexander's brigades, and Dodge's companies had arrived at Helena, which, like most white settlements in the lead mining region, was a collection of fewer than a dozen log cabins. The tiny hamlet was deserted, for all the settlers fled toward the forts and blockhouses once the war started. Posey and the army's quartermaster ripped apart the abandoned cabins in order to make the necessary rafts. By July 27th, part of the army had been transferred over the river, but there was still considerable equipment and the process was not completed until noon the next day. The army had marched only about four miles on July 28th when it struck the trail of the British Band. By now, Black Hawk had had a week's head start, and Atkinson knew that this was his last chance to catch him with the troops he had at his disposal. The horses they rode were the last of those that could still bear up under the strain. By the time he reached the Mississippi, those horses would also be too fatigued and worn-out to go any farther. If Black Hawk managed to get across the river, Atkinson would need fresh horses and probably new men.[3] Indeed, the journey to the Mississippi would be the last that this army of Atkinson's was likely to make.

The trail pushed west into yet more long stretches of country that few white Americans had ever seen. The relatively flat country to the east, where the army had operated earlier, now gave way to towering cliffs and high hills; several men even ventured to call the country "mountainous." Although no member of the army had a clear idea of where he was, the soldiers were comforted by the fact that as long as they kept finding the enemy's trail and moving west, they would eventually see the Mississippi. Several regular officers noted that the narrow defiles through which the army passed would have been excellent ambush positions where a few well-placed warriors could easily have stopped the army in its tracks. However, they also sensed the desperation of the British Band and why it was not stopping to fight. Every day, the army usually passed two of the encampments of the British Band; it was obvious that Black Hawk and his followers were moving much more slowly now and that the army was gaining on them. One reason for this lack of speed was the loss of horses, for the starved members of the British Band were now slaughtering and eating them.[4]

On August 1st, the army crossed the Kickapoo River and the country opened up into prairie. The horses, which had had inadequate fodder along the way, moved at such a slow pace that the regular infantrymen on foot had no problem keeping up with their mounted comrades. By dusk, the army encamped and was only five or six miles from the Mississippi. During the march on August 1st, the army came upon additional evidence that it was closing in on the British Band. Eleven corpses lay along the line of march where members of the British Band had dropped and died from starvation. The volunteers of Henry's brigade found one dead warrior who had been properly interred in the Sauk manner: his body was painted red and laid above ground in a log coffin covered with bark. The volunteers immediately tore it apart. The scouts at the front of the army found an old Sauk man who was taken prisoner and interrogated. He told the scouts that the British Band was then at the eastern bank of the Mississippi only a few miles ahead and that it planned to cross the next morning. After receiving this valuable intelligence, the volunteers shot the old Sauk. One of Henry's men justified the murder by saying that "no doubt, he had been at the massacre of a number of our citizens, and deserved to die for the crimes he had perpetrated."[5]

As Atkinson continued his march from the east, additional preparations were underway on the Mississippi River, where Gustavus Loomis and Indian agent Joseph Street worked to cut off other avenues of escape. Loomis and Street knew that members of the

British Band had been making their escape downriver in makeshift canoes ever since the Battle of Wisconsin Heights. Some of them ultimately did cross the Mississippi and managed to find their way back to the Sauk and Fox country. One woman entered the Mississippi near the mouth of the Wisconsin River with her baby girl strapped to her back as she maintained a grip on her horse. Miraculously, she and her baby made it to the opposite shore, although the horse drowned in the process. Others were not so lucky, for Loomis had a six-pound cannon and a twenty-five-man detachment mounted on a flatboat anchored at the mouth of the Wisconsin River under the command of Lieutenant Joseph Ritner, one of the officers of the Fourth Infantry Regiment who had arrived from Baton Rouge Barracks at Fort Crawford on July 25th. By August 5th, Ritner and his men had killed fifteen men, made prisoners of another four, and captured thirty-two women and children. Loomis also placed eight regulars at a ferry six miles up the Wisconsin River. The detachment there shot at a group of makeshift canoes that passed by its position on the night of July 28th and killed one member of the British Band. As a final precaution, Loomis also hired out the steamboat *Enterprise* (which had brought the two companies from Baton Rouge), and deployed a detachment of thirty soldiers on board along with a six-pound cannon mounted on the bow.[6]

The same day that the *Enterprise* arrived, Street ordered his subagent, Thomas Burnett, to instruct all the Winnebagos of the Mississippi bands to assemble at Prairie du Chien. North of Prairie La Crosse, Burnett found Washington Decorah and a group of Winnebagos who agreed to comply with the order, and for sound reasons. First, Street refused to pay them their treaty annuities if they did not. Just as significant was their desire to stay clear of the British Band and the army that was pursuing it. Burnett and Street were less concerned with the Winnebagos than with their canoes, for those could have been used to ferry the British Band across the Mississippi. About 250 men, women, and children left in between thirty-five and forty canoes and arrived on July 26th at Prairie du Chien. There they joined the Winnebagos under the civil chief Carrymaunee the Lame and the speaker Waukon Decorah, who had arrived the previous day. On July 27th, Burnett again ascended the Mississippi and visited Prairie La Crosse, but the majority of the Prairie La Crosse band was out hunting. Burnett told the few Winnebagos he met there that it was of the utmost importance they leave in their canoes and head to Prairie du Chien. Despite Burnett's demands, the Winnebagos asserted that they could not leave with so many people out hunting but would try to leave in three or four days. This was actually a minor setback since the majority of the Mississippi Winnebagos were assembled at Prairie du Chien by this time. While there, they formed search parties that assisted in capturing members of the British Band.[7]

Prairie du Chien was not the only place where Indians collected in order to stay clear of both the British Band and Atkinson's army. Of course, the United States recruited warriors to fight against Black Hawk, but in most cases, Indian agents and military commanders were content to see the Indians simply assemble at the major Indian agencies and stay out of the conflict. The major assembly points were at Chicago and Ottawa, where the Potawatomis of northern Illinois and southeastern Wisconsin gathered; and Prairie du Chien and Fort Winnebago, where the Winnebagos of the Rock, Wisconsin, and Mississippi River bands assembled. Indian agents issued rations as an incentive for the Indians to assemble at these places. It was a successful, albeit expensive strategy, and though the number of Indians who gathered at these various locations is difficult to determine, it was in the thousands.[8]

Although assembling the Mississippi River Winnebago bands at Prairie du Chien was a priority for both Street and Loomis, they had additional ideas concerning how to prevent the escape of the British Band. By July 30th, the *Enterprise* had been released from its duties and Loomis hired the *Warrior* as his new armed steamboat. He outfitted the vessel with a detachment of sixteen regulars and a six-pound artillery piece. Loomis had James Kingsbury, the young lieutenant who commanded the detachment, ascend the river and meet with Chief Wabasha of the Santee Sioux. Kingsbury's primary objective was to warn Wabasha that the British Band would soon attempt to cross the Mississippi. It is unclear whether Kingsbury asked Wabasha to have his warriors intercept Black Hawk's fleeing band or whether Wabasha assumed this task himself. Nevertheless, he eagerly agreed to supply 150 warriors for the purpose. Indeed, his warriors began to depart even before Kingsbury left. Unlike the fiasco back in June when the Santee Sioux warriors who assembled under Hamilton at Prairie du Chien did little more than march through northern Illinois, now there was the real possibility of a fight.[9]

The *Warrior* left the next day on August 1st, and in addition to the regulars, it had a twenty-man crew and six self-styled citizen volunteers from Prairie du Chien who were, according to one of them, eager to "get a pop at the Indians."[10] As the boat descended the Mississippi, it passed a group of Santee Sioux who told the *Warrior*'s captain, Joseph Throckmorton, that they had seen the British Band near the mouth of the Bad Axe River. By 4:00 p.m., the *Warrior* had arrived in the vicinity of the river's mouth and found the British Band. Black Hawk and his followers had just arrived and were beginning preparations to cross the Mississippi, using whatever makeshift rafts could be assembled on the spot. Black Hawk knew Throckmorton and was convinced that if he flew a white flag, he could surrender what remained of his hungry band. However, Throckmorton was as anxious as everyone else on the *Warrior* to engage the enemy, even if Black Hawk was an old acquaintance. Throckmorton thought the white flag was a ruse and refused to land the *Warrior* near shore. The details differ between the several white accounts and those of Black Hawk and one of his followers concerning what happened next. White accounts say that Throckmorton ordered the Indians on shore to get a small vessel and come out to the *Warrior* so he could determine whether they were Winnebagos (which is how they had initially identified themselves) or members of the British Band. Black Hawk had no transport, and he called out several times to the captain to send out some small vessel but received no response. Part of the problem was that the conversation was conducted in Winnebago through translators. Black Hawk had a Winnebago with him (one of the five who conducted the British Band to the Mississippi), and someone on the boat spoke Winnebago (although who it was and how well they spoke the language remains unknown). There was also a woman who was probably either Indian or Métis who knew at least some of the Sauk and Fox language.[11]

Black Hawk was convinced that whoever spoke Winnebago on board the *Warrior* garbled his message, for he asserted that Throckmorton "would not have fired upon us, if he had known my wishes."[12] However, white accounts make it clear that even if Black Hawk could have met with Throckmorton, it would not have mattered. Such a meeting would have simply confirmed sooner to

Throckmorton, the regulars, and everyone on the steamboat that they were face to face with the British Band rather than a group of Winnebagos. The woman on board who spoke Sauk and Fox ultimately identified the Indians on shore as the British Band, and the crew members, regulars, and volunteers on the *Warrior* immediately prepared for an attack. Throckmorton asserted that he gave the British Band fifteen minutes to remove the women and children, but the delay occurred not because of any humanitarian impulse on Throckmorton's part; it simply took that long to confirm that the Indians on shore were not Winnebagos. Black Hawk immediately had his women and children find cover. The regulars loaded canister shot into the cannon (essentially making it a large shotgun) and fired into the British Band. Over the course of the next two hours, the regulars fired two more canister rounds (there were only three rounds on board), and the regulars, crewmen, and volunteers on board fired their rifles and muskets. Only one man on the *Warrior* was wounded. Both Indian and white sources agree that the British Band lost a total of twenty-three members. Throckmorton broke off the attack and returned to Prairie du Chien only when the *Warrior* began to run out of fuel.[13]

After the *Warrior* departed, Black Hawk tried to persuade his followers to go north and find refuge among their traditional allies, the Ojibwas. Most refused and demanded instead to cross the Mississippi and make their way back to their own country. Only three lodges (or about sixty people) decided to travel with Black Hawk. Black Hawk was completely unaware that Atkinson was only one day's march away.

About ten miles to the east, Atkinson's army made camp at dusk on August 1st and did not get to eat dinner until about 10:00 p.m. Atkinson issued orders that the army, after only a few hours of sleep, would wake at 2:00 a.m. and be ready to march. However, Henry and Alexander did not receive these instructions until their men had already let their horses loose to graze. Thus, when reveille sounded, it was too dark for their men to find their mounts, and both brigades had to wait until it was light before they could march. Atkinson had to move forward in the early morning darkness with only Dodge's battalion, the regulars, and Posey's brigade.[14]

Dodge's battalion was the lead element that morning, and Dodge had his spy company under the command of Captain Joseph

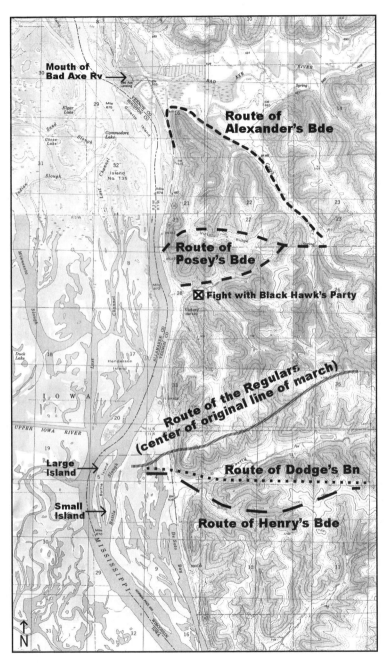

Map 6. Battle of Bad Axe

167

Dickson out in front of his main body. Behind Dodge were the regulars, and behind them was Posey's brigade. Alexander and Henry eventually caught up after sunrise; Alexander marched behind Posey, and Henry brought up the rear. Dickson had scouted a trail heading north on the evening of August 1st, and he pursued it further on the morning of August 2nd. By 6:00 a.m. it was sunrise, and Dickson's men engaged with a party of Indians for about an hour and killed fourteen of them. Once Atkinson received word of this skirmish, he began to deploy his forces for an assault. Dodge's battalion dismounted and formed the center. To Dodge's right, Zachary Taylor had ten companies of regulars deploy in line while he kept another three companies to the rear in reserve. Posey's brigade took its place to the right of the regulars, and on the extreme right was Alexander's brigade. Atkinson deployed his troops to the right because he believed that the British Band would attempt a retreat to the north. Moreover, the initial engagement indicated that the main body was somewhere to the north (and thus to the right) of Atkinson's line of march. However, Atkinson soon learned that the enemy was actually farther to the south. Atkinson had surmised that Dickson's short engagement had been with a guard element that Black Hawk had posted immediately to the rear of the British Band's main body. Upon advancing with his army, he found that this was not the case.[15]

White observers (and later historians) assumed that this party of Indians served as a rear guard detachment calculated to draw Atkinson's army farther to the north. However, the group killed by Dickson's men was not intentionally posted as either a rear guard or as a feint. Black Hawk had been heading north with his party during the early morning of August 2nd when, at about sunrise, he was overtaken by one of his warriors who had stayed with those attempting to cross the Mississippi. The young warrior communicated to Black Hawk that a number of people had already made it across and that Atkinson's army was closing in on them. Black Hawk decided to head back with the small group he led. While his autobiography is somewhat sketchy regarding his motives, the evidence strongly suggests that Black Hawk did not know that Atkinson had pursued the British Band after the Battle of Wisconsin Heights. He most likely assumed that the messenger sent to the hilltop on the night of July 23rd had, indeed, succeeded in relaying the message that the British Band would cause no more trouble if it was allowed to cross the Mississippi unmolested. This, of course, explains why Black Hawk posted no guards or harassing forces during the march to the Mississippi, as well as why he believed that the followers he left at the Mississippi would be able to cross unhindered. When he learned that morning that Atkinson's army had, in fact, pursued the British Band, he understood the gravity of the situation and decided to return to the main body at the Mississippi. He did not think that he could defeat Atkinson's army, but he nevertheless "concluded to return, and die with my people, if the Great Spirit would not give us another victory!"[16]

Black Hawk and his party immediately headed south to rejoin the main body of the British Band attempting to cross the Mississippi. While making their way south, Black Hawk and those with him made contact with Dickson's troops near present-day Victory, Wisconsin, roughly two miles to the north of where the main body was attempting to cross. As Dickson's men approached, those with Black Hawk hid in a thicket. Black Hawk and a Sauk woman both noted that a number of white volunteers passed by their position without noticing them, but another group that was part of Black Hawk's party was not so lucky and became engaged with Dickson's men; it was fourteen members of this group that Dickson's men killed. The remaining members of Black Hawk's party retreated north after the small battle and continued with their original plan to head toward the Ojibwa country rather than south toward the main body crossing the Mississippi. Although the small battle was not an intentional feint, the effect was the same, for Atkinson deployed the bulk of his army to the right and north toward the Bad Axe River rather than south toward the main body of the British Band.[17]

Atkinson had the army deploy by dismounting and forming ranks that ran roughly parallel to the Mississippi. The nature of the terrain made staying in neat ranks difficult, and as the regulars and volunteers moved forward, the ranks began to collapse into columns that followed the ravines down toward the river bottom. As the army moved forward and made no contact, Atkinson began to realize his mistake; the enemy was farther to the south. He ordered Dickson's men to the left and sent a messenger to hasten Henry's brigade forward. Henry and his men served as the reserve because they started so late that morning, and they probably would not have seen any action if Atkinson had not deployed the other units so far to the north. Henry was now going to be in the thick of the fight. Atkinson ordered him to move forward with one regiment while the remainder of his brigade was to be in reserve. After taking a trail down a narrow ravine, Henry's men began to engage the actual rear guard of the main body of the British Band. It was now about 9:00 a.m., and Henry immediately brought his entire brigade forward.[18]

Dodge's battalion and the regulars were in the best position to join the battle, and they pushed forward at a double-time pace. The regulars soon came to a steep bluff, which they slid down using their hands and rifle butts to retard their speed. Many of Dodge's men stayed at the top of the river bank and shot down at the warriors below. Dodge had most of his command down at the river bottom before the regulars arrived, and he was angered by the regulars' slow pace. The movement along the river bottom was slow partly because the ground was a labyrinth of high grass, deadfall, and sloughs that sliced across the marshy ground. It was here that many of Black Hawk's followers attempted to swim across the main slough to one of two islands that stood in the main channel of the river. Others had fashioned makeshift rafts from the available timber so they could float to the west bank of the Mississippi. The arrival of the volunteers and regulars led to pandemonium as the Indians continued their attempts to cross the river while their warriors harried and shot at the white troops closing in on them. Because of the high grass, the volunteers and regulars frequently could not see what they were shooting. Most simply fired at the flashes that they saw when the warriors fired, but others shot anything they saw moving through the grass. This resulted in many women and children being shot in addition to warriors. Dodge's battalion, Henry's brigade, and the regulars bore the brunt of the fighting that day, while Alexander and Posey were too far to the north to have any significant effect. Thus, as with the Battle of Wisconsin Heights, Alexander and Posey failed to earn the laurels of battle. However, Dodge, Henry, and Taylor had such an overwhelming superiority in manpower that it was quite a lopsided battle. Indeed, the British Band was down to about 500 members by this time, only about 150 of them warriors.[19]

As the volunteers and regulars slowly gained ground along the river bottom, the desperate women and children increasingly began to plunge into the Mississippi and held onto the backs of their horses. One volunteer saw at least six people clinging to a single horse. One Sauk mother saved herself and her baby by tightly bundling the child in a blanket that she held in her teeth while she firmly grasped with both hands the tail of a horse. Many of the escaping Indians went first across the main slough to one of the two islands. Soon, the regulars began to take a large volume of fire from the larger of the two islands. Taylor had six companies of regulars and some of Henry's and Dodge's men wade across the chest-deep water to the larger island. Five of the regulars crossing the slough were killed by warriors who turned as they and their women and children tried to cross the main channel of the river. Many managed to cross, but more would have made it had not the *Warrior* arrived at about noon, three hours after the battle had started along the river bottom. While at Prairie du Chien, a contingent of Menominee warriors, eager to attack their enemies, went aboard the steamboat. The regulars on board the *Warrior* began to use the artillery piece on board to sweep the larger island. Several warriors attempted to cross the river by exposing only their mouths and nostrils above the surface of the water but were shot by the Menominees aboard the vessel.[20]

After raking the west side of the island with cannon fire, Taylor had the *Warrior* bring the remainder of his regulars and two or three companies of volunteers onto the larger island. By this time, most of the Indians on the island had crossed the main channel or had been killed. Three or four warriors on the island were killed as the additional troops scoured it. When the volunteers discovered two warriors in a tree, virtually everyone began shooting at the same time, and both men were riddled by the discharge of more than one hundred guns. One of the regular officers who witnessed the event stated, "I saw them drop from limb to limb, clinging . . . like squirrels; or like the Indian in the 'Last of the Mohicans.'"[21] A few of the Menominees from the *Warrior* were on the island as well. When a young Menominee ran forward to scalp one of the Sauk warriors who had just been killed, one of the volunteers mistook him for a member of the British Band and shot and killed him. The young warrior was buried with full military honors alongside the regular soldiers who also died that day. A few troops were also landed on the smaller of the two islands, where a few more warriors of the British Band were also slain. One volunteer on the smaller island found a small sack with a piece of red cloth in it. He opened the sack and found a British flag in mint condition.[22]

By about 2:00 p.m., what came to be known as the Battle of Bad Axe was over, and, not surprisingly, the British Band suffered the heaviest casualties. Roughly 500 members of the British Band were at the battle, and Atkinson and other white participants estimated, based upon the corpses found, that about 150 Indians died (mostly warriors but also a number of women and children) while another 40 (all but one of whom were women and children) were taken as prisoners. Athough the number of prisoners was accurate, the estimated number of dead was too low since many members of the British Band were known to have drowned and their bodies were carried downstream. A little more than 200 people made it across the Mississippi that day, and, based upon these numbers, it can be safely assumed that at least another 110 people died in the river. Thus, at least 260 members of the British Band died that day, and possibly more. The total number of those who died in the British Band during the spring and summer of 1832 will never be known, but estimates range from as low as 442 to as high as 592; the average of these figures is about 520, which is probably the most accurate number that can be determined.

White losses at the Battle of Bad Axe were negligible. Atkinson lost 5 regulars during the fighting and another later died of wounds. Dodge lost 5 men, Henry lost 3, and, along with the Menominee warrior killed accidentally, a total of 14 men from Atkinson's army died. Total white fatalities—including volunteers, regulars, and civilians—totaled 77 during the war, of which 45 were killed by the British Band and the other 32 by Winnebagos, Potawatomis, and possibly members of other tribes.[23] Thus, it was the British Band that shed the vast majority of blood and suffered the greatest number dead during the war.

Moreover, many members of the British Band were needlessly and ruthlessly slaughtered at the Battle of Bad Axe, and this made it less of a battle and more of a massacre. The volunteers scalped many of the dead just as they had at the Battle of Wisconsin Heights; a few even took strips of flesh off the backs of dead warriors and used them to make razor straps. Several white observers noted that both the volunteers and regulars made valiant attempts to avoid shooting women and children that day. Nevertheless, many women and even children were intentionally targeted by those volunteers who cared little about sparing those usually characterized as noncombatants. One of Dodge's men had become particularly enraged after rounds went through his whiskers and the rim of his hat. He saw a woman with a child on her back and reportedly said, "See me kill that d[am]n squaw." He shot and killed the woman, and in the process hit the child's arm and shattered the bone. Later, Dr. Addisson Philleo amputated the arm without any kind of anesthetic while the child lay quietly and ate a biscuit. Another of Dodge's men noted that he and his comrades "killed everything that didn't surrender," which included "three squaws [who] . . . were naked." He also asserted that Joseph Dickson, the commander of Dodge's scouts, killed one Indian woman who attempted to surrender. Despite these acts, the volunteer still had the audacity to later insist: "We have been accused of inhumanity to those Indians. It is false as hell, we never did it."[24]

Other volunteers also described seeing naked Indian women along the shore of the river that day. Some women apparently had stripped themselves of their clothes in order to swim across the river. Others may have had little clothing left after their exhausting and demanding trek over the past four months. There is no direct evidence that any regulars or volunteers sexually assaulted female members of the British Band at the Battle of Bad Axe, but there are some sketchy bits of information that strongly suggest that sexual assaults may have occurred. One regular officer, while on the larger island, found a naked Sauk girl whom he described as being in "very uncomfortable circumstances," possibly a Victorian euphemism for her being a victim of sexual assault. He wrote that her body aroused in him "some rising symptoms of romance." However, in good Victorian form, he resisted, mostly because of her race, and he noted that the "fire, mud, and water, or rather I believe her complexion" soon cooled whatever sexual ardor he felt.[25] Nevertheless, if a well-disciplined regular officer could be tempted to commit sexual assault, it can easily be imagined what Indian-hating volunteers might do.

The most bloodthirsty volunteer at the Battle of Bad Axe was a Dutchman named John House, also called "Big Tooth John" because his eye teeth protruded over his lower lip like tusks. When Joseph Dickson ordered one volunteer to shoot an Indian child, the man refused and stated that he could not, in good conscience, shoot a child. House, on the other hand, eagerly shot the young boy through the heart as he leaped from behind a piece of driftwood. Shortly thereafter, a second young boy jumped from the same hiding spot, and House shot him in the head. During the course of the battle, a young Sauk mother had tied her baby to a piece of wood and sent the child into the current in the hope that it would be safe. House reportedly saw the young baby, coolly loaded his rifle, and shot the infant dead. When reproached by other volunteers for his unnecessary cruelty, House merely replied, "Kill the nits, and you'll have no lice."[26] If such behavior seems unfathomable today, House's comrades, even if they did not approve, could offer a clear rationale for such atrocities. One volunteer considered it God's providence and noted that "the Ruler of the Universe . . . takes vengeance on the guilty" and while he considered it a "great misfortune" that Indian women and children were killed, he glossed over this inconvenient fact by reminding posterity that "they were of the savage enemy, and the common enemy of the country."[27]

The large number of Indians killed during the war is one gauge of the preponderance of military strength that Atkinson possessed over Black Hawk, but there are other criteria as well. One of the most significant is the number of Indians that both sides managed to attract as allies. In the end, Black Hawk faced an overwhelming force of white volunteers and federal soldiers, but he faced a large number of Indians as well. It is safe to estimate that at least 752 Indians served on the side of the United States. This included Hamilton's 225-man force, the 95 Potawatomis under Caldwell, another 50 Potawatomis who served as scouts around Chicago, the 232 members of the Menominee battalion, and the 150 Santee Sioux warriors of Chief Wabasha. Black Hawk, on the other hand, managed to attract only about 50 Potawatomis and 50 Rock River Winnebagos to his standard, and they did not really fight with the British Band but instead used the conflict as an excuse to settle old scores with whites in their respective localities. Moreover, the thousands of Indians who remained neutral by sitting out the war at Ottawa, Chicago, Fort Winnebago, and Prairie du Chien ultimately helped the United States more than they did the British Band.[28]

With his victory at the Battle of Bad Axe on August 2nd, Atkinson considered the war to be over, but there was still some unfinished business. He still did not have Black Hawk or the Winnebago

Prophet, and many members of the British Band had made it across the river during the battle. The next day, the *Warrior* ferried about 150 volunteers to the west bank of the Mississippi so they could continue the pursuit. The volunteers went only about eight miles and determined that it would be impossible for them to catch up with those who made it across the river. They also were fatigued and had no desire to continue hunting down what remained of Black Hawk's followers. Atkinson decided to let them return and let the enemies of the Sauks and Foxes finish rounding up those who remained in what had been the British Band. From August 2nd to the 4th, Atkinson had the *Warrior* take the wounded, the prisoners, the regulars, and those volunteers without horses to Fort Crawford. The volunteers with horses conducted a thirty-five-mile march to Prairie du Chien. On the voyage down to Prairie du Chien, those on the steamboat saw dead horses, human corpses, and various bits of clothing and equipment lost by the British Band. Upon arriving at Prairie du Chien, one volunteer noted that the Menominees there "were rejoicing at the defeat of the Sacs and Foxes" and were dancing over the scalps taken at the Battle of Bad Axe.[29]

The Santee Sioux, Menominees, and Mississippi Winnebagos hunted down the roughly 200 members of the British Band who had made it across the Mississippi. Wabasha's 150 Santee Sioux warriors arrived too late in the day on August 2nd to participate in the battle, but the next morning Atkinson ordered them to pursue those who fled across the Mississippi. The Santee Sioux found a camp of Black Hawk's followers along the Cedar River in present-day Iowa and attacked them at dawn on either August 9th or 10th. The Sauks and Foxes were too tired and confused to put up a fight; the Santee Sioux killed most of the party and took the others captive. One woman who was taken prisoner during the raid noted that many of those with her yelled in desperation that they were Winnebagos, but this failed to persuade any members of the Santee Sioux war party. The Santee Sioux had accounted for another ninety members of the British Band, for they brought sixty-eight scalps and twenty-two prisoners to Prairie du Chien by August 22nd. Between thirty and forty members of the British band managed to escape from the Santee Sioux during the attack at the Cedar River.[30]

The Menominee battalion under Samuel Stambaugh also did not arrive in time to fight in the Battle of Bad Axe. The Menominee battalion had made it as far as Fort Winnebago by August 2nd, and Atkinson subsequently instructed Stambaugh that the services of the Menominees were no longer needed. The Menominees were eager to engage their enemies, and Stambaugh sent his adjutant to Prairie du Chien to meet with Scott and convince him to give the Menominees some role in the war. Scott allowed the Menominees to assist in capturing the remnants of the British Band on the east side of the Mississippi. Stambaugh gave his two Menominee companies explicit orders to make prisoners of all who surrendered. They could only shoot at armed warriors, and all women and children were to be spared. The Menominees generally followed Stambaugh's instructions, but he did not command them as much he wanted to believe. Indeed, the Menominees, although organized as a battalion, had little inclination to fight like white soldiers and instead practiced their own martial customs. One of the Menominee chiefs, A-co-mot, served as the expedition's prophet, and he conducted rituals each night with the purpose of discerning the location of the Menominees' enemies. Stambaugh stated that he found these "absurd . . . ceremonies . . . fatigueing and sometimes not a little annoying," but he did not interfere with them.[31]

An even more significant illustration of the Menominees' autonomy was the manner in which they fought. On August 10th, near the mining settlement of Cassville in present-day southwestern Wisconsin, the battalion picked up the trail of a small Sauk party that had most likely escaped down the Wisconsin River after the Battle of Wisconsin Heights. Once on the trail, the Menominees moved so fast on foot to find the Sauks that the officers, who were on horseback, had problems keeping up with them. When they were finally near the small party, the Menominees immediately stripped off their clothes, greased their bodies, painted their skin, and prepared to fight in the Indian manner. Stambaugh begged the Menominees to pursue what he believed was the most honorable course and simply take the entire party prisoner since it was so small compared to the battalion. However, the Menominees had a strong desire to avenge their dead relations and were not going to let the Sauk party escape unscathed. He asked them, at least, to spare any women or children. The Menominees respected Stambaugh's wishes and shot only the party's two armed Sauk warriors. The other eight members of the party, all of whom were either women or children, were taken as prisoners, although one young child was hit by some buckshot and died the next day. These were not the only casualties. There was an intense amount of firing and one of the Métis lieutenants, Robert Grignon, was accidentally shot in the arm by one of his men. Although the Menominee battalion played only a small role, the Menominee nation was very pleased with the outcome of the war and the destruction of the British Band. Stambaugh noted that the tribe was "entirely satisfied with the chastisement inflicted upon the Sac & Foxes" by the United States and that "the promise made them, that their enemies should be punished, has been redeemed to the very letter by our government."[32]

The majority of the Winnebagos assembled at Prairie du Chien were from the Mississippi River bands (although some from the Wisconsin River bands had assembled there as well), and they also assisted in rounding up stray members of the British Band. The Mississippi River Winnebagos had exhibited a distinct lack of support for Black Hawk's cause. Indeed, as several of them made their way down to Prairie du Chien prior to the Battle of Bad Axe, they saw the British Band along the east bank of the Mississippi on the evening of August 1st. The members of the British Band pleaded with the passing Winnebagos to ferry them across the river in their canoes, but the Winnebagos refused. On July 29th, the Winnebagos and the small number of Menominees who lived in the vicinity of Prairie du Chien began capturing prisoners they found fleeing down the Wisconsin River. One Winnebago was killed on August 2nd by two Sauk warriors who had managed to slip down the Wisconsin River; ironically, it was White Pawnee, who had been faithfully serving the Americans ever since Pierre Paquette recruited him. This loss did little to dampen the enthusiasm of the Winnebagos, and by August 22nd, they had taken a total seventy-seven prisoners and had brought in between fifty and sixty scalps.[33]

This was not evidence that all of the Mississippi River Winnebagos were necessarily enthusiastic for the American cause. Walking Cloud, the son of the village chief at Prairie La Crosse named, coincidentally, Black Hawk (and who is usually differentiated as Winnebago Black Hawk) noted that his father, older brother, and other Mississippi Winnebagos assisted in attacking those members of the British Band who escaped down the Wisconsin River after the Battle of Wisconsin Heights. White Cloud's narrative is a bit sketchy concerning the exact location, but his father and brother most likely were stationed at or near the ferry on the Wisconsin River where Loomis had posted a party of regulars. Walking Cloud noted that his father and brother undertook this responsibility only after experiencing heavy-handed American coercion. Moreover, Winnebago Black Hawk, despite calls by other Mississippi River Winnebagos, also refused to engage in warfare against the remnants of the British Band after the Battle of Bad Axe.[34]

The Wisconsin River bands were more evenly divided concerning their support for the British Band. While some like White Pawnee fought with the Americans, others rendered what assistance they could to the British Band. As they were fleeing down the Wisconsin River after the Battle of Wisconsin Heights, many members of the British Band were assisted by the Winnebagos along the river, who provided them with better canoes to replace their makeshift bark ones. While the Menominee battalion was at the portage of the Fox and Wisconsin Rivers, some of the Winnebagos there even threatened to attack the families of the Menominees. They told the Menominees that "the Americans were enemies of all red men, & that the Sacs would yet be victorious."[35]

The Rock River Winnebagos continued to be the staunchest supporters of the British Band, but even this support wavered once it was clear that Black Hawk had been defeated. Some members of the British Band found refuge among the Rock River Winnebagos who lived at Lake Koshkonong and the Four Lakes region. How many managed to avoid capture by remaining among the Winnebagos is impossible to determine, but the number was probably not insignificant. The regular army officer left in command of Fort Koshkonong noted that two entire lodges of Sauks, or about forty people, remained in the area after the British Band departed and stayed until early September. They probably continued to hide among either the Rock River Winnebagos or the local Potawatomis until they were able to secret themselves back across the Mississippi at a later date. At least a few Rock River Winnebagos decided to turn against the British Band and hunt down those stragglers who remained in the Rock River Valley. By August 26th, Winnebago warriors who lived in the region of Lake Koshkonong had killed three Sauk warriors in the area and brought a young Sauk girl to the fort as a prisoner.[36]

Some members of the British Band managed to find their way back to their country and miraculously evaded Atkinson's army as well as the Winnebago, Menominee, and Santee Sioux war parties that scoured both sides of the Mississippi. However, even this was not a guarantee of freedom, for Keokuk had agreed to turn over all those members of the British Band who had returned to the tribe. By August 19th he and his followers had transferred to the United States over fifty half-starved members of Black Hawk's band who had made their way back to the Sauk villages, including Napope. The exact number of Black Hawk's followers who survived the holocaust of the Black Hawk War is impossible to determine since some, like those who hid among the Winnebagos at Lake Koshkonong, were never captured. Also, the army did not keep exact records on all the captured prisoners brought to Rock Island. Nevertheless, a relatively accurate estimate is possible. By late August, 129 prisoners had been accounted for at Rock Island (this included those secured by Keokuk). About one hundred others were either at Prairie du Chien awaiting transport to Rock Island or still being held by the Winnebagos and Santee Sioux. In addition, roughly forty Sauks found refuge among the Winnebagos around Lake Koshkonong. Moreover, these forty were not the only followers of Black Hawk who successfully avoided capture, for there was also a party of thirty-seven Kickapoos that abandoned the British Band after crossing the Mississippi in April 1832 and found refuge among the Potawatomis of northeastern Illinois. Thus, roughly three hundred members of the British Band were known to have survived the carnage of the war.[37]

Of course, Black Hawk started with about 1,100 followers; if about five hundred died and another three hundred were known to have survived, that leaves three hundred persons unaccounted for. What happened to these three hundred is speculative, but a likely explanation is that as the war dragged on during the summer of 1832, many members abandoned the British Band and found refuge in the surrounding Indian communities until, after the war, they could infiltrate back to their home villages in small parties that escaped the notice of the army and their Indian enemies. For example, Winfield Scott noted that in addition to the thirty-seven Kickapoos who found refuge among the Potawatomis, there were several other Kickapoo lodges (he did not provide an exact number) that deserted the British Band and went to the Kickapoo villages along the Wabash River. Assuming this story was true (for, like the two lodges of Sauks around Fort Koshkonong, these Kickapoos were never captured), these lodges would have contained as few as forty Kickapoos and possibly as many as one hundred. Moreover, there are scattered references to small parties that were known to have deserted Black Hawk during the war.[38] So several hundred persons probably disappeared into the numerous tribal communities of the upper Great Lakes and upper Mississippi Valley, where they may have had familial relations or at least found sympathetic Indians and remained in these havens until it was safe to return to their homeland.

Those who were captured did not remain in captivity for long; ultimately, all except a handful of prisoners were turned over to their tribes. Those who returned were not allowed to have a separate political existence as a band. The army delivered all Sauk prisoners to Keokuk while those who were Foxes were given to Wapello. By September 4th, Joseph Street had convinced the Winnebagos and Santee Sioux to deliver the last of their prisoners to Prairie du Chien, and all of them were loaded onto the steamboat *Winnebago* and taken to Rock Island. The most prominent prisoners on the steamboat were the principal leaders of the British Band: Black Hawk and the Winnebago Prophet.[39]

Black Hawk intended to return to the main body of the British Band during the Battle of Bad Axe, and although he was within about two miles of the battle, his autobiography makes it clear that he never arrived at the battle site. He was angry about the fact that the volunteers and regulars had killed "helpless women and little children," but he learned of the gruesome details of the battle from one of his warriors who was there and managed to escape; Black Hawk did not die there or even fight there as he said that he would.[40] Instead, he headed north with the Winnebago Prophet. His autobiography becomes somewhat self-serving at this point, for he states that he went to the Winnebago village at Prairie La Crosse and asked the Winnebagos there to escort him to Prairie du Chien so that he could give himself up to the Americans. He had, of course, originally been headed toward the Ojibwa country where he had relations; he provides no account of why he would have changed his mind. Moreover, the fact that he and a small party left the main body of the British Band after the first battle with the *Warrior* on August 1st did not sit well with his followers. The civil chief Weesheet and others who remained at the Mississippi River said after he and the Winnebago Prophet departed, "Now they have brought us to ruin and lost us our women and children, they have run to save their own lives."[41] In Black Hawk's defense, he had invited anyone who wanted to join him and head toward the Ojibwa country to do so. Moreover, when he left, he did not know that Atkinson had pursued him, and he did make a sincere, albeit belated, attempt to return to the battle site when he learned that the army was near.[42]

However, Black Hawk did not give himself up of his own free will but was forced to do so by the Mississippi River Winnebagos. In fact, Black Hawk was not at Prairie La Crosse (nor at the Wisconsin Dells, as many earlier histories have claimed) when he and those followers who fled with him were found by a Winnebago named Hishoog-ka (Big Gun) at a camp near the headwaters of the La Crosse and Lemonweir Rivers (southwest of present-day Tomah, Wisconsin). Black Hawk was definitely on his way to the Ojibwa country and probably would have made it had Hishoog-Ka and his party not stumbled upon Black Hawk's camp. Hishoog-Ka was the brother of Winnebago Black Hawk of Prairie La Crosse. He reported his discovery to his brother, who immediately called a council of the local Winnebago leadership to discuss the situation. One-Eyed Decorah, who later claimed a larger role in the capture of Black Hawk than he actually played, suggested annihilating Black Hawk's camp since, he argued, the Mississippi bands had pledged their services to Atkinson. Winnebago Black Hawk refused, stating, "We are not gathered here to counsel war against our friends," particularly since the Winnebago Prophet was a relation to some of those who lived at Prairie La Crosse.[43] However, this did not mean that Winnebago Black Hawk was simply going to allow Black Hawk and his party to flee to the Ojibwa country, for the reward for capturing Black Hawk was significant: one hundred dollars and forty horses. Winnebago Black Hawk sent a party under a young warrior named Chaashjan-ga (whose name meant Wave and who was mistakenly called Chaetar in white sources), who was a relation of the Winnebago Prophet, with a mission of calling for a cessation in the war.[44]

When Chaashjan-ga arrived at Black Hawk's camp on or about August 20th, he offered Black Hawk and the Winnebago Prophet a pipe of peace. He spoke on behalf of Winnebago Black Hawk and the local Winnebago leaders who had sent him and told Black Hawk that the war he was fighting had caused much hardship to the women and children of the British Band. Chaashjan-ga offered the pipe of peace. By smoking it, Black Hawk would have made a solemn promise to end the war and, by extension, surrender himself and the remainder of his band over to the Americans. According to Winnebago sources, Black Hawk refused the pipe of peace offered by Chaashjan-ga, as did the Winnebago Prophet, who asserted that he and those with him intended to keep fighting. Everyone assembled with Black Hawk also refused to accept the peace pipe, everyone except a young boy. He took the pipe, pressed it to his lips despite angry shouts by his elders, and smoked the tobacco. Such an act was not something that was undertaken lightly, and among the Indians of the Great Lakes, if one member of a community accepted the pipe of peace, all did. According to the grandson of Winnebago Black Hawk, the assembled members of the British Band "wailed and cried, for this meant complete surrender and cessation of the war."[45] Thus, one small boy, fatigued from what must have seemed an endless four months of war and hunger, sealed the fate of Black Hawk, the Winnebago Prophet, and their entire party.

The Winnebagos took Black Hawk and the Winnebago Prophet back to Prairie La Crosse, where the women made them outfits of white deer skin. Before departing for Prairie du Chien, Black Hawk gave one of the local Winnebago chiefs (possibly Winnebago Black Hawk) his war bundle, long a symbol of what it meant to be a member of the Sauk nation. The Winnebago chief promised to safeguard it and return it to Black Hawk if the Americans allowed him to live. On August 27th, Chaashjan-ga appeared at the Indian agency house in Prairie du Chien with Black Hawk and the Winnebago Prophet. Joseph Street and Zachary Taylor were present, as were many of the officers from Fort Crawford, all of whom were eager to get a glimpse of the two men against whom they had fought. Chaashjan-ga, who was not a chief or an orator, made a short speech and told Street and Taylor that since the Winnebago Prophet was a relation of his, he did not wish to be present if the Americans were going to hurt or kill him. Indeed, Chaashjan-ga stated, "Soldiers some times stick the ends of their Guns (bayonets) into the backs of Indians . . . when they are going about in the hands of the guard. I hope this will not be done to these men."[46] One-Eyed Decorah accompanied Chaashjan-ga and attempted to take some of the credit for the capture of Black Hawk and the Prophet, but he had nothing to do with it. Street obviously saw through his ruse, for the reward of one hundred dollars and forty horses went to Winnebago Black Hawk and his brother Hishoog-Ka. However, Winnebago Black Hawk soon learned that the horses were those confiscated from the British Band, and he did not even receive all forty. He later complained: "We have received but 20 horses, and they are so poor that we can't get them along."[47]

Black Hawk and the Winnebago Prophet stayed for a short while in the stockade at Fort Crawford until they departed on September 4th aboard the steamboat *Winnebago.* Along with Black Hawk were his eldest son, Nashaweskaka (Loud Thunder or Whirling Thunder) and his younger son Wathametha (Roaring Thunder). Two of the Winnebago Prophet's sons were also with him, as was his brother. In what was one of the great ironies of American history, the two army officers who accompanied Black Hawk were Lieutenant Jefferson Davis and Lieutenant Robert Anderson, who would play significant roles on opposing sides of the Civil War thirty years later. Davis was absent on furlough in Mississippi during the entire duration of the Black Hawk War. Later in his life he attempted to make claims to the contrary, but in truth he returned from Mississippi after the war ended, and escorting the defeated leader of the British Band was his only contribution.

Before leaving Prairie du Chien, Black Hawk talked with Street. He noted that he did not initiate the war and that others (most likely he meant the Rock River Winnebagos under White Crow) urged its continuance once it started. In a pointed criticism of the Americans, he told Street that he tried to surrender twice. When his attempt to surrender to the captain of the *Warrior* was rebuffed on August 1st, he decided that he would not surrender again. He hinted that his capture by the Winnebagos was the event that forced him to surrender. He also promised to provide the full story regarding his role in the war to General Winfield Scott when he arrived at Rock Island.[48]

The *Winnebago* stopped at Galena, where a large crowd gathered to catch a glimpse of Black Hawk. Some even tried to get into his cabin, but Lieutenant Davis forbid it. Black Hawk and the other prisoners were supposed to land at Rock Island so they could be put with the other Indian prisoners held at Fort Armstrong, but cholera had broken out there and the captain of the *Winnebago* refused to land. Black Hawk had wanted to talk to Scott, but the *Winnebago*'s captain refused to dock the vessel as it approached Rock Island on September

5th. Scott even took a small boat out and attempted to talk to Black Hawk on board the steamboat, but the captain did not allow anyone from Rock Island onto the *Winnebago*. Instead, he took the vessel a little bit below Rock Island so that the prisoners could be let off and handed over to Keokuk. However, Black Hawk and the other leaders of the British Band were not allowed to go, for they were to be kept as prisoners. The *Winnebago* proceeded to Jefferson Barracks, where it arrived on September 10th. At Jefferson Barracks, Black Hawk once again met Napope, Weesheet, and two other civil chiefs from the British Band who had arrived only about a week and half earlier. A total of twenty members of the British Band—virtually all the civil chiefs, war leaders, and warriors of note—were, according to Scott, to be held as "hostages for the good conduct of the remainder of the Band."[49]

There was no stated length of time that Black Hawk and his comrades were to remain prisoners, although Scott had suggested a sentence of at least ten years. Fortunately for Black Hawk, President Andrew Jackson had different ideas and his incarceration lasted only about a year. Fourteen of the prisoners were released in April 1833. The remaining six—Black Hawk, his eldest son, the Winnebago Prophet and one of his sons, Napope, and the civil chief Pamaho—gained their freedom in early August 1833. Black Hawk and the others were not mistreated during their time as prisoners, at least not by white standards. Henry Atkinson had returned to Jefferson Barracks during September and insured that Black Hawk and his fellow prisoners were comfortable and well fed, although each man had to wear a ball and chain around his foot to prevent escape. Atkinson did not quite understand how humiliating this was for Black Hawk, for among the Indian communities of the upper Great Lakes and upper Mississippi Valley, there was no honor in being a prisoner. Whereas a warrior could die a glorious death in battle, he could live only a miserable, embarrassing existence in confinement. Black Hawk stated as much when he asserted that "a brave war chief would prefer *death* to *dishonor*," and that he found wearing the ball and chain "extremely mortifying . . . confinement, and under such circumstances, could not be less than torture!"[50]

As Black Hawk and his compatriots languished in the stockade, Scott and Governor John Reynolds of Illinois negotiated treaties that were designed to make the Winnebagos, as well as the Sauks and

Foxes, pay a steep price in land for the belligerent actions by minorities of their tribes. Indeed, the most significant consequence of the Black Hawk War was that it gave the federal government a great deal of leverage over the regional tribes, particularly the Winnebagos and Sauks and Foxes. Andrew Jackson had signed the Indian Removal Act into law in 1830, and this required all Indians east of the Mississippi to be removed to the trans-Mississippi West. Of course, the government was still required to negotiate individual treaties with each tribe, but now their new homes would be across the Mississippi.

Prior to the Black Hawk War, the government had focused most of its efforts in the South, where tribes such as the Cherokees, Choctaws, Chickasaws, and Creeks were larger, and thus politicians in Washington perceived a more pressing need to remove them. The Black Hawk War brought the region that is today the upper Midwest into the spotlight. Of course, there had been a few previous land cession treaties in this region, but these had occurred due to special circumstances. After the Black Hawk War, the pace of land cession treaties picked up significantly, and within two decades virtually the entire region passed into the hands of the federal government. Indeed, the Black Hawk War was the watershed event in the region's history. It marked the end of an era that began when the French first penetrated the region in small numbers in the seventeenth century and lived alongside the tribes, all of whom retained their cultural, economic, and political autonomy even through the British and early American regimes. The war marked the beginning of a new era in which the United States not only stripped the regional tribes of their land bases but of their cultural, economic, and political independence as well.[51]

The first treaty council took place with the Winnebagos and opened at Rock Island on September 10th. Winfield Scott started the council by allowing the Wisconsin River Winnebagos to make their opening speeches. Konoka Decorah (also known as Old Decorah) ended his speech by giving the names of eight Winnebagos, all members of the Rock River bands, who were involved in the various attacks committed during the war. However, much to Scott's chagrin, none of them had been brought along as he had ordered in his initial instructions. The next day, White Crow spoke, and in many cases he either stretched the truth or fabricated it. Despite evidence that illustrated otherwise, he denied urging the young warriors of the Rock River bands to commit their attacks and instead blamed the Winnebago Prophet. He denied harboring Napope after the Battle of Wisconsin Heights (despite Napope's testimony to the contrary), and he attempted to prove his loyalty by recounting his services to Dodge and Atkinson during the war.[52]

Scott spoke and singled out the Rock River Winnebagos for their perfidy. He had earlier accepted the arguments of Joseph Street that the Rock River bands should be forced to cede their lands and moved west into the Neutral Ground. Street believed that moving the Winnebagos there also would put a damper on intertribal warfare between the Santee Sioux and the Sauks and Foxes. Scott latched onto both of these ideas and proposed that the Rock River Winnebagos and a significant number of the Wisconsin River bands sell their land and remove to the Neutral Ground. After discussing the matter, the Winnebagos agreed, although many of them had doubts about moving to the Neutral Ground since they feared being caught between the Sauks and Foxes and the Santee Sioux if they fought each other. The Rock River Winnebagos were hardly eager to sell their lands, but their speeches made at the treaty council suggested a sense of fatalism. Whites had long coveted their lands, and sooner or later whites would get them. Moreover, the treaty meant additional annuity monies for all the Winnebago bands. The provisions seemed generous, so on September 15th, the Winnebagos ceded the Rock River country, which included all the territory between the Four Lakes and Lake Winnebago as well. In exchange, they received the Neutral Ground (which many Winnebagos later abandoned when warfare between the Santee Sioux and the Sauks and Foxes resumed) and an annuity of $10,000 per year for twenty-seven years.[53]

Scott and Reynolds opened a second council with the Sauks and Foxes on September 19th, at which Keokuk and Wapello served as the principal representatives of the two tribes. Scott's opening address left little doubt about his intentions. He stated that the Americans had spent "immense sums" of money to put down Black Hawk's band, and "as conquerors we would have a right to help ourselves; to enter your country and mark off, for seizure, that portion which belonged to Black Hawk's band." Scott did not fail to mention that the chiefs and warriors present remained at peace, but he asserted that "if a particular part of a nation goes out of their country, and makes war, the whole nation is responsible." He assured the

Sauk and Fox leadership that the federal government, wedded as it was to the ideas of treating its vanquished enemies with "moderation, and temper[ing] justice with humanity" would not take the land of the Sauks and Foxes, however justified it was in doing so. Instead, the United States would fully compensate the two tribes. The proposed cession encompassed a large portion of the west bank of the Mississippi, including Dubuque's Mines. The cash annuity for the sale was to be $20,000 a year for thirty years.[54]

The Sauks and Foxes believed that as long as the land cession was inevitable, they would press for the best possible deal. Keokuk told Scott that the two tribes would agree to the land cession if the United States was willing to end the perpetual—and paltry—annuity of $1,000 in goods from the 1804 treaty and raise the annuity of the current treaty to $30,000 for the thirty years. They also wanted forty kegs of tobacco and an identical quantity of salt each year for thirty years. The tribe had about $40,000 in debts with the American Fur Company (more specifically, the Rock Island merchants George Davenport and Russell Farnham), and Keokuk asked that the government assume these debts and also provide a year's worth of provisions for the poor families among the two tribes, especially those who had been with Black Hawk and had not planted or hunted that summer. Keokuk revised the boundaries of the land cession so it was smaller and asked for a reservation of about thirty square miles of land within the cession. The Sauks and Foxes negotiated much more aggressively than the Winnebagos, and in the end they were successful. The only point that Scott and Reynolds could not meet was an alteration in the annuity; the perpetual annuity of $1,000 in goods and the proposed annuity of $20,000 for thirty years had to remain.[55]

The treaty between the United States and the Sauks and Foxes was signed September 21, 1832. Prior to signing the treaty, Scott spoke in glowing terms about Keokuk and how his faithfulness to the United States had prevented the army from overrunning the country of the two tribes earlier that summer. Scott even went so far as to compare Keokuk to President Andrew Jackson. So impressed were Scott and the president with Keokuk that he was elevated, essentially by presidential fiat, to the position of head chief among the Sauks and Foxes. As a symbol of this new authority, Scott presented Keokuk with a medal to wear around his neck that bore the

Figure 18. A sketch of Keokuk made in 1833 by George Catlin. Reprinted from Catlin, *Letters and Notes on the Manners, Customs, and Condition of the North American Indians*, vol. 2

image of Andrew Jackson. Keokuk, who was not born into a chiefly clan, had reached the pinnacle of his career and was now the undisputed leader of the two tribes. Keokuk asked that all the annuity money in the future be given to him and the other chiefs each year rather than doled out to individuals in the tribe. He did this so that he could consolidate his power and control much of the economic and political affairs of the two tribes. The Sauks and Foxes had to leave their ceded land on the west side of the Mississippi (a tract referred to as the Black Hawk Purchase) by June 1, 1833. The treaty also stipulated that Black Hawk, the Winnebago Prophet, and ten of their principal lieutenants were to remain in custody until released by the president.[56]

Not all of the Sauks and Foxes were happy with the elevation of Keokuk. A white observer noted in 1835 that many of the chiefs believed that Scott and Reynolds "usurped more power . . . than belongs to [the Sauks' and Foxes'] whole nation" when they elevated Keokuk to the position of principal chief in 1832, particularly since it was the custom of the two tribes that "a man *must be born a chief*, or never can become one!" One old Sauk summed up the feelings of the tribe when he stated, "The *whites* would have been displeased, no doubt, had *we* made Gen. Scott their Great Chief and Great Father!"[57] Nevertheless, Keokuk controlled the annuity money from the 1832 treaty as well as the annuities from later treaties for the next ten years, and this did much to ensure his continued leadership. Black Hawk's humiliation was reinforced by the fact that his only hope for leaving his confinement at Jefferson Barracks was to have Keokuk successfully petition the government for his release. In December 1832, Black Hawk and the Winnebago Prophet also asked Atkinson to intervene on their behalf and petition for their release.[58] However, it was not to be, for Black Hawk, the Winnebago Prophet, and the other prisoners first had to make a long journey to the East.

8

THE CALM
AFTER THE STORM

But all my folks had suffered much,—
(We will leave that behind,)
When I get back the words you speak,
Shall be fixed in my mind.
I will not go to war again,
But I will live in peace;
And as I hold you by the hand,
Our friendship shall not cease.
—AMER MILLS STOCKING

Originally, Black Hawk and nineteen others were placed in confinement, but over the course of the succeeding months, the number was whittled down as many of the lower-ranking members of the British Band were deemed innocuous enough to be released to Keokuk. The treaty signed on September 21st specified only twelve persons to be detained (although one of them, a son of the Winnebago Prophet, had been released by Atkinson before he received word that the boy was to be held). In November 1832, Winfield Scott suggested to Secretary of War Lewis Cass that the remaining eleven prisoners be transferred to Fort Monroe in Virginia. Like all frontier posts, Jefferson Barracks did not have the facilities needed to hold prisoners for any great length of time. Scott noted that Black Hawk and his companions could be kept at Fort Monroe without a sentinel having to be posted to guard them at all times, unlike at Jefferson Barracks; Fort Monroe was also more secure and the prisoners could have the relative freedom to walk about the entire post without fear of them escaping. Since it was late in the season when Scott made his recommendation, Black Hawk and the others had to wait until spring. Their remaining time at Jefferson Barracks was not uneventful, for they had been visited by George Catlin, the renowned painter of North American Indians. Catlin painted the portraits of Black Hawk, his eldest son Nashaweskaka, the Winnebago Prophet, and Weesheet.[1]

In March 1833, Black Hawk also received a visit from his wife, Asshewqua (Singing Bird), and his daughter, both of whom were accompanied by Keokuk and several Sauk chiefs. Black Hawk and the other prisoners were cheered by the visit, particularly since Keokuk planned to discuss their release with William Clark. Keokuk petitioned for the release of their tribesmen, but Clark was not fully able to grant their wish. Scott had received word that four of the prisoners could go free, but Black Hawk, Nashaweskaka, the civil chiefs Napope and Pamaho, and the Winnebago Prophet and his adopted son were to remain in confinement. Weesheet, who also was supposed to remain, became ill and was turned over to Keokuk. Moreover, Black Hawk and his five companions were to be sent to Washington and then to Fort Monroe. Thus, in early April 1833, a year after they had crossed the Mississippi in order to save their homeland, Black Hawk and his fellow prisoners left Jefferson Barracks by steamboat and headed south down the Mississippi River and then east on the Ohio River.[2]

The small party also included an interpreter, Charles St. Vrain (the brother of Felix St. Vrain), an army lieutenant, and two sergeants. The steamboat ascended the Ohio all the way to Wheeling, Virginia, where Black Hawk and his party debarked and took a stagecoach. Black Hawk was amazed by the National Road and the immense amount of labor required to construct it. As the stagecoach made its way east, Black Hawk noted that he was "astonished to find so many whites living on the hills!"[3] He continued, as his trip progressed, to express surprise and even shock at the vast number of white persons who lived in the United States. And that, of course, was the trip's purpose. The federal government sought to impress him with the large population of the United States and the futility of resisting American expansion. Prior to his trip east, Black Hawk had seen only small frontier settlements of a thousand persons or less such as St. Louis and Detroit. Seeing cities like Baltimore, Philadelphia, and New York opened his eyes to the true size of the nation's white population. Black Hawk also noticed that people in the East were fundamentally different from those on the frontier. Indeed, westerners tended to see Indians as almost subhuman. Easterners, on the other hand, rarely had contact with Indians and thus treated them as novelties and even as romantic "noble savages." Black Hawk concluded that the principle of Christianity, as he understood it, was "to do unto others as you wish them to do unto you" and that the people in the East acted on this principle while settlers in the West "seem never to think of it."[4]

On April 22, 1833, Black Hawk and his comrades arrived in Washington and, as cheering crowds gathered on the streets to greet them, they toured the city for several days and met with a variety of important officials. On April 26th, Black Hawk finally met the "Great Father": President Andrew Jackson. The day began when Black Hawk and his companions walked first to the War Department and the Office of Indian Affairs, where they were shown the many portraits of famous chiefs and warriors that graced the walls. The members of Black Hawk's party were able to identify both friends and enemies among the portraits. They then walked a short distance to the president's mansion. Jackson, who was six feet, one inch tall, would have been a commanding presence as he met with the delegation, particularly since its leader, Black Hawk, was only about five feet, five inches tall. Black Hawk was impressed by the man who stood in front of him, and noted that he looked to be a man who had "seen as many winters as I have, and seems to be a *great brave!*"[5] In fact, both men had been born in 1767 and had had long careers in frontier warfare, although always fighting on opposite sides. It is doubtful whether Black Hawk ever said to Jackson during the course of their meeting, "I am a man and you are another." Like other quotes attributed to Black Hawk, this one is of dubious provenance. Nevertheless, the extant sources make it clear that Black Hawk was not about to cower in front of Jackson, and he maintained his dignity even as he expressed humility.[6]

Black Hawk gave the president a Sauk war headdress as a sign of friendship; Jackson then asked him why he had gone to war. Both Black Hawk and the Winnebago Prophet recounted their reasons, which were consistent with those they provided a year earlier. They asserted that the British Band had had a right to live on the east side of the Mississippi and raise corn at the Winnebago Prophet's village. Both men also stated that they wanted to return immediately to their people. Indeed, Black Hawk noted that when Keokuk visited Washington several years earlier, he had been allowed to return after meeting with the president. However, Black Hawk did not seem to understand that when Keokuk went east in 1824 he did so as part of a treaty delegation; Black Hawk and his companions went as prisoners. Jackson told them that they would remain prisoners at Fort Monroe until he was certain that the Sauks and Foxes were disposed to remain at peace and abide by the terms of the recent treaty. Black Hawk started to talk the president out of his decision, but he noted that "as our interpreter [St. Vrain] could not understand enough of our language to interpret a speech, I concluded it was best to obey our Great Father, and say nothing contrary to his wishes."[7]

After shaking the president's hand, Black Hawk and his companions departed for Fort Monroe, which was far more comfortable than Jefferson Barracks. There, Black Hawk did not have to wear a ball and chain, but Jackson ordered him to wear white men's clothes for the remainder of his confinement since he would be meeting many dignitaries. Black Hawk had to wear a white cotton shirt, silk tie, and a blue army frock coat. Surprisingly, he did not mind the change in attire and wore it not only for the remainder of the trip but for the rest of his life. The officer in charge of Black Hawk and his fellow prisoners during their time at Fort Monroe was Colonel Abraham Eustis, who commanded Scott's regulars during the war. The War Department went to great lengths to insure that Black Hawk and his companions were comfortable, and Lewis Cass directed that they have access to the entire fort and its environs. Black Hawk and his comrades were treated more like honored guests than prisoners, and they had their portraits painted several more times while at Fort Monroe by the well-known artists Charles Bird King, Robert Matthew Sully, Samuel L. Brookes, and John Wesley Jarvis.[8]

Jackson most likely did not have a firm idea concerning how long he was going to have Black Hawk and his companions stay at Fort Monroe. Regardless of what he may have thought, there were many voices that called for allowing the prisoners to return to their homes. William Clark noted that the Sauks and Foxes were impressed with the folly of ever resisting the United States again, and he also believed that releasing Black Hawk and his fellow prisoners would be

Figure 19. A lithograph of Black Hawk in the army frock coat that he regularly wore in his later years, based on a portrait by James Otto Lewis and reprinted from Armstrong, *The Sauks and the Black Hawk War.*

a gesture of good will that would bolster Keokuk's political position among the Sauks and Foxes. Henry Atkinson also believed that the prisoners should return to their people, but only after seeing the cities of Baltimore, Philadelphia, and New York. Even the newspapers began to offer opinions on the matter. The *National Intelligencer,* one of the most stridently anti-Jackson newspapers in the country, believed that "it may be deemed compatible with a just and humane policy, to make their duress of short duration."[9]

Since the British Band had ceased to exist (at least for the time being), and Keokuk had repeatedly pledged that the Sauks and Foxes would remain at peace, Jackson decided to release Black Hawk and his companions after they had been at Fort Monroe for about a month. Cass directed that on their way back home they see the major cities of the eastern seaboard—particularly Norfolk, Philadelphia, New York, and Boston—so they could appreciate the size of the United States. Major John Garland was charged with escorting Black Hawk and his party for the remainder of the trip. Eustis and the other officers at Fort Monroe treated Black Hawk and his fellow prisoners to a feast before they left. Black Hawk had been more of a celebrity than a prisoner at Fort Monroe, but he soon found that his celebrity had spread much farther.[10]

Black Hawk and his companions departed Fort Monroe on June 4th. Although it was dark when they arrived by steamboat at Norfolk, an immense crowd gathered at the dock to catch a glimpse of the Indians. The next day they visited the nearby naval yard and were astounded by the size of the seventy-four-gun *Delaware*. Black Hawk was particularly pleased when he saw the bow of the ship and noticed that the carved figurehead was an Indian warrior. When Black Hawk and his companions arrived back at their hotel, they were besieged by a crowd of local citizens so large that not everyone could squeeze into the room where Black Hawk and the Winnebago Prophet were receiving visitors. They decided instead to address the crowd from the hotel balcony. Through their interpreter, Black Hawk promised that in the future he would exhibit only a peaceful disposition toward his white brothers. A mob of people later followed Black Hawk and his party as they departed their hotel and made their way to the docks to board a steamboat that took them from Norfolk.[11]

Although the next stop should have been Philadelphia, Garland decided that Black Hawk, constantly pressed by crowds wherever he went, needed a rest and made an unplanned stop in Baltimore. At the time, Jackson was making his own tour of eastern cities, and he happened to arrive in Baltimore on the same day as Black Hawk. Both men attended the same theater on the night of June 6th, and while they sat in separate boxes, the theatergoers in attendance that night buzzed with excitement at the spectacle of seeing both Jackson and Black Hawk. The next day, Jackson had a second, impromptu meeting with Black Hawk. He admonished Black Hawk to remain at peace because the Americans were as numerous "as the leaves in the woods. What can you do against us? You may kill a few women and children, but such a force would be soon sent against you, as would destroy your whole tribe." Black Hawk responded by making a sincere promise to Jackson; he pledged: "I won't go to war again. I will live in peace."[12]

Black Hawk did not get any respite in Baltimore. The newspapers gave his trip so much publicity that virtually everyone in every city he visited knew when he and his companions would arrive. Many young women even kissed Nashaweskaka, whose tall frame and well-proportioned features attracted their attention. Black Hawk was impressed with the size of Baltimore and found it hard to believe that Philadelphia would be even larger and New York larger still. He arrived in Philadelphia on June 10th, two days after Jackson had arrived. The fact that the two men were visiting the same cities was purely coincidental, but once again Black Hawk attracted large crowds at the president's expense. On June 14th, Black Hawk and his companions arrived in New York; the president had arrived two days earlier. Jackson attracted great crowds the day he arrived, but many people expressed disappointment when they did not see Black Hawk with him. Jackson was clearly becoming annoyed at the seemingly undue attention that the crowds paid to a defeated Indian leader rather than their president, "Old Hickory," the victor at the Battle of New Orleans. On the day they arrived in New York, Black Hawk and his companions were taken to Castle Garden to witness the flight of a hot air balloon. Jackson was also supposed to attend the event, but he claimed fatigue and did not go. One young New Yorker noted that the crowds that lined up for Black Hawk's arrival were so large that the steamboat could not dock as planned. He also noted, as Jackson had correctly surmised, that, to the citizens of New York City "Black Hawk and his companions . . . now occupy the place in the public curiosity which Gen. Jackson so recently filled."[13]

The tours, theaters, and sightseeing continued in New York. Black Hawk and his companions were completely awestruck upon seeing the hot air balloon ascend into the heavens and fly off until it could no longer be seen. According to Black Hawk, "[O]ne of our young men asked the *prophet*, if he [the balloon's pilot] was going up to see the Great Spirit?"[14] The residents of the nation's eastern seaboard were so engrossed in Black Hawk's trip that several newspapers began to carry columns labeled "Blackhawkiania," covering details of the tour. By mid-June, many newspapers were publishing outright fabrications. One paper reported that Nashaweskaka had fallen in love with a prominent woman from New York, while another reported that Black Hawk had stroked a woman's head and commented on how fine it would be for scalping.[15]

The constant crowds and unrelenting schedule began to take their toll, and soon the novelty of the trip began to fade. The party was slated to see Boston, but Black Hawk objected and asked Garland to begin the journey toward the Mississippi instead. Garland relented and noted that by the time Black Hawk and his companions had reached New York, they had been sufficiently impressed with the size of the United States. He later noted: "It was with difficulty they could believe their own senses" when they saw the "populous cities and the immense crowds of people, assembled in them . . . they had not formed even a distant conception of the extent and population of the United States."[16]

Upon arriving at Detroit, Black Hawk was eager to see the friends he had there, particularly Lewis Cass. Black Hawk was obviously not aware that Cass had left Detroit more than a year earlier to assume the post of secretary of war in Washington, D.C. While in Detroit, Black Hawk and his companions continued to draw crowds, albeit far smaller and often less friendly ones. Detroit was a frontier city, and according to the Detroit newspapers, one crowd burned effigies of the visiting Indians. Black Hawk and his companions stayed only a few days in Detroit before they departed by steamboat for Green Bay. From there, they took the familiar Fox-Wisconsin waterway to Prairie du Chien, where they arrived during the last days of July 1833. At Prairie du Chien, the Winnebago Prophet, and his adopted son were released to the Winnebagos, and Black Hawk met with Joseph Street and mentioned that he wanted to recover property that the Winnebagos took from him when they made him a captive. This included four horses, some kettles, and, most importantly, his war bundle. Street had allowed the Winnebagos to keep these items, and he was not sure if he could get them back. He promised Black Hawk he would try. Black Hawk had not completely rid himself of his distrust toward the Americans, for he noted: "I hope he [Street] will not forget his promise, as the whites generally do."[17]

Black Hawk and his remaining three companions were taken to Rock Island, where they arrived on August 3rd, one year and one day after the Battle of Battle Axe. Keokuk and the other Sauk and Fox chiefs arrived the next day, and Garland made a short and rather threatening speech to Black Hawk to remain at peace under Keokuk's leadership. The tone of the speech was quite unnecessary in Black Hawk's view because he had given his word to the president; Garland's speech did little more than humiliate him in front of a group of chiefs and warriors he had not seen in many months. Black Hawk berated Garland, and Colonel William Davenport, the commandant at Fort Armstrong, spoke in order to ease the tension. Davenport praised Black Hawk as an old friend and reminded him (firmly but politely) of the populous cities he had seen on his tour of the East, and he hoped that Black Hawk would see the futility of ever making war against the United States again. Davenport's speech worked perfectly, and Black Hawk left the meeting in happier spirits. He later noted that Garland's speech had been "uncalled for, and did not become him," while Davenport's talk "sounded like coming from a *brave!*"[18]

Thus ended the career of the greatest warrior of the Sauk nation. Black Hawk retired to a site on the Iowa River near Keokuk's village. He lived there for the remaining days of his life with his two sons, his daughter, and his wife. He frequently entertained white guests at his lodge and went out of his way to be hospitable. In September 1836, George Catlin attended a treaty council between the United States and the Sauk and Fox tribes. Black Hawk attended but remained silent since Keokuk did not permit him to speak. Black Hawk still wore the frock coat he had received three years earlier. Catlin described him as a "poor dethroned monarch" and "an object of pity" who wore "an old frock coat and brown hat . . . and [carried] a cane in his hand." Along with his two sons, Black Hawk was accompanied by "his *quondam* aide-de-camp, Nah-pope, and the prophet."[19]

The 1836 treaty transferred to the United States the small reservation of land that the Sauks and Foxes had demanded in their 1832 treaty. However, this was not the last treaty cession that Black Hawk witnessed. In October 1837, he was allowed to travel once again to Washington, D.C., with Keokuk. There, the Sauks and Foxes sold an additional 1.25 million acres of land in present-day Iowa. Black Hawk did not attract nearly as much attention during his second trip to the East, and he did not speak during the treaty negotiations. Indeed, the man who had once zealously fought to retain the lands of his tribe stood by in silence as his greatest political rival sold them away. Black Hawk died before the next series of land cessions and removals, but in his autobiography, he issued a cautionary tale. He said that he was "very much afraid, that in a few years, they [white settlers] will begin to drive and abuse our people, as they have formerly done. I may not live to *see* it, but I feel certain that the day is not distant."[20] His words were prophetic.

Black Hawk lived the last years of his life on the new tribal lands of the Sauks farther to the west along the Des Moines River.

Figure 20. Painting of Black Hawk by Charles Bird King, 1837. Reprinted from
McKenney and Hall, *The History of the Indian Tribes of North America.*

Although he did not have any power within the tribe, he still had
quite a bit of prestige within the Sauk nation. A white settler saw
Black Hawk and a group of other Sauks on a steamboat that was heading north after leaving St. Louis in July 1837. He noted that Black
Hawk continued to wear a frock coat and hat and carried a cane. He
also used a knife and fork and ate his meals in the manner of whites.
He even drank brandy, although apparently only when invited to do
so by white passengers. He did all these things, according to the settler, so that "his influence with his Braves may be exerted in the

course which he professes to pursue," and that course was one of peace with the whites. The settler also noted that "the whole Band appears to pay him deference even in his present Situation."[21]

White settlers who began to move into the Black Hawk Purchase also continued to demonstrate a sense of respect and even awe for the former Sauk warrior. The next year, in 1838, those who had settled near the former site of Fort Madison invited Black Hawk to their July 4th celebration. During his speech, he related how much he had loved the Rock River Valley and how he had been willing to fight for it six years earlier. He told the audience how rich and beautiful it was; he told them that now that they owned it, they should take care of it as he and his people had done. The speech demonstrated that Black Hawk was a man of his word; he had promised to be at peace with the whites and treat them as brothers, and he did so in the final years of his life. Nevertheless, he still had fire in his soul, although now he reserved his anger and bitterness for Keokuk rather than for whites. During the course of his speech, he noted: "I was once a great warrior, I am now poor. Keokuk has been the cause of my present situation."[22]

Black Hawk passed away three months later on October 3, 1838, at seventy-two years of age. Even in death, his celebrity did not diminish; newspapers as far away as London printed his obituary. However, death did not bring him peace. Black Hawk was buried in the Sauk manner in an above-ground coffin made of logs. He wore the frock coat he had received in Washington six years earlier, although expensive gold epaulettes and a belt and sword were added for his funeral. He also wore on his neck all the medals he had received during his career from important dignitaries and leaders: one had the image of President Andrew Jackson, another had the image of President James Madison, and a third he had received from the British in Canada. Within a year, a white doctor and his accomplices stole Black Hawk's corpse. They first took Black Hawk's head (which had fallen off at the neck) and later took the remainder of the body. The doctor then removed the remaining pieces of flesh from the bones and planned to sell the complete skeleton. Black Hawk's family petitioned the governor of Iowa Territory, Robert Lucas, to demand the skeleton back, but he had no idea where it was. When one of the accomplices had a falling out with the doctor, he contacted Lucas and told him where it could be recovered. Lucas had Black Hawk's bones deposited at the Geological and Historical Society building in Burlington for safekeeping until his family could claim them. However, the Sauks and Foxes were moving yet again, and Black Hawk's family decided to leave them in the building until they were settled in their new home farther west. Why they never went back to Burlington to get the remains is unknown. Black Hawk's bones were still in the building when it burned down in 1855, destroying what remained of the Sauk nation's most famous warrior.[23]

After Black Hawk's death, Keokuk remained the most powerful political figure in the two tribes, primarily because he and a few other chiefs controlled the annuity money that the Sauks and Foxes received from their various treaties. One of the key challengers to Keokuk's management of the annuities as well as to the legitimacy of his leadership came from a hereditary civil chief named Hardfish, who, by 1836, had emerged as the principal leader of the faction opposing Keokuk. He went so far as to set up a separate village, which attracted many of those who had been members of the British Band. This did not sit well with John Beach, the federal Indian agent of the Sauks and Foxes. He believed that Hardfish's faction, containing as it did former members of the British Band, was in flagrant violation of the 1832 treaty. Territorial Governor Robert Lucas denied such allegations, for he, too, had become concerned with Keokuk's near dictatorial control over the two tribes. Black Hawk had had nothing to do with the constitution of this band, but clearly it arose in large part because of his earlier example, and the fact many former members of the British Band joined Hardfish's band did much to present a clear line of continuity. As early as 1834, a white missionary among the Sauks noted that "[Black Hawk] has been degraded and is not permitted to hold any office amongst his people, yet he has a very respectable band who follow him and are much attached to him." The missionary went on to say, "[I]t is quite questionable whether . . . he is not quite as much respected as the haughty and high-minded Ke-o-kuck who now holds the reins of government in his own hands."[24] Thus, the tribe continued to exhibit a division between factions; while the issues were different than they had been forty years earlier, the parties that constituted them generally remained the same.

In 1842, the federal government purchased from the two tribes the last of their Iowa lands. They were allowed to stay on the western portion of the cession until 1845, but after that year, all Sauks and

Foxes had to remove to a new reservation in present-day Kansas. During this period, the Foxes, traditionally the smaller and politically weaker of the two tribes, began to resent Keokuk's control over the annuities. They had also lived on some of the most desirable lands in Iowa and were loath to remove. The majority of the Foxes stayed behind when the two tribes moved to the new reservation in October 1845. Both Keokuk's and Hardfish's factions participated in the exodus that year. In Kansas, the Sauks and the few Foxes who went with them shared a 435,200-acre reservation with several other tribes that had been moved west. It turned out to be a rather miserable twenty-four-year period, particularly since those who moved faced competition from other tribes that had been removed as well as from the resident plains Indians. Throughout the 1850s, the majority of the Foxes returned to Iowa where their kinsmen had remained. By 1856, they had legalized their residence there through an act of the Iowa legislature, and the Foxes purchased a three-thousand-acre settlement near Tama, Iowa, with annuity money and funds raised from the sale of horses and jewelry.[25]

A smaller number of Foxes stayed with the Sauks in Kansas, and by the 1850s the two groups had become, for all practical purposes, a single tribe called the Sac and Fox tribe. Nevertheless, it was overwhelmingly Sauk in composition. The population of the Sac and Fox tribe in Kansas was about 2,700 immediately after the removal; eight years later in 1853 it was down to about 2,100. This decline occurred despite the fact that many Sauks from the Missouri River, who had had a separate political existence since the War of 1812, joined them. The Sauks of the Missouri had received their own reservation in Kansas, but many of them left to join their kin among the Sac and Fox tribe eighty miles to the south. In 1848, Keokuk died and passed his office down to his son, Moses Keokuk, who generally practiced the same brand of leadership as his father: siding with the government and controlling the tribal annuity funds. Hardfish had also died, and the leadership of his band passed to another civil chief, Mokohoko (Jumping Fish), who was originally a member of the Missouri River Sauks. In 1861, Mokohoko led an exodus of those Missouri River Sauks who desired to practice their traditional culture and live with their kin among the Sac and Fox tribe. Mokohoko's Missouri River Sauks left their reservation, and upon arriving at the Sac and Fox reservation, they were joined by other Sauk traditionalists and the followers of Hardfish. By the 1860s, the issue that maintained the split between the two factions was one of culture: Mokohoko led the traditionalists while Moses Keokuk pushed for assimilation into white culture. Thus, Moses Keokuk's followers had white schools and Christian missionaries; Mokohoko's did not.[26]

The government promised the Sac and Fox members that their journey to Kansas would be their final move, but white settlers cast covetous eyes upon their lands. In February 1867, the Sac and Fox tribe sold its lands in Kansas and conducted a final removal to Indian Territory (present-day Oklahoma). Mokohoko and about 240 members of his band refused to leave. In language reminiscent of his ideological grandfather, Black Hawk, he said that he had not "touched a feather" to the treaty and thus did not join the exodus to Indian Territory in 1869. The army removed Mokohoko and his followers to Indian Territory in 1878, but, once again, in the spirit of the British Band, they promptly returned to Kansas. Mokohoko died in 1878, and leadership of his band passed to a hereditary civil chief named, ironically, Pashipaho, whose name was the same as that of the civil chief who had sided with Keokuk against Black Hawk more than forty years earlier. The army finally removed the band permanently to the Indian Territory in 1886, but it maintained its separate political existence.[27]

In the Indian Territory, Pashipaho's band persisted in its resistance. In 1891, the Sac and Fox members became the victims of the federal Dawes Act, which required family heads to take land allotments of 160 acres. Thus, the tribal reservation would not be owned in common, as had been the traditional practice. Of course, there would be surplus land after each family received its allotment, and this would be sold to white settlers. The Sac and Fox was not the only tribe subject to the Dawes Act; virtually every tribe with a reservation suffered from its effects. The rationale behind the law was to "civilize" the Indians through individual land ownership. This, the government believed, would spur them to practice the white man's brand of agriculture. Selling surplus lands to whites would also put them into closer contact with white neighbors who could offer them good examples of how civilized, Christian people lived. Like most government programs, the Dawes Act was a complete disaster; few Indians who received their allotments farmed them, and most sold their lands to white farmers and ranchers.

Thus, the tribal reservations, which constituted what remained of their once sprawling land bases, were themselves whittled down in size. The majority of the members of the Sac and Fox tribe took land allotments, as did those persons in Pashipaho's band. However, Pashipaho's followers pooled their individual allotments together to create a small reservation for themselves, where they practiced the traditional Sauk way of life. By 1903, these Indians were known as the Kansas Sauk Band, and except for their horses, they owned everything in common at their village along the Cinnamon River.[28] Thus, well after the Black Hawk War and Black Hawk's death, the idea of resistance to American cultural and political domination continued in an unbroken lineage among a faction of the Sauks.

The split between the Sauk tribal factions was a continuity that carried over from the prewar period, and resistance to American expansion, although in a much muted form, also continued to be evident. As early as November 1832, there were rumors that the Indians of the upper Great Lakes and upper Mississippi Valley would renew their campaign against the whites the next year. Keokuk took the rumors seriously enough that he issued a proclamation published in several papers denying that the Sauks and Foxes planned another war against the United States in 1833. Whites were far more worried about the Winnebagos than the Sauks and Foxes, for the rumors that spread throughout the region in November 1832 indicated that the members of the Rock River bands were unhappy about having to remove from their ceded lands the next year. Also, the Winnebago perpetrators of the killings committed in the lead mining region during the war remained at large, and this did much to fuel the rumors of renewed violence. Undoubtedly, there were Winnebagos sullen about having to leave the Rock River Valley, and though panic-stricken whites with fresh memories of the war spread most of the rumors, at least a few Winnebagos intentionally planted such ideas in the minds of white settlers. Several Winnebagos circulated wampum among the neighboring tribes to feel them out for the possibility of an alliance, but these were rather feckless efforts made by young warriors who did not have a realistic chance of leading a new pan-Indian uprising.[29]

The rumors of another Indian war in 1833 did not come to pass, and while the idea of using warfare as a means of countering white expansion did not die, opportunities to employ warfare effectively against the United States rapidly began to vanish after the Black Hawk War. The number of warriors in the various tribes of the region was simply not enough to counter the sheer numbers of men—both regulars and especially volunteers—that the Americans could muster. This was particularly true because of the huge rush of white settlers that arrived in the region after the war. The 1836 census for Wisconsin Territory listed more than 11,000 persons while the 1840 census listed over 30,000. By 1850, the population of the state of Wisconsin swelled to more than 300,000 persons. However, despite this overwhelming superiority in numbers, anti-Americanism and the dream of a pan-Indian federation did not end in 1832, and the events of 1836 provide evidence of this. In December 1835, the Seminoles in Florida killed 109 regulars in what became known as the Dade Massacre. By April 1836, there were reports of Seminole war wampum circulating among the Winnebagos. At the time, it looked as though another pan-Indian uprising that would stretch from the Gulf of Mexico to the headwaters of the Mississippi was in the making. The reports of wampum circulating among the Winnebagos were most likely true, although the chances of any uprising occurring, much less succeeding, were slim. Nevertheless, the governor of Wisconsin Territory, Henry Dodge, and Secretary of War Lewis Cass took no chances and ordered additional arms and ammunition sent to the army posts in the region.[30]

The principal military force that patrolled the frontier after the Black Hawk War was the new U.S. Mounted Rangers. Although the battalion did not come together in time to fight in the Black Hawk War, its utility and its continued existence was guaranteed by the conduct of the war and the events that transpired afterward. The War Department realized that the slow pace of the war could not be pinned solely upon Henry Atkinson and his mediocre tactical skills. Lewis Cass, in the end, was satisfied with Atkinson's execution of the war, as was President Andrew Jackson, whose only complaint was that Atkinson was too cautious in his approach. What was questioned by federal policymakers was not Atkinson's prosecution of the Black Hawk War but the constitution of the army itself. Both Jackson and Cass praised the efforts of the volunteers, but both were forced to admit that their employment had been an inefficient way to fight hostile Indians. Cass believed that the lack of mounted regulars had been the foremost problem. He strongly supported the idea of a mounted battalion of regulars, but as early as November 1832 he began to press Congress to expand the battalion into a regiment. Cass rightly believed that mounted regulars were essential to fighting any future Indian wars. History proved him correct, for the Black Hawk War was the turning point in how the United States Army fought against a mounted foe. From 1832 onward, the army always had mounted regulars organized as dragoons or cavalry. The Mounted Ranger Battalion had not even been in existence for a year when, in March 1833, Congress followed Cass's advice and increased the battalion to a full regiment of mounted dragoons. Henry Dodge retained his command and was promoted from a major commanding the battalion to a colonel commanding the regiment. The reason was financial, for it was less expensive to prevent Indian wars than fight them. Cass estimated that maintaining a full regiment of dragoons would cost $143,598 annually. The final cost of the Black Hawk War, once all the various claims for pay and lost property were approved by Congress, came out to a little over a million dollars.[31] Thus, an ounce of prevention truly was better than a pound of cure.

Under orders from Winfield Scott, Dodge first employed the Mounted Ranger Battalion in the autumn of 1832. He sent three of his companies down to the South while the other three were to patrol the area from the Wabash River to the Wisconsin River. In the spring of 1833, Dodge aggressively employed the latter three companies to supervise the removal of the Winnebagos from the Rock River Valley. Having mounted regulars in their country caused the Winnebagos no small amount of consternation. Dodge also sought to capture the eight Winnebagos who committed depredations during the war. They had actually been captured earlier but had escaped from Fort Winnebago. Dodge not only recaptured seven of the eight men but managed to round up several Rock River Winnebagos who had not left the ceded lands. By July, most of his men had served their one year of service and were discharged, and Dodge was without a command until the new dragoon regiment could be organized. The Mounted Ranger Battalion was hardly a crack force; it did not even have uniforms and had not received any specialized training. Nevertheless, it proved once again that mounted troops on the frontier, even those who were poorly trained, were better than well-drilled infantrymen who moved slowly on foot. Many observers credited Dodge's battalion with preventing an uprising among the

Winnebagos in 1833, although it is doubtful that any new Indian uprising would have occurred without the presence of Dodge's troops. Nevertheless, the Winnebagos were concerned about the presence of the battalion and even believed Dodge would attack Winnebago villages without provocation.[32]

Capturing the escaped prisoners in 1833 was probably the most significant service that Dodge's troops provided that year, but in the end it did not matter, for none of the Winnebagos was ever sentenced. Both the Winnebagos and Potawatomis had to produce the guilty individuals who spilled blood during the Black Hawk War. Although there were certainly more Winnebagos and Potawatomis involved in the various attacks in northern Illinois and the lead mining region than were turned over for prosecution, federal officials were content to take into custody those deemed to be the most responsible. The Winnebagos surrendered their eight perpetrators at Fort Winnebago in late October 1832; by early December of that same year they had escaped the guardhouse. The seven men recovered by Dodge were brought back to Fort Winnebago during the summer of 1833, but they did not stay in confinement very long. James D. Doty, a former federal judge in Michigan Territory, agreed to take their case. He first had all seven men released with a writ of habeas corpus since the government had not charged them with any specific crimes. The attorney assigned to prosecute the case was unable to find any Winnebagos or white persons who had witnessed any of the seven men commit the murders for which they were to be tried. While a grand jury indicted all seven men in October 1833, none of them ever went to trial for any crime, and in 1837 the prosecuting attorney finally dropped all the charges.[33]

There also had been three other prisoners who Atkinson initially believed were Potawatomis responsible for the attack at Big Indian Creek. Atkinson had them held at Jefferson Barracks before he transferred them to the civil authorities in LaSalle County, Illinois, to await trial. LaSalle County did not have a jail at the time, so the sheriff put the three prisoners in Fort Johnson, which had been built during the war. It was not much better than the Fort Winnebago guardhouse, for by December 1832, the three men had escaped. The sheriff managed to recapture them almost immediately. Upon questioning them, he found out that they were not Potawatomis at all; the three men—Kewassee, Toquamee, and Comee—were brothers who claimed to be

Sauks and former members of the British Band. Shabonna assured the sheriff that the three men were definitely Sauks and not Potawatomis. They almost certainly were the three Sauks who had accompanied the Potawatomis during their attack on the Big Indian Creek the previous year. However, there was no solid proof to support such an assertion, and the three men were certainly not willing to make confessions. Moreover, neither Sylvia nor Rachel Hall were able to positively identify the three men in court. There was not even enough evidence available for a grand jury to produce an indictment, and by October 1834 all the charges against the three were dropped.[34] Thus, except for relatively short confinements, no Indians were convicted of any crimes, served any extended sentences, or were hanged for any of the killings committed during the war. This, of course, included Black Hawk, whose year in confinement was hardly onerous, and during his tour of the East, was probably quite entertaining at times.

Although the Black Hawk War was the last Indian war fought in Illinois and Wisconsin, it was not the last Indian war fought east of the Mississippi. Less than three years after the guns went silent at the Battle of Bad Axe, the Dade Massacre became the first battle of another war in the South that showed the nativist ideology of anti-Americanism and resistance to United States expansion and Indian removal had not died that fateful day in August 1832. From 1835 to 1842, the United States fought a far longer and bloodier struggle in Florida known as the Second Seminole War. In this conflict, Osceola picked up the torch that had been passed down by Indian leaders such as Pontiac, Tecumseh, and the Shawnee Prophet; that same torch had been briefly carried by Black Hawk. Not surprisingly, white observers saw similarities between Osceola and Black Hawk. One Florida newspaper in 1836 noted that Osceola was "a savage of great tact, energy of character, and bold daring. The skill with which he has for a long time managed to frustrate the measures of our government for the removal of the Indians beyond the Mississippi entitle him to be considered as superior to *Black Hawk*."[35]

Black Hawk and Osceola certainly shared the common goal of resisting white expansion and removal from their homelands, but there were also other parallels between the two wars they led. In February 1838, after more than two grueling years, the War Department published a list of the numbers of men that had been employed in removing the Seminoles from Florida. Almost 5,000 regulars, more than 14,000 white militia volunteers, and about 900 Indian warriors from various tribes had participated in the conflict up to that point. Thus, resistance to white expansion and pan-Indian nativism were the foundation for both the Black Hawk War and the Second Seminole War, and the army continued to utilize the same methods in its execution of Indian wars by relying upon white volunteers and Indian auxiliaries to assist regular forces. The difference was primarily in the final outcome, for while all of Black Hawk's followers were forced west across the Mississippi, a small and tenacious number of Seminoles managed—thanks to the difficult terrain of Florida—to resist removal westward and maintained a residence in Florida that has continued to the present day.[36]

Although Black Hawk may not have succeeded in his quest to retain his beloved homeland in the Rock River Valley, he did not have to be ashamed about what he had attempted. He did not seek to make war when he crossed the Mississippi River with his band, and once the fighting started, there was little he could have done to stop it. He had been forced to fight, and he did it well. This was particularly true of his greatest moment during the war, the Battle of Wisconsin Heights, where, with a mere 120 warriors, he held off a force several times larger long enough to allow the main body of his band to conduct a river crossing. After he returned from the East in 1833, Black Hawk recited his autobiography to Antoine LeClaire, the government interpreter at Rock Island, and a young newspaper editor named John B. Patterson. He dedicated his autobiography to Henry Atkinson, his foe during the war, because of the kind treatment that Atkinson had extended to him during his confinement. In his dedication, Black Hawk warned Atkinson: "The path to glory is rough, and many gloomy hours obscure it. May the Great Spirit shed light on your's—and that you may never experience the humility that the power of the American government has reduced me to."[37] Now, more than 170 years later, it appears, in retrospect, that Black Hawk spoke these words too soon; during his life, he successfully walked his own path to glory, and a very rough path it was.

Appendix

Forts during
the Black Hawk War

Although the following list is complete concerning the names and locations of federal and volunteer forts, it should not be considered definitive for settler forts. There were undoubtedly others in Illinois and Wisconsin, but many were simply preexisting structures such as houses and barns that were hastily reinforced and called "forts." Moreover, those in lower Michigan and Indiana are not included in this list. The following sources were used to compile this appendix: Perry A. Armstrong, *The Sauks and the Black Hawk War* (Springfield, Ill.: H. W. Rokker, 1887); Ellen C. Whitney, ed. *The Black Hawk War, 1831–1832*, 2 vols., *Collections of the Illinois Historical Library*, vols. 35–38 (Springfield: Illinois Historical Library, 1970–78); William R. Smith, *The History of Wisconsin, In Three Parts*, vols. 1 and 3 (Madison, Wisc.: Beriah Brown, 1854); William F. Stark, *Along the Black Hawk Trail* (Sheboygan, Wisc.: Zimmerman Press, 1984).

Settler Forts	Present-day Location
Apple River Fort	Elizabeth, Ill.
Blockhouse at Galena	Galena, Ill.
Buffalo Grove Fort	Polo, Ill.
Butler's Fort	Monmouth, Ill.

Crane's Fort	Lanark, Ill.
De Seelhorst's Fort	Elk Grove, Wisc.
Des Plaines River Fort (also known as Orr's Blockhouse)	West Joliet, Ill.
Fort Beggs (also known as Fort Walker)	Plainfield, Ill.
Fort Blue Mounds	Blue Mounds
Fort Defiance (Mich. Terr.)	Willow Springs Township, Wisc.
Fort Defiance (Ill.)	Edelstein, Ill.
Fort Gratiot	Gratiot, Wisc.
Fort Hamilton	Wiota, Wisc.
Fort Jackson	Mineral Point, Wisc.
Fort Payne	Naperville, Ill.
Fort Union	Dodgeville, Wisc.
Funk's Fort	Monticello, Wisc.
Gum's Fort	Galesburg, Ill.
Parrish's Fort	Wingville Township, Wisc.
Pence's Fort	Oquawka, Ill.
Plum River Fort	Savanna, Ill.
Fort at Cassville	Cassville, Wisc.
Fort at Diamond Grove	Diamond Grove, Wisc.
Fort at Hennepin	Hennepin, Ill.
Fort at New Diggings	New Diggings, Wisc.
Fort at Platteville	Platteville, Wisc.
Fort at Schullsburg	Shullsburg, Wisc.
Fort at Sinsinawa Mound	Sinsinawa, Wisc.
Fort at White Oak Springs	White Oak Springs, Wisc.

Volunteer Forts

Fort Johnson	Ottawa, Ill.
Fort Wilbourn	LaSalle, Ill.
Fort at Kellogg's Grove	Kent, Ill.

Federal Forts (Permanent)

Fort Armstrong	Rock Island, Ill.
Fort Brady	Sault Ste. Marie, Mich.
Fort Crawford	Prairie du Chien, Wisc.
Fort Dearborn	Chicago, Ill.

Fort Howard	Green Bay, Wisc.
Fort Mackinac	Mackinac Island, Mich.
Fort Snelling	Minneapolis, Minn.
Fort Winnebago	Portage, Wisc.
Jefferson Barracks	St. Louis, Mo.

Federal Forts (Temporary)

Fort at Dixon's Ferry	Dixon, Ill.
Fort Koshkonong	Fort Atkinson, Wisc.

Notes

BHW	Ellen C. Whitney, ed., *The Black Hawk War, 1831–1832*, 2 vols., *Collections of the Illinois Historical Library*, vols. 35–38 (Springfield: Illinois Historical Library, 1970–78).
Forsyth Papers	Thomas Forsyth Papers, Series T, Lyman C. Draper Manuscript Collection, State Historical Society of Wisconsin, Madison, Wisconsin. (References are to volume and page numbers.)
HI	Douglas L. Wilson and Rodney O. Davis, eds., *Herndon's Informants: Letters, Interviews, and Statements about Abraham Lincoln* (Urbana: University of Illinois Press, 1998).
HOW	William Smith, ed., *The History of Wisconsin. In Three Parts*, vol. 3 (Madison: Beriah Brown, 1854).
M-1	Records of the Michigan Superintendency of Indian Affairs, 1814–1851, Microfilm Publication M-1, Record Group 75, Records of the Bureau of Indian Affairs, National Archives, Washington, D.C. (References are to reel, volume, and page numbers or to reel and frame numbers.)
M-6	Letters Sent by the Secretary of War Relating to Military Affairs, 1800–1889, Microfilm Publication M-6, Record Group 107, Records of the Office of the Secretary of War,

National Archives, Washington, D.C. (References are to reel, volume, and page numbers.)

M-234   Letters Received by the Office of Indian Affairs, 1824–1881, Microfilm Publication M-234, Record Group 75, Records of the Bureau of Indian Affairs, National Archives, Washington, D.C. (References are to reel and frame numbers.)

M-617   Returns from U.S. Military Posts, 1800–1916, Microfilm Publication M-617, Record Group 94, Records of the Office of the Adjutant General, National Archives, Washington, D.C. (References are to reel numbers.)

MPHC   J. C. Holmes, et al., eds., *Collections of the Michigan Pioneer and Historical Society*, 40 vols. (Lansing: Michigan Pioneer and Historical Society, 1877–1929).

RG   Record Group

Sen. Doc. 512 *Correspondence on the Subject of the Emigration of Indians*, 23rd Cong., 1st sess., 1834, Sen. Doc. 512 (Serials 244–48). (All references include volume serial numbers.)

T-494   Documents Relating to the Negotiation of Ratified and Unratified Treaties with Various Tribes of Indians, 1801–1869, Microfilm Publication T-494, Record Group 75, Records of the Bureau of Indian Affairs, National Archives, Washington, D.C. (References are to reel and frame numbers.)

TPUS   Clarence E. Carter and John P. Bloom, eds., *The Territorial Papers of the United States*, 28 vols. (Washington, D.C.: Government Printing Office, 1934–1975).

WHC   Lyman C. Draper, et al., eds., *Collections of the State Historical Society of Wisconsin*, 31 vols. (Madison: State Historical Society of Wisconsin, 1855–1931).

WHH   Logan Esarey, ed., *Messages and Letters of William Henry Harrison*, 2 vols., *Indiana Historical Collections*, vols. 7 and 9 (Indianapolis: Indiana Historical Commission, 1922).

INTRODUCTION

1. It is unnecessary to list every work here, particularly since historiographical assessments can be found in Nichols, "Black Hawk War in Retrospect," 244–45; and Nichols, *Black Hawk and the Warrior's Path*, 160–68.

2. Dowd, *Spirited Resistance*, 23–201.

3. Whitney, *The Black Hawk War* (hereafter cited as *BHW*).

4. Stocking, *Saukie Indians*, viii.

CHAPTER ONE: SOWING THE SEEDS OF FURY

1. Black Hawk, *Autobiography*, 1–18, 31–35, 171–76, 180.

2. *Ibid.*, 181–82.

3. *Ibid.*, 60–62.

4. Callender, "Sauk," *Handbook of North American Indians* (hereafter cited as *HBNI*), 648; Callender, "Fox," *HBNI*, 636; Edmunds and Peyser, *Fox Wars*, 9–30, 65–77, 119–70, 174–95.

5. Edmunds and Peyser, *Fox Wars*, 198–211; Black Hawk, *Autobiography*, 47; Kay, "Fur Trade," 275–77.

6. White, *Middle Ground*, 269–314; Trask, "In the Name of the Father," 3–21; Gorrell, "Journal," *WHC*, 1:25–32.

7. Nasatir, "Anglo-Spanish Frontier in the Illinois Country," 292–93; Cummings, "Burning of Sauk-E-Nuk," 53–62.

8. Kurtz, "Economic and Political History of the Sauk and Mesquakie," 18–48.

9. Horsman, *Expansion and American Indian Policy*, 3–52, 86, 95, 97.

10. White, *Middle Ground*, 413–24, 453–68, 472–74; Sugden, *Blue Jacket*, 103, 134, 144, 186, 227–28; quoted from Black Hawk, *Autobiography*, 58.

11. Wallace, *Jefferson and the Indians*, 206–24.

12. *Ibid.*, 224, 248–51; quoted from Henry Dearborn to William Henry Harrison, 27 June 1804, Letters Sent by the Secretary of War Relating to Indian Affairs, 1800–1824, Microfilm Publication M-15, Reel 2, vol. B, p. 7.

13. Hagan, "Sauk and Fox Treaty of 1804," 1–3; Wallace, "Prelude to Disaster," *BHW*, 1:16–18; Black Hawk, *Autobiography*, 58–59; Warren Cattle to James Bruff, 9 September 1804, TPUS, 13:62–63; quoted from Bruff to James Wilkinson, 29 September 1804, Ibid., 13:56–58. For an example of a work that asserts sexual advances toward Sauk women were the cause, see Cole, *I Am a Man*, 30–31.

14. Black Hawk, *Autobiography*, 58–59; Mackay Wherry to Amos Stoddard, 12 September 1804, TPUS, 13:63; Bruff to Wilkinson, 29 September 1804, Ibid., 13:56–58; Bruff to Wilkinson, 5 November 1804, Ibid., 13:76–80; Thomas Forsyth, Original Causes of the Troubles With a Party of Sauk and Fox Indians, Forsyth Papers, 9:54–59.

15. Michelson, Notes on Sauk Ethnography, p. 1; Jones, *Ethnography of the Fox Indians*, 82–84; Wallace, "Prelude to Disaster," *BHW*, 1:4–6; Callender, "Great Lakes–Riverine Sociopolitical Organization," *HBNI*, 616–20.

16. Quoted from Bruff to Wilkinson, 5 November 1804, TPUS, 13:76.

17. Black Hawk, *Autobiography*, 60; Forsyth, Original Causes, Forsyth Papers, 9:55; Bruff to Wilkinson, 5 November 1804, TPUS, 13:76–77.

18. Hagan, "Sauk and Fox Treaty of 1804," 4–7; William Jones, "Notes on the Fox Indians," 109; quoted from Black Hawk, *Autobiography*, 61.

19. Treaty with the Sauk and Foxes, 3 November 1804, in Kappler, *Indian Affairs: Laws and Treaties*, 74–77 (hereafter cited as *Indian Treaties*); Wallace, "Prelude to Disaster," 1:19–21.

20. Black Hawk, *Autobiography*, 61–64, 111; Pierre Chouteau aux chefs des nations Sakias et Renards, 18 October 1804, Pierre Chouteau Letter

Book, 1804–1819, p. 2, Chouteau Family Papers; Talks between Edmund P. Gaines and the Sauk, 4–7 June 1831, *BHW*, 2:28; George Davenport to Joseph Duncan, 11 February 1832, Ibid., 2:211; Tanner, *Atlas of Great Lakes Indian History*, 98–99; Harrison to Dearborn, 27 May 1805, *WHH*, 1:134.

21. Quoted from Wilkinson to Dearborn, 27 July 1805, *TPUS*, 13:168.

22. Wilkinson to Dearborn, 8 October 1805, Ibid., 13:234.

23. James Many to Wilkinson, 20 May 1806, Ibid., 13:513; Nicolas Boilvin to William Eustis, 11 February 1811, Ibid., 14:439–40.

24. William Clark, et al., to William Crawford, 16 July 1815, *American State Papers: Indian Affairs*, 2:8 (hereafter cited as *ASP:IA*); quoted from Forsyth to Clark, 3 June 1817, *WHC*, 11:348.

25. Forsyth, Original Causes, Forsyth Papers, 9:55; Potawatomi Chief to the President, 1 September 1815, *TPUS*, 17:227–28; Sauk and Fox Chiefs to Forsyth, September 1821, Forsyth Papers, 4:109–11; Forsyth to Clark, 17 May 1829, Ibid., 6:97–98; Clark, Indian council with Keokuk, 27 March 1830, M-234, 749:1229; Wallace, "Prelude to Disaster," *BHW*, 1:23–24, 27–30.

26. Dowd, *Spirited Resistance*, 23–201.

27. Ibid., 91–115; Edmunds, *Shawnee Prophet*, 28–37, 78.

28. Edmunds, *Shawnee Prophet*, 42–93; Willig, "Prophetstown on the Wabash," 115–58; Harrison to Eustis, 15 June 1810, *WHH*, 1:427; Harrison to Eustis, 7 August 1810, Ibid., 1:456; Black Hawk, *Autobiography*, 66.

29. Edmunds, *Tecumseh and the Quest for Indian Leadership*, 32–44, 94–95, 120–25; Dowd, *Spirited Resistance*, 139.

30. Edmunds, "Main Poc," 259–72; Clifton, *Prairie People*, 193–94.

31. Hamilton, "Elements of the Concept of Ideology," 18–38; Geertz, "Ideology as a Cultural System," 47–76; Converse, "Nature of Belief Systems in Mass Publics," 206–61; Rudé, *Ideology and Popular Protest*, 27–38.

32. Nichols, *Black Hawk and The Warrior's Path*, 31–34; Jackson, "William Ewing," 3–7; Foley, "Different Notions of Justice," 2–13; Meriwether Lewis to Dearborn, 1 July 1808, *TPUS*, 14:202–3; Clark to Eustis, 5 April 1809, Ibid., 14:260; Harrison to Eustis, 25 July 1810, *WHH* 1:449; Clark to Eustis, 12 September 1810, *TPUS*, 14:412–14.

33. William Wells to Harrison, 20 August 1807, *WHH*, 1:242; Clark to Eustis, 20 July 1810, Ibid., 1:449; John Johnson to Eustis, 7 August 1810, Ibid., 1:459; Extract of a Letter to the War Department, 17 September 1811, *ASP:IA*, 1:801; Forsyth to Lewis, 7 September 1812, *TPUS*, 16:264; Allen, *His Majesty's Indian Allies*, 54–56, 83–84, 110–15.

34. Gilpin, *The War of 1812*, 3–22; Harrison to Eustis, 18 November 1811, *WHH*, 1:618–31; Rising, "White Claims for Indian Depredations," 281–304.

35. Black Hawk, *Autobiography*, 64n, 64–68; Jackson, "Old Fort Madison—1808–1813," 11–20, 47–53.

36. Black Hawk, *Autobiography*, 68.

37. Ibid., 68–93; Hagan, *Sac and Fox Indians*, 80–81, 233; Clark to John Armstrong, 12 September 1813, *TPUS*, 14:697–98.

38. Stevens, "Illinois in the War of 1812–1814," 97; Horsman, "Wisconsin and the War of 1812," 3–15; Taylor, "Zachary Taylor in Illinois," 84–91; Allen, *His Majesty's Indian Allies*, 160–61; Black Hawk, *Autobiography*, 89–90.

39. Dwight L. Smith, "North American Neutral Indian Zone," 56–59; quoted from Robert McDouall to Alfred Bulger, 2 May 1815, *WHC*, 13:143.

40. Quoted from McDouall to the Military Secretary, 17 June 1816, *MPHC*, 16:464.

41. Fisher, "Treaties of Portage des Sioux," 495–503; *Missouri Gazette and Illinois Advertiser*, 8 July 1815, 15 July 1815; *Missouri Gazette*, 16 September 1815, 15 June 1816; Black Hawk, *Autobiography*, 73, 78–86; Stevens, *Black Hawk War*, 43–44, 55–59; George Graham to Jacob Brown, 25 August 1815, M-6, 8:8:291–92.

42. Fisher, "Portage des Sioux," 504–5; Treaty with the Foxes, 14 September 1815, *Indian Treaties*, 121–22; Report of LaRoche and Chevalier, 4 April 1813, *TPUS*, 14:654; *Missouri Gazette*, 15 June 1816; Hagan, *Sac and Fox Indians*, 81–82; Prucha, *Sword of the Republic*, 126–28; Treaty with the Sauk, 13 May 1816, *Indian Treaties*, 126–28; quoted from Clark, et al., to Crawford, 17 June 1816, *TPUS*, 17:353.

43. Black Hawk, *Autobiography*, 98.

44. Forsyth to William Lee, 3 July 1823, Forsyth Papers, 6:25–26; Forsyth to Clark, 7 July 1823, Ibid., 4:170; quoted from Forsyth to Clark, 3 April 1823, Ibid., 4:159–60.

CHAPTER TWO: THE STORM CLOUDS GATHER

1. Return of the Number of Troops, 6 June 1812, *American State Papers: Military Affairs*, 1:320 (hereafter cited as *ASP:MA*); Prucha, *Sword of the Republic*, 123–28, 134–37, 147–51; Fort Howard Post Return, December 1822, M-617, 488; Fort Dearborn Post Return, December 1822, Ibid., 300; Fort Crawford Post Return, December 1822, Ibid., 264; Fort Armstrong Post Return, December 1822, Ibid., 41; Fort Snelling Post Return, December 1822, Ibid., 1193.

2. Prucha, *Sword of the Republic*, 151–53; Jacob Brown to James Barbour, 11 January 1826, *ASP:MA*, 3:215–16; Position and Distribution of Troops in the Eastern Department, November 1826, Ibid., 3:339–40; Position and Distribution of Troops in the Western Department, November 1826, Ibid., 3:341–42; Prucha, *Broadax and Bayonet*, 120–29; Fort Dearborn Post Returns, April 1817, October 1817, M-617, 300; Fort Snelling Post Return, September 1822, Ibid., 1193; quoted from David Twiggs to Thomas Jesup, 15 July 1828, Quartermaster General's office Consolidated Correspondence File, 1794–1915, Box 856 (hereafter cited as CCF).

3. Quoted from George Croghan, 1826 Inspection Report, Inspection Reports of the Office of the Inspector General, 1814–1842, Microfilm Publication M-624, Reel 2, Frames 29–52, (hereafter cited as M-624).

4. Lewis Cass to John C. Calhoun, 17 April 1818, *TPUS*, 10:744–46; Cass to Calhoun, 11 June 1823, M-1, 5:4:162–68; Croghan, 1826 Inspection Report, M-624, 2:35–36, 51–52; Calhoun to Brown, 11 March 1819, M-6,

10:10:272; Willoughby Morgan to Jesup, 12 April 1824, CCF, 430; Cass to the Secretary of War, 20 March 1825, *TPUS*, 11:663–66.

5. Calloway, "End of an Era," 6–19; Sims, "Algonkian-British Relations in the Upper Great Lakes Region," 1–64, 85–91; Cass to Calhoun, 3 August 1819, *TPUS*, 10;852–55; Armour, "From Drummond Island," 17–22.

6. Robert McDouall to unknown, 19 June 1816, *MPHC*, 16:468–69; Return of Indians, 1818–1820, Ibid., 23:108; William Puthuff to Cass, 20 August 1817, *WHC*, 19:472; Sims, "Algonkian-British Relations," 40–41, 136–37; William Lee, Persons to Whom Money . . . Have Been Delivered, 19 February 1824, *ASP: IA*, 2:444–45; Lee, Persons to Whom Money . . . Have Been Delivered, 18 February 1825, Ibid., 2:561–62; quoted from Thomas Forsyth to Calhoun, 23 September 1823, Forsyth Papers, 4:178.

7. Sims, "Algonkian-British Relations," 55–58, 81–91; Anderson's Remarks, 13 July 1828, *MPHC*, 23:147–48; Alexander Wolcott to Cass, 14 November 1819, M-1, 6:212–13; Black Hawk, *Autobiography*, 132.

8. Everhart, "Leasing of Mineral Lands in Illinois and Wisconsin," 117–23; M. Thomas to George Bomford, 30 September 1826, *Message from the President of the United States . . . in Relation to the Lead Mines . . . .,* 19th Cong., 2nd sess., 1826, Ho. Exec. Doc. 7 (Serial 149): 7–8; John Marsh to Cass, 20 November 1826, M-1, 19:106; Kuhm, "Mining and Use of Lead by the Wisconsin Indians," 25–31; Nicolas Boilvin to William Eustis, 5 March 1811, *TPUS*, 11:156; Forsyth to Calhoun, 24 June 1822, Forsyth Papers, 4:128–31; Forsyth to William Clark, 1 June 1825, Ibid., 4:232–35; Forsyth to Clark, 15 August 1826, Ibid., 4:258–59.

9. Guha, *Elementary Aspects of Peasant Insurgency*, 5–12.

10. Wolcott to Cass, 14 November 1819, M-1, 6:212–13; Joseph Smith to Brown, 5 January 1820, *WHC*, 20:139–42; quoted from William Maddison, to unknown, 5 October 1819, Ibid., 20:126.

11. Smith to Brown, 5 January 1820, *WHC*, 20:140.

12. William Henry Harrison to the Secretary of War, 25 July 1810, *WHH*, 1:449; quoted from Harrison to the Secretary of War, 28 August 1810, Ibid., 1:470–71.

13. Clark to Barbour, 11 July 1827, M-234, 748:89; William Puthuff to Cass, 17 October 1815, M-1, 2:1:148; Boilvin to Calhoun, 11 June 1819, Nicholas Boilvin Letters, Box 3, vol. 1, pp 105–7; John Kinzie to Cass, 24 July 1819, M-1, 6:92.

14. Zanger, "Conflicting Concepts of Justice," 265–75; Henry Leavenworth, Interrogation of the Winnebago Prisoners, William Clark Papers, vol. 2, pp 182–94.

15. Boilvin, Depositions, 6–7 July 1826, M-234, 931:4–26; Tanner, *Atlas of Great Lakes Indian History*, 140, 144; Morgan to G. W. Bulter, 9 July 1826, M-234, 931:1–3; Lockwood, "Early Times and Events in Wisconsin," *WHC*, 2:155–56; Mahan, *Old Fort Crawford*, 100–4; quoted from Cass to John Q. Adams, 10 April 1827, *MPHC*, 36:541–42.

16. Zanger, "Red Bird," 69–70.

17. *Ibid.*, 70; Forsyth to Clark, 9 July 1827, Forsyth Papers, 4:274–76; Joseph Street to Barbour, 15 November 1827, *Letter from the Secretary of War . . . In Relation to the Hostile Disposition of the Indian Tribes on the*

Northwestern Frontier, 20th Cong., 1st sess., 1828, Ho. Doc. 277 (Serial 175): 14–15 (hereafter cited as Ho. Doc. 277); Marsh to Clark, 20 July 1827, M-234, 748:138–40.

18. Zanger, "Red Bird," 70–72; McKenney, *Memoirs*, 127–31; Marsh to Cass, 4 July 1827, *TPUS*, 11:1096–97; Lawrence Taliaferro to Clark, 8 August 1827, M-234, 757:20–21.

19. Marsh to Thomas L. McKenney, 10 July 1827, M-234, 419:937–38; Forsyth to Clark, 28 July 1827, Forsyth Papers, 6:66; Taliaferro to Clark, 17 August 1827, Lawrence Taliaferro Papers, vol. 4, pp 101–2 (hereafter cited as Taliaferro Papers); Eid, "'National' War among Indians," 125–54; quoted from Cass to Clark, 11 July 1827, M-234, 748:98.

20. Butte des Morts Treaty Journal, 1827, T-494, 2:3–4; Cass to Marsh, 4 July 1827, M-234, 748:103–4; McKenney to Barbour, 4 August 1827, Ibid., 419:952.

21. Fort Howard Post Returns, July and August 1827, M-617, 488; Fort Snelling Post Return, July 1827, Ibid., 1193; Fort Armstrong Post Return, July 1827, Ibid., 41; Nichols, "General Henry Atkinson," 321–22; Nichols, *Henry Atkinson*, 116–27, 135–36; Henry Atkinson to Edmund P. Gaines, 28 September 1827, *Annual Report of the Secretary of War for 1827*, 20th Cong., 1st sess., 1827, Ho. Doc. 2 (Serial 169): 156–57 (hereafter cited as Ho. Doc. 2); McKenney to Cass, 18 August 1827, M-1, 21:61; Cass to Barbour, 17 August 1827, M-234, 419:779; Childs, "Recollections of Wisconsin since 1820," *WHC*, 4:172–73; Ourada, *Menominee Indians*, 83–84, 232–35.

22. McKenney, *Memoirs*, 95–100, 108–13; Atkinson to Gaines, 17 September 1827, Ho. Doc. 2, 151; Atkinson to Gaines, 28 September 1827, Ibid., 157–58; Nichols, *Henry Atkinson*, 131–35.

23. Quoted from McKenney to Barbour, 17 September 1827, Ho. Doc. 277, 11.

24. Zanger, "Red Bird," 72–74; Cass to Barbour, 10 July 1827, *TPUS*, 11:1101–4; Marsh to Cass, 31 July 1827, M-1, 21:27.

25. Jung, "To Extend Fair and Impartial Justice to the Indian," 40–42; Royce, "Indian Land Cessions in the United States," 722–25.

26. Captain Doyle to Clark, 12 May 1828, M-234, 748:416; Forsyth to Clark, 1 July 1828, Forsyth Papers, 6:91–92; Cass to Barbour, 17 August 1827, M-234, 419:780; Barbour to Ninian Edwards, 10 September 1827, M-6, 12:12:313; Alexander Macomb to Peter B. Porter, November 1828, *Annual Report of the Secretary of War for 1828*, 20th Cong., 2nd sess., 1828, Sen. Doc. 1. (Serial 181): 157; Turner, "History of Fort Winnebago," *WHC*, 14:69–73; Fort Winnebago Post Return, October 1828, M-617, 1454.

27. Lurie, "In Search of Chaetar," 166–67; Forsyth to Clark, 15 June 1827, Forsyth Papers, 4:271; Forsyth to Clark, 9 July 1827, Ibid., 4:274; Forsyth to Cass, 10 September 1827, M-1, 21:102; Forsyth to Clark, 15 October 1827, Forsyth Papers, 6:78; Hickerson, *Chippewa and Their Neighbors*, 66, 76–90; Kurtz, "Economic History of the Sauk and Mesquakie," 37–54.

28. Henry Schoolcraft to George B. Porter, 15 August 1832, *BHW*, 2:1008; Forsyth to Clark, 30 September 1818, Forsyth Papers, 4:61–62; Forsyth to Clark, 11 May 1825, Ibid., 4:227–28; Forsyth to Clark, 6 May 1830, Ibid., 6:125–26; Clark to John H. Eaton, 17 May 1830, M-234, 749:943;

Hickerson, *Chippewa and Their Neighbors*, 83–88; Joseph Street to Clark, 21 September 1830, M-234, 696:215; Forsyth to Calhoun, 3 June 1823, Forsyth Papers, 4:165–66; John Marsh to Clark, 30 May 1827, M-234, 748:94; Robert Stuart to Eaton, 9 February 1830, *TPUS*, 12:125–26; Messengers of Ta-oman, 17 May 1830, M-234, 749:945–46.

29. Treaty with the Sioux, etc., 19 August 1825, *Indian Treaties*, 2:250–55; quoted from Cass and Clark to Barbour, 1 September 1825, T-494, 1:750–51.

30. Josiah Snelling to Atkinson, 31 May 1827, *TPUS*, 11:1082–83; Forsyth to Clark, 15 June 1827, Forsyth Papers, 4:271–72; Street to Clark, 25 August 1828, M-234, 696:97; Taliaferro, Daily Journal, 4 January 1829, Taliaferro Papers, 8:211; Clark to Eaton, 18 August 1829, M-234, 749:726–27; Taliaferro to Clark, 3 May 1830, Ibid., 749:935.

31. Eid, "'National' War," 125–37; Wallace, "Prelude to Disaster," *BHW*, 1:7–9; Black Hawk, *Autobiography*, 52–53; Journal of a Council with the Sauk and Fox, 5 September 1831, *BHW*, 2:156.

32. Clark to McKenney, 27 April 1830, M-234, 749:911–12; Van der Zee, "The Neutral Ground," 311–12; Hagan, *Sac and Fox Indians*, 116–17; Forsyth to Clark, 7 May 1830, Forsyth Papers, 6:126–27; Talk of Clark to the Sacs and Foxes, 16 June 1830, Sen. Doc. 512 (Serial 245), 71–74; quoted from Minutes of a Council at Prairie du Chien, 1830, T-494, 2:249–53.

33. Van der Zee, "Neutral Ground," 312–31; Clark to McKenney, 23 July 1830, T-494, 2:268–69.

34. Street to Clark, 2 February 1831, M-234, 749:1151; Street to Cass, 12 July 1831, Ibid., 696:355; Schoolcraft to Cass, 17 July 1831, Ibid., 420:691–92; Samuel Stambaugh to Cass, 16 August 1831, Ibid, 315:527–29; Street to Gustavus Loomis, 31 July 1831, *BHW*, 2:114–115; quoted from Cass to Clark, 25 August 1831, Letters sent by the Office of Indian Affairs 1824–1881, Microfilm Publication M-21, Reel 7, Vol. 7, p. 338 (hereafter cited as M-21).

35. Clark to Eaton, 17 January 1831, M-234, 749:1126; Thomas Burnett to Street, 5 June 1832, *BHW*, 2:524–25; Stambaugh to Cass, 10 June 1832, *TPUS*, 12:485–87.

CHAPTER THREE: RUMORS OF WAR

1. James Barbour to Ninian Edwards, 9 October 1827, M-6 12:12:321; quoted from Thomas Forsyth to William Clark, 24 May 1828, Forsyth Papers, 6T:81–82.

2. Forsyth to Clark, 10 June 1828, Forsyth Papers, 6T:83–85; Wallace, "Prelude to Disaster," *BHW*, 1:29.

3. Black Hawk, *Autobiography*, 110; Stevens, *Black Hawk War*, 77–78.

4. Stevens, *Black Hawk War*, 79; Black Hawk, *Autobiography*, 112.; Wallace, "Prelude to Disaster," *BHW*, 1:29–30; quoted from Forsyth to Clark, 17 May 1829, Forsyth Papers, 6T: 97–99.

5. Black Hawk, *Autobiography*, 111–12, 115; Forsyth to Clark, 22 May 1829, Forsyth Papers, 6T: 100–101.

6. Quoted from Journal of the Prairie du Chien Treaty, 1829, T-494, 2:193.

7. Nichols, *Black Hawk and the Warrior's Path*, 78–85; Hagan, *Sac and Fox Indians*, 94–96; Katharine C. Turner, *Red Men Calling*, xiv–xv.

8. Wallace, "Prelude to Disaster," *BHW*, 1:4–5; Black Hawk, *Autobiography*, 53–54, 81–83, 93; Speech of Black Hawk, 3 August 1815, *MPHC*, 16: 196–97; Blair, *Indian Tribes of the Upper Mississippi Valley*, vol. 2, 156–57, 192–93.

9. Wallace, "Prelude to Disaster," *BHW*, 1:4; Clark to John H. Eaton, 17 January 1831, M-234, 749:1126; Metcalf, "Who Should Rule at Home?," 660–61.

10. Black Hawk, *Autobiography*, 113; *Niles Weekly Register*, 4 May 1833; Atwater, *Remarks on a Tour to Prairie du Chien*, 65, 90, 134; Clark to the Secretary of War, 12 August 1831, *BHW*, 2:136; Forsyth to Clark, 7 August 1827, Forsyth Papers, 6T:71–72; quoted from Forsyth to Clark, 15 October 1827, Ibid., 6T:76.

11. Forsyth to Clark, 10 June 1828, Forsyth Papers, 6T:83–85; Forsyth to Clark, 22 June 1828, Ibid., 6T:88–89.

12. Black Hawk, *Autobiography*, 113, 115–20; Lloyd Dunlap, Sale of Lands in Royce Area 50, Docket 83, Sac and Fox Indians, Exhibit 146, pp. 2–3, RG 279, Records of the Indian Claims Commission.

13. Forsyth to Clark, 28 April 1830, Forsyth Papers, 6T:118–20; Forsyth to Clark, 30 April 1830, Ibid., 6T:121–22; Forsyth to Clark, 25 May 1830, Ibid., 6T:132; Gibson, *Kickapoos*, 80–87; Minutes of an Examination of Prisoners, 19 August 1832, *BHW*, 2:1028; Kay, "Fur Trade," 275.

14. Clark to Thomas L. McKenney, 2 August 1828, M-234, 748:465; Van der Zee, "Early History of Lead Mining," 39–46; quoted from George Davenport to Joseph Duncan, 11 February 1832, Sen. Doc. 512 (Serial 246), 221–23.

15. Quoted from Black Hawk, *Autobiography*, 120.

16. Felix St. Vrain to Clark, 6 April 1832, *BHW*, 2:231; Wallace, "Prelude to Disaster," Ibid., 1:46; Nichols, *Black Hawk and the Warrior's Path*, 91–92.

17. St. Vrain to Clark, 8 October 1830, M-234, 749:1217; St. Vrain to Clark, 15 May 1831, *BHW*, 2:7; Street to Eaton, 12 July 1831, M-234, 696:355; John Reynolds to Andrew Jackson, 2 August 1831, Ibid., 2:122n; Clark to Lewis Cass, 12 August 1831, Ibid., 2:135–37; Reynolds to Clark, 26 May 1831, Ibid., 2:13; quoted from Reynolds, *My Own Times*, 208.

18. Clark to Edmund P. Gaines, 28 May 1831, *BHW*, 2:16–17; Gaines to Reynolds, 29 May 1831, Ibid., 2:22–23; Gaines to Roger Jones, 14 June 1831, Ibid., 2:48; Jefferson Barracks Post Returns, May–June 1831, M-617, 545; Fort Crawford Post Return, June 1831, Ibid., 264; Fort Winnebago Post Return, April 1831, Ibid., 1454; quoted from Gaines to Roger Jones, 30 May 1831, *BHW*, 2:25–26.

19. Quoted from Black Hawk, *Autobiography*, 124.

20. Treaty of Ghent, 24 December 1814, in Haswell, *Treaties and Conventions*, 404; Black Hawk, *Autobiography*, 124, 136–37.

21. George McCall to Archibald McCall, 17 June 1831, *BHW*, 2:55; Black Hawk, *Autobiography*, 124–27; Talks between Gaines and the Sauk, 4–7 June 1831, *BHW*, 2:27–31; Gaines to Jones, 8 June 1831, Ibid., 2:36.

22. Deposition of Riggs Pennington, 24 October 1831, *BHW*, 2:172; Gaines to unknown, 20 June 1831, Ibid., 2:63; quoted from Black Hawk, *Autobiography*, 127–28.

23. Reynolds, *My Own Times*, 211; Reynolds to Edwards, 18 June 1831, *BHW*, 2:59; Letter from Rushville, 20 June 1831, Ibid., 2:64–66; Armstrong, *Sauks and the Black Hawk War*, 160–64; Returns of the Brigade of Mounted Volunteers, 13 June–2 July 1831, *BHW*, 1:54–119; Gaines to unknown, 20 June 1831, Ibid., 2:63; McCall to McCall, 23 June 1831, Ibid., 2:74–75; Fort Armstrong Post Return, June 1831, M-617, 41; McCall to McCall, 1 July 1831, *BHW*, 2:90–93.

24. Gaines to Hugh White, 6 July 1831, *BHW*, 2:102–3; McCall to McCall, 1 July 1831, Ibid., 2:92–93; Staff Officer to unknown, 1 July 1831, Ibid., 2:93–95; Quaife, *Early Day*, 44–48; Return of Benjamin Pike's Company, 16 June–2 July 1832, *BHW*, 1:113–15; quoted from Black Hawk, *Autobiography*, 128–29.

25. Quoted from Reynolds, *My Own Times*, 215.

26. Hagan, *Sac and Fox Indians*, 131–34; St. Vrain to Clark, 23 July 1831, *BHW*, 2:112; quoted from Quaife, *Early Day*, 49.

27. Articles of Agreement and Capitulation, 30 June 1830, *BHW*, 2:85–88; quoted from McCall to McCall, 5 July 1831, Ibid., 2:98.

28. St. Vrain to Clark, 23 July 1831, *BHW*, 2:112; Hagan, *Sac and Fox Indians*, 132–34; quoted from Black Hawk, *Autobiography*, 129–30.

29. Nichols, *Black Hawk and the Warrior's Path*, 100; Journal of a Council, 5 September 1831, *BHW*, 2:155–59; Black Hawk, *Autobiography*, 130–32; Wallace, "Prelude to Disaster," *BHW*, 1:40.

30. Answer of Black Hawk, 26 April 1832, *BHW*, 2:312–13; Minutes of an Examination of Prisoners, 20 August 1832, Ibid., 2:1034–35; Black Hawk, *Autobiography*, 132–33; Wallace, "Prelude to Disaster," *BHW*, 1:46–47.

31. Minutes of an Examination of Prisoners, 20 August 1832, *BHW*, 2:1034; quoted from Black Hawk, *Autobiography*, 133, 140.

32. Wallace, "Prelude to Disaster," *BHW*, 1:45–46; Joseph Street to Eaton, 12 July 1831, M-234, 696:355; Reynolds to Andrew Jackson, 2 August 1831, *BHW* 2:122n; Gaines to Jones, 14 June 1831, Ibid., 2:47; Clark to Cass, 12 August 1831, Ibid., 2:135–37, 138n.

33. Henry Gratiot to Gaines, 11 June 1831, *BHW*, 2:46; Street to Cass, 12 July 1831, M-234, 696:355; Gratiot to Clark, 25 June 1831, *BHW*, 2:76; Winnebago Chiefs to Gratiot, 1 July 1831, Ibid., 2:95–96; quoted from John Kinzie to Cass, 28 September 1831, M-234, 696:345–46.

34. John Dixon to James Soulard, 19 June 1831, *BHW*, 2:60; Clark to Cass, 12 August 1831, Ibid., 2:135–37.

35. Thomas Burnett to Clark, 29 June 1831, *BHW*, 2:81.

CHAPTER FOUR: THE THUNDERBIRDS' FIRST ROAR

1. Black Hawk, *Autobiography*, 133–35; John Dougherty to William Clark, 3 February 1832, *BHW*, 2:210; Drake, *Life and Adventures of Black Hawk*, 121–23; George Davenport to Joseph Duncan, 11 February 1832, *BHW*, 2:211–13; Lewis Cass to Duncan, 15 March 1832, Ibid., 2:218.

2. William Clark to Cass, 6 December 1831, *BHW*, 2:205–6; John Kinzie to Cass, 1 March 1832, M-234, 696:402–3; Fort Dearborn Post Return, April 1831, June 1832, M-617, 300; Wentworth, *Fort Dearborn*, 47–49; Cass to Daniel Wardwell and Charles Dayan, 7 April 1832, M-6, 13:13:174–76.

3. Henry Atkinson to Alexander Macomb, 3 April 1832, *BHW*, 2:224; Atkinson, Orders, 5 April 1832, Ibid., 2:225–26; Thian, *Notes Illustrating the Military Geography*, 107; Silver, *Edmund Pendleton Gaines*, 132, 146, 160–61; Nichols, *Henry Atkinson*, 3–68, 169; Eby, *Black Hawk War*, 29–30.

4. Nichols, *Henry Atkinson*, 169–75.

5. John Bliss to Atkinson, 30 March 1832, *BHW*, 2:222–23; Nichols, *Black Hawk and the Warrior's Path*, 106–8; quoted from Taimah and Apenose to Clark, 22 July 1832, *BHW*, 2:852.

6. Atkinson to Macomb, 7 April 1832, *BHW*, 2:232.

7. Felix St. Vrain to Clark, 6 April 1832, *BHW*, 2:230–31; quoted from Black Hawk, *Autobiography*, 136.

8. Black Hawk, *Autobiography*, 124–25, 136; Matson, *Memories of Shaubena*, 105–6; Thomas Forsyth, Original Causes of the troubles with a party of Sauk and Fox Indians, Forsyth Papers, 9:54–59; Bliss to Atkinson, 9–12 April 1832, *BHW*, 2:237; Andrew Hughes to Atkinson, 13 April 1832, Ibid., 2:248.

9. Minutes of an Examination of Prisoners, 27 August 1832, *BHW*, 2:1056–57; Samuel Stambaugh to George Boyd, 13 August 1832, Ibid., 2:1074; Nathan Smith to Atkinson, 13 April 1832, Ibid., 2:249; John Dixon to Isaiah Stillman, 28 April 1832, Ibid., 2:325; Matson, *Memories of Shaubena*, 105.

10. Black Hawk, *Autobiography*, 136–37, 136n, 146; Davenport to Atkinson, 13 April 1832, *BHW*, 2:247; Wallace, "Prelude to Disaster," Ibid., 1:39–40; Bliss to Atkinson, 9–12 April 1832, Ibid., 2:237–39.

11. Black Hawk, *Autobiography*, 137; Nichols, *Henry Atkinson*, 157–58; Bliss to Atkinson, 30 March 1832, *BHW*, 2:222–23; Fort Armstrong Council, 13 April 1832, Ibid., 2:253–54.

12. Atkinson to Macomb, 13 April 1832, *BHW*, 2:244–45; Fort Armstrong Council, 13 April 1832, Ibid., 2:251–54; Nichols, *Henry Atkinson*, 158; quoted from Atkinson to John Reynolds, 13 April 1832, *BHW*, 2:245–46.

13. Trask, *Black Hawk*, 158–61; Reynolds to Atkinson, 16 April 1832, *BHW*, 2:263.

14. Atkinson to William Ferguson, 14 April 1832, *BHW*, 2:256; quoted from Atkinson to Henry Dodge, 14 April 1832, Ibid., 2:255.

15. Albert S. Johnston, Journal, 14–19 April 1832, *BHW*, 2:1308.

16. Atkinson to Macomb, 19 April 1832, *BHW*, 2:278–79; Fort Armstrong Council, 13 April 1832, Ibid., 2:253–54, 255n; quoted from St. Vrain to Clark, 18 April 1832, Ibid., 2:277.

17. Atkinson to Black Hawk, 24 April 1832, *BHW*, 2:301–2; quoted from Answer of Black Hawk's Band, 26 April 1832, Ibid., 2:312–14.

18. Atkinson to Henry Gratiot, 15 April 1832, *BHW*, 2:257; Gratiot, Journal, 16–22 April 1832, Ibid., 2:1302–3.

19. Gratiot to Cass, 26 April 1832, *BHW*, 2:314–15; Gratiot, Journal, 24–25 April 1832, Ibid., 2:1302–3; quoted from Black Hawk, *Autobiography*, 138–39.

20. Black Hawk, *Autobiography*, 138–38; Gratiot, Journal, 26 April 1832, *BHW*, 2:1303; Washburne, "Col. Henry Gratiot," *WHC*, 10:253–54.

21. Kellogg, "Winnebago Visit to Washington in 1828," 347–54; Lurie, "In Search of Chaetar," 166–67; Kinzie to Cass, 28 September 1831, M-234, 696:345–46; Porter's Grove Council, 3–4 June 1832, *BHW*, 2:507–12; Street to Atkinson, 13 August 1832, Ibid., 2:997–99; Minutes of an Examination of Prisoners, 19 August 1832, Ibid., 2:1028–33.

22. Reynolds to Atkinson, 16 April 1832, 2, *BHW*, 2:263; Reynolds, Orders, 16 April 1832, Ibid., 2:265–67; Reynolds, Orders, 20 April 1832, Ibid., 2:284–85; quoted from Speech of Abraham Lincoln, 27 July 1848, in Basler, *Collected Works of Abraham Lincoln*, 1:509–10.

23. Pratt, "Abraham Lincoln in the Black Hawk War," 18–19, 21; Temple, "Lincoln's Arms and Dress," 145–49; Company of Abraham Lincoln, 27 May 1832, *BHW*, 1:176–78; Muster Roll of Capt. David W. Barnes, 30 August 1832, Black Hawk War Records, 1832–1891 RG 301.007; quoted from Moore, "Mr. Lincoln as a Wrestler," 433–34.

24. Quoted from Richard Young, et al., to Reynolds, 20 April 1832, *BHW*, 2:288–89.

25. Reynolds, Orders, 23 April 1832, *BHW*, 2:298–99; Thomas Taylor to Reynolds, 25 April 1832, Ibid., 2:312; Stevens, *Black Hawk War*, 116; Returns of Whiteside's Brigade, 16 April–28 May 1832, *BHW*, 1:123–224.

26. Atkinson to Dodge, 25 April 1832, *BHW*, 2:304–5; Atkinson to James Strode, 25 April 1832, Ibid., 2:305; Atkinson, Orders, 25 April 1832, Ibid., 2:306; quoted from Answer of Black Hawk, 26 April 1832, Ibid., 312; quoted from Gratiot to Atkinson, 27 April 1832, Ibid., 2:317–18.

27. Quoted from Black Hawk, *Autobiography*, 138–39.

28. Ibid., 139.

29. Quoted from Atkinson to Reynolds, 27 April 1832, *BHW*, 2:320.

30. Atkinson to Kinzie, 16 April 1832, *BHW*, 2:257; Atkinson to Reynolds, 18 April 1832, Ibid., 2:275; Bliss to Atkinson, 12 April 1832, Ibid., 2:238; quoted from Nathan Smith to Atkinson 13 April 1832, Ibid., 2:249.

31. Quoted from Bliss to Atkinson, 12 April 1832, *BHW*, 2:238–39.

32. Thwaites, "Story of the Black Hawk War," *WHC*, 12:232; Bliss to Atkinson, 11–12 April 1832, *BHW*, 2:237–39; quoted from Reynolds, *My Own Times*, 225.

33. Atkinson to Reynolds, 27 May 1832, *BHW*, 2:320; Atkinson to Reynolds, 5 May 1832, Ibid., 2:348; quoted from Benjamin F. Irwin to Herndon, 22 September 1866, *HI*, 353.

34. Royal Clary to Herndon, October 1866, *HI*, 372; quoted from Greene to Herndon, 30 May 1865, Ibid., 18–19.

35. Young, et al., to Neale and James D. Henry, 20 April 1832, *BHW*, 2:288; Stillman to Elias Foster, 29 April 1832, Ibid., 2:332; William Headon to his brother, 1 May 1832, Ibid., 2:341.

36. Quoted from Black Hawk, *Autobiography*, 137, 137n, 139, 140.

37. Ibid., 140–41.

38. Orville Browning, Journal, 26 April–3 May 1832, *BHW*, 2:1297–98; Reynolds, *My Own Times*, 226–28; Atkinson to Gaines, 3 May 1832, *BHW*, 2:343–44; Atkinson to Reynolds, 5 May 1832, Ibid., 2:348; Johnston, Journal, 4–8 May 1832, Ibid., 2:1310; Atkinson, Orders, 9 May 1832, Ibid., 2:360;

Return of Odd Infantry Battalion, 28 May 1832, Ibid., 1:217–23; Atkinson to Macomb, 10 May 1832, Ibid., 2:362; Adams, *General William S. Harney*, 39.

39. Quoted from Atkinson to Macomb, 10 May 1832, *BHW*, 2:362.

40. Hagan, "General Henry Atkinson," 195; Samuel Whiteside to Atkinson, 12 May 1832, *BHW*, 2:366–67; Whiteside to Atkinson, 18 May 1832, Ibid., 2:386–87.

41. Wakefield, *Black Hawk War*, 41–46; Reynolds, *My Own Times*, 229–31; Dodge to Reynolds, 8 May 1832, *BHW*, 2:357–58; Whiteside to Atkinson, 18 May 1832, Ibid., 2:386, 387n; Armstrong, *Sauks and the Black Hawk War*, 310–12; quoted from [Backus], "A Brief History of the War with the Sac & Fox Indians," *MPHC*, 12:426.

42. For examples, see Nichols, "Black Hawk War in Retrospect," 239–40; Prucha, *Sword of the Republic*, 211–12; Wallace, "Prelude to Disaster," *BHW*, 1:51.

43. Wakefield, *Black Hawk War*, 46–48; Black Hawk, *Autobiography*, 140–41; quoted from Matson, *Memories of Shaubena*, 92–94, 106–11.

44. Black Hawk, *Autobiography*, 45–50, 55, 141; Matson, *Memories of Shaubena*, 112–15. Although Black Hawk's autobiography refers to them as "medicine bags," this is a mistranslation as Black Hawk is clearly referring to war bundles. See Harrington, *Sacred Bundles*, 125–212, 239–40; Skinner, "War Customs," 303–4.

45. Wakefield, *Black Hawk War*, 45–47; Black Hawk, *Autobiography*, 141–43; Militia Officer's Report, 18 May 1832, *BHW*, 2:387–88.

46. Whiteside to Atkinson, 18 May 1832, *BHW*, 2:386, 387n; Militia Officer's Report, 18 May 1832, Ibid., 2:388; War News from Galena, 23 May 1832, Ibid., 2:426; Asher Edgerton to Elisha Edgerton, Ibid., 2:464; Stillman to the *Missouri Republican*, 19 June 1832, Ibid., 2:635–36; Minutes of an Examination of Prisoners, 20 August 1832, Ibid., 2:1034; Wakefield, *Black Hawk War*, 47–51; John Hanks to Herndon, 1865–66, *HI*, 458; Trask, *Black Hawk*, 183–86; Black Hawk, *Autobiography*, 144.

47. Hauberg, "Black Hawk War, 1831–1832," 118; quoted from Black Hawk, *Autobiography*, 144–46.

48. Atkinson to Dodge, 17 May 1832, *BHW*, 2:377; War News from Galena, 16 May 1832, Ibid., 2:377; Nichols, *Henry Atkinson*, 164–65; quoted from Macomb to Atkinson, 22 May 1832, *BHW*, 2:409.

49. Nichols, *Henry Atkinson*, 144–45; Atkinson to Jones, 19 November 1832, *BHW*, 2:1204–12; Distribution of Troops in the Eastern and Western Departments, 3 December 1831, *ASP: MA*, 4:722–25; Stubbs and Connor, *Armor-Cavalry Part I: Regular Army*, 4–8; *National Intelligencer*, 2 June 1832, 15 June 1832; *Register of Debates in Congress*, 8:991–92, 1070, 1075–78, 3388–98; *U.S. Statutes at Large*, 4:532–33; Patrick Galt, Order No. 14, 28 August 1832, Military Order Book and Letters, 1832–1834, p. 3, Henry Dodge Papers.

CHAPTER FIVE: THE EYE OF THE STORM

1. Quoted from Black Hawk, *Autobiography*, 144–47.

2. Joseph Street to Henry Atkinson, 6 June 1832, *BHW*, 2:536–38; quoted from Black Hawk, *Autobiography*, 147–48, 153.

3. Starkey, *European and Native American Warfare*, 17–56; Edmunds, "Indian-White Warfare," 35–45; Gleach, *Powhatan's World*, 4, 42–54.

4. James Strode to John Reynolds and Atkinson, 23 May 1832, *BHW*, 2:421–23; Oliver Kellogg to James Johnson, 19 May 1832, Ibid., 2:390–91; Matson, *Memories of Shaubena*, 117–27, 149–53; Statement of Rachel Hall Munson, 10–11 October 1834, *BHW*, 2:1287–92; Black Hawk, *Autobiography*, 151–53; Minutes of an Examination of Prisoners, 27 August 1832, *BHW*, 2:1055; George E. Wacker to Atkinson, 17 January 1833, M-234, 728:316; La Salle County Circuit Court Order, 21 May 1834, *BHW*, 2:1283; Clifton, *Prairie People*, 233.

5. Black Hawk, *Autobiography*, 153; Statement of Munson, 10–11 October 1834, *BHW*, 2:1288–92; Skinner, *Ethnology of the Sauk Indians*, 71–73.

6. War News from Galena, 23 May 1832, *BHW*, 2:427–28; Birmingham, "Story of Fort Blue Mounds," 47–57; Thomas J. V. Owen to George B. Porter, 18 May 1832, *BHW*, 2:383; Roster of Cook County Volunteers, May 1832, Ibid., 1:447–54; John Robb to Samuel Bayard, 8 June 1832, M-6, (both lines); 13:13:204 quoted from Stephen Mack to Lovicy Cooper, 13 June 1832, *BHW*, 2:583.

7. War News from Galena, 23 May 1832, *BHW*, 2:426; War News from Galena, 30 May 1832, Ibid., 2:488–89; Robert Anderson, Memoranda, 27 August 1832, Ibid., 2:1057; Black Hawk, *Autobiography*, 147.

8. Owen to John Hogan and Almanzan Huston, 24 May 1832, *BHW*, 2:431–32; Winfield Scott to Cass, 19 August–21 August 1832, Ibid., 2:1025; Owen to Porter, 18 September 1832, Ibid., 2:1162; Atkinson to Johnson, 20 May 1832, Ibid., 2:395; Atkinson to Alexander Macomb, 30 May 1832, Ibid., 2:478; Tanner, *Atlas of Great Lakes Indian History*, 140, 152–53.

9. Wakefield, *Black Hawk War*, 49–55; Black Hawk, *Autobiography*, 143; quoted from Reynolds, *My Own Times*, 235–36.

10. Ibid., 236–37; Samuel Whiteside to Atkinson, 18 May 1832, *BHW*, 2:386.

11. Muldoon, *Alexander Hamilton's Pioneer Son*, 89–95; Atkinson to William S. Hamilton, 18 May 1832, *BHW*, 2:378–79; Atkinson, Orders, 18 May 1832, Ibid., 2:380; Isaiah Stillman to Reynolds or Atkinson, 21 May 1832, Ibid., 2:400–401; Atkinson to Macomb, 23 May 1832, Ibid., 2:412; Atkinson to Macomb, 25 May 1832, Ibid., 2:435; Albert S. Johnston, Journal, 19 May–29 May 1832, Ibid., 2:1311–13, 1311n–12n.

12. Reynolds, *My Own Times*, 237; Atkinson, Orders, 22 May 1832, *BHW*, 2:403–4; quoted from Black Hawk, *Autobiography*, 146–47.

13. Quoted from Atkinson, Orders, 22 May 1832, *BHW*, 2:404.

14. Zachary Taylor to Atkinson, 26 May 1832, *BHW*, 2:453; quoted from William Orr to John Sawyer, 1 July 1832, Ibid., 2:726.

15. Johnston, Journal, 23 May–24 May 1832, *BHW*, 2:1312; Whiteside to Atkinson, 27 May 1832, Ibid., 2:461; Reynolds, *My Own Times*, 237–39.

16. Atkinson to Macomb, 25 May 1832, *BHW*, 2:435–37; Atkinson to Macomb, 30 May 1832, Ibid., 2:477–78; quoted from Atkinson to Roger Jones, 19 November 1832, Ibid., 2:1212.

17. Johnston, Journal, 28 May–29 May 1832, *BHW*, 2:1312–13; Atkinson to Reynolds, 29 May 1832, Ibid., 2:469; Rosters of Jacob Fry's Twenty-Day Interim Regiment, 27 May–21 June 1832, Ibid., 1:225–42; Suppiger, "Private Lincoln in the Spy Battalion," 46–49; quoted from Herndon and Weik, *Abraham Lincoln*, vol. 1, 91.

18. Pelzer, *Henry Dodge*, 8–54, 67; Atkinson to Henry Dodge, 14 April 1832, *BHW*, 2:255; Atkinson to Dodge, 25 April 1832, Ibid., 2:304–5.

19. Hugh Brady to Atkinson, 1 May 1832, *BHW*, 2:340; [Backus], "A Brief History of the War with the Sac & Fox Indians," *MPHC*, 12:428–29; Atkinson to Brady, 27 May 1832, *BHW*, 2:457; Fort Winnebago Post Return, June 1832, M-617, 1454; Fort Howard Post Return, May 1832, Ibid., 489; Brady to Scott, 30 May 1832, *BHW*, 2:481–82; Fort Leavenworth Post Returns, May–July 1832, M-617, 610; Return of United States Army Troops, 3 August 1832, *BHW*, 1: 576–77.

20. Atkinson to Brady, 27 May 1832, *BHW*, 2:457; Atkinson to Street, 26 May 1832, Ibid., 2:445–46.

21. Johnston, Journal, 26 May–28 May 1832, *BHW*, 2:1312; Thomas Burnett to Street, 5 June 1832, Ibid., 2:524–25; Lyman C. Draper, ed., "Winnebagoes and the Black Hawk War," *WHC*, 5:306–9; Street to Clark, 7 June 1832, *BHW*, 2:547; quoted from Street to Atkinson, 6–7 June 1832, Ibid., 2:535.

22. Hamilton to Atkinson, 13 June 1832, *BHW*, 2:582; Taylor to Atkinson, 13 June 1832, Ibid., 2:585; Pratt, "Abraham Lincoln in the Black Hawk War," 26; William Campbell to Andrew Jackson, 17–19 June 1832, *BHW*, 2:612; Dodge to Atkinson, 18 June 1832, Ibid., 2:622–23; Hamilton to Atkinson, 24 June 1832, Ibid., 2:663–64; quoted from Talk between Street and Sioux, 22 June 1832, Ibid., 2:653.

23. Chicago Residents to James Stewart, 29 May 1832, *BHW*, 2:475; Atkinson to Owen, 31 May 1832, Ibid., 2:491; Owen to Atkinson, 6 June 1832, Ibid., 2:534; Brady to Scott, 21 May 1832, Ibid., 2:398; Kinzie to Cass, 3 August 1827, M-1, 21:40–41; Owen to Atkinson, 3 June 1832, *BHW*, 2:506.

24. Jipson, "Winnebago Villages and Chieftains," 125–39; Four Lakes Council, 26 May 1823, *BHW*, 2:454–56; Blue Mounds Council, 28 May 1832, Ibid., 2:467–68; Statement of Munson, 10–11 October 1834, Ibid., 2:1289–90; Henry Gratiot, Journal, 2–7 June 1832, Ibid., 2:1303–4; Minutes of an Examination of Prisoners, 20 August 1832, Ibid., 2:1035–36; Council at Porter's Grove, 2–4 June 1832, Ibid., 2:507–13; quoted from Gratiot to Clark, 12 June 1832, Ibid., 2:578.

25. Strode to Atkinson, 10 June 1832, *BHW*, 2:566–69; Council with the Rock River Winnebago, 11 September 1832, Ibid., 2:1133.

26. Gratiot, Journal, 14–27 June 1832, *BHW*, 2:1304; quoted from Report of Oliver Emmell and White Crow, 27 June 1832, Ibid., 2:694.

27. Quoted from Report of Emmell and White Crow, 27 June 1832, *BHW*, 2:695–96.

28. Statement of Munson, 10–11 October 1834, *BHW*, 2:1288–89; Black Hawk, *Autobiography*, 143–49; Porter's Grove Council, 3–4 June 1832, *BHW*, 2:511–13; Strode to Atkinson, 10 June 1832, Ibid., 2:566; Iles, *Sketches of Early Life*, 49; Eby, *Black Hawk War*, 183.

29. Atkinson, Orders, 6 June 1832, *BHW*, 2:530–31; Pratt, "Abraham Lincoln in the Black Hawk War," 26; John T. Stuart to William H. Herndon, 1865–66, *HI*, 481; Iles, *Sketches*, 45–51.

30. John Sherman to Dodge, 30 May 1832, *BHW*, 2:487; Strode to Atkinson, 10 June 1832, Ibid., 2:566–67; Ebenezer Brigham to John Kinzie, 16 June 1832, Ibid., 2:605; *Galenian*, 27 June 1832.

31. Dodge to Sherman, 16 June 1832, *BHW*, 2:607–8; Francis Gehon to John Sherman, 17 June 1832, Ibid., 2:614; Charles Bracken and Peter Parkinson, Jr., "Pekatonica Battle Controversy," *WHC*, 2:366–72, 377–78; quoted from Dodge to Atkinson, 18 June 1832, *BHW*, 2:622–25.

32. Trask, *Black Hawk*, 235–36; quoted from Citizens of Prairie du Chien to Dodge, 3 July 1832, *BHW*, 2:737.

33. Taylor to Atkinson, 9 June 1832, *BHW*, 2:558; Militia Officer's Report, 16 June 1832, Ibid., 2:609–11.

34. Report of James Stephenson, 19 June 1832, *BHW*, 2:633–34; William Campbell to Atkinson, 23 June 1832, Ibid., 2:658; Black Hawk, *Autobiography*, 150–51; Daniel Parkinson, "Pioneer Life in Wisconsin," *WHC*, 2:351; Edward Beouchard, "Beochard's Narrative," *HOW*, 212; Council with the Rock River Winnebago, 11 September 1832, *BHW*, 2:1133–34.

35. Campbell to Jackson, 17–19 June 1832, *BHW*, 2:612–14; Williams to Porter, 17 June 1832, Ibid., 2:598; William Gordon to James Edwards, 25 June 1832, Ibid., 2:669–70; Owen to Atkinson, 13 June 1832, Ibid., 2:584; Matson, *Memories of Shaubena*, 194–204, 226–34.

36. Black Hawk, *Autobiography*, 149; Company of Clack Stone, 6 September 1832, *BHW*, 1:520–21; Strode to Atkinson, 25 June 1832, Ibid., 2: 673–74; *Galenian*, 27 June 1832, 4 July 1832; Starkey, *European and Native American Warfare*, 24, 27.

37. Stevens, *Black Hawk War*, 188–89; quoted from Cooke, *Scenes and Adventures in the Army*, 158.

38. Reynolds, *My Own Times*, 244–45; Stevens, "Forgotten Hero," 77–94; Return of Illinois Mounted Volunteers, June 1832, *BHW*, 1:572–73; Return of United States Army Troops, 2 August 1832, Ibid., 1:576–77; Atkinson to Jones, 19 November 1832, Ibid., 2:1209; Atkinson to Scott, 9 July 1832, Ibid., 2:753; quoted from Bryant, *Prose Writings*, vol. 1, 20.

39. Rosters of odd battalions and companies, *BHW*, 1:447–79, 534–59; Reynolds, *My Own Times*, 245–46; Pratt, "Abraham Lincoln in the Black Hawk War," 26; Armstrong, *Sauks and the Black Hawk War*, 726; Pelzer, *Henry Dodge*, 53–54; Hollman, "Autobiography," 223–24; Atkinson to Dodge, 11 June 1832, *BHW*, 2:571; Illinois Companies Attached to Michigan Territory Volunteers, May–September 1832, Ibid., 1:526–33; Atkinson to Scott, 9 July 1832, Ibid., 2:753; Bracken, "Further Strictures," *WHC*, 2:404; Dodge to Atkinson, 18 July 1832, *BHW*, 2:820.

40. Atkinson to Owen, 11 June 1832, *BHW*, 2:571; Potawatomi Indians in United States Service, 22 June–22 July 1832, Ibid., 1:560–62; Clifton, "Case of Billy Caldwell," 69–94.

41. Atkinson to Taylor, 7 June 1832, *BHW*, 2:538; Porter's Grove Council, 4 June 1832, Ibid., 2:511–13; Street to Atkinson, 6 June 1832, Ibid., 2:536; Owen to Atkinson, 11 June 1832, Ibid., 2:574; Atkinson to Milton K.

Alexander, 28 June 1832, Ibid., 2:697; quoted from Atkinson to Macomb, 15 June 1832, Ibid., 2:589.

42. Quoted from Robb to Atkinson, 12 June 1832, M-6, 13:13:221–22.

43. Atkinson to Cass, 6–7 July 1832, *BHW*, 2:742–43; Skelton, "The Commanding General and the Problem of Command," 119–21; *National Intelligencer*, 7 July 1832, 26 July 1832; Remini, *Andrew Jackson*, 345–73, 377–79; Cass to Scott, 15 June 1832, *BHW*, 2:590–91.

44. Quoted from Robb to Jackson with Jackson's response, 12 June 1832, *BHW*, 2:579–80.

45. Stein, "Indian-White Hostility," 173–87; Horatio Newhall to Isaac Newhall, 19 May 1832, *BHW*, 2:393; Street to Atkinson, 20 May 1832, Ibid., 2:397; Scott to Cass, 15 July 1832, Ibid., 2:806; Macomb to Cass, November 1832, *Annual Report of the Secretary of War for 1832*, 22nd Cong., 2nd sess., 1832, Ho. Doc. 2. (Serial 233): 58–59; John Russell, "The Black Hawk War," Russell Family Papers, p. 9, Box 1, Folder 16; Atkinson to Jones, 19 November 1832, *BHW*, 2:1206–7; quoted from Cass to Clark, 22 May 1832, Ibid., 2:405.

46. Atkinson, Orders, 20 June 1832, *BHW*, 2:637–38; *General Regulations for the Army*, 92–124; Johnston, Journal, 20–25 June 1832, *BHW*, 2:1313–15; Atkinson, Orders, 21 June 1832, Ibid., 2:640.

47. Johnston, Journal, 25 June 1832, *BHW*, 2:1315; Atkinson, Orders, 19 June 1832, Ibid., 2:629; Company of Captain Adam W. Snyder, 21 June 1832, Ibid., 1:237–39; quoted from *Recollections of the Pioneers*, 249.

48. Reynolds, *My Own Times*, 247; *Vandalia Whig and Illinois Intelligencer*, 11 July 1832; Jacob Early to Atkinson, 26 June 1832, *BHW*, 2:678–79; quoted from John Dement, Report of Battle at Kellogg's Grove, 26 June 1832, Ibid., 2:681.

49. Quoted from Black Hawk, *Autobiography*, 149–50.

50. Dement, Report, 26 June 1832, *BHW*, 2:681–82; Reynolds, *My Own Times*, 247–50; Rosters of Dement's Spy Battalion, 28 May–16 August 1832, *BHW*, 1:286–94; quoted in Black Hawk, *Autobiography*, 150.

51. Strode to Atkinson, Brady, and Reynolds, 30 June 1832, *BHW*, 2:722–24; Joshua Pilcher to Atkinson, 6 August 1832, Ibid., 2:946; quoted from Reynolds to Ninian Edwards, 22 June 1832, Ibid., 2:649. The numbers of casualties are taken from those presented in the text; also see Ibid., 2:613.

52. Quoted from Atkinson to Macomb, 23 June 1832, *BHW*, 2:656.

53. Black Hawk, *Autobiography*, 137–40, 150–54; Report of Emmell and White Crow, 27 June 1832, *BHW*, 2:694; Minutes of an Examination of Prisoners, 19 August 1832, Ibid., 2:1029, 1031–33.

54. Reynolds, *My Own Times*, 249; Alexander Posey to Atkinson, 26 June 1832, *BHW*, 2:679; Atkinson to Jones, 19 November 1832, Ibid., 2:1208; Johnston, Journal, 25 June 1832, Ibid., 2:1315; Early to Atkinson, 26 June 1832, *BHW*, 2:678–79; *Illinois Herald*, 12 July 1832; *Sangamo Journal* (Springfield, IL), 19 July 1832; quoted from Atkinson to Posey, 25 June 1832, *BHW*, 2:665.

55. Atkinson to Alexander, 26 June 1826, *BHW*, 2:676; Atkinson to Posey, 25 June 1832, Ibid., 2:665; George Harrison to Herndon, 1866, *HI*,

327–28; Atkinson to Posey, 28 June 1832, *BHW*, 2:697; quoted in Early to Atkinson, 26 June 1832, Ibid., 2:678.

56. Atkinson to Jones, 19 November 1832, *BHW*, 2:1209.

Chapter Six: The Silence and the Fury

1. *General Regulations for the Army*, 85; Henry Atkinson, Orders, 26 June 1832, *BHW*, 2:677; Atkinson to Winfield Scott, 9 July 1832, Ibid., 2:753; quoted from Hugh Brady to Scott, 26 June 1832, Ibid., 2:685.

2. James D. Henry to Atkinson, 26 June 1832, *BHW*, 2:685–86; Cooke, *Scenes and Adventures in the Army*, 161–62.

3. Atkinson to Milton K. Alexander, 28 June 1832, *BHW*, 2:697; Atkinson to Henry Dodge, 28 June 1832, Ibid., 2:698–99; Atkinson to Alexander Posey, 28 June 1832, Ibid., 2:697; Albert S. Johnston, Journal, 28 June 1832, Ibid., 2:1315.

4. Posey to Atkinson, 29 June 1832, *BHW*, 2:710; Daniel M. Parkinson, "Pioneer Life in Wisconsin," *WHC*, 2:352–53; quoted from Parish, *George Wallace Jones*, 120–22.

5. Johnston, Journal, 28 June–3 July 1832, *BHW*, 2:1315–16; Atkinson to Roger Jones, 19 November 1832, Ibid., 2:1209; Wakefield, *Black Hawk War*, 76–79; [Backus], "Brief History," *MPHC*, 12:429; Nineveh Shaw, Journal, 26 June–4 July 1832, *BHW*, 2:1333–34; Henry Gratiot, Journal, 5–15 July 1832, Ibid., 2:1304; Parkinson, "Pioneer Life," *WHC*, 2:353.

6. Atkinson, Orders, 5 July 1832, *BHW*, 2:741; Wakefield, *Black Hawk War*, 80–81; Minutes of an Examination of Prisoners, 19 August 1832, *BHW*, 2:1030; Atkinson to Lewis Cass, 6 July 1832, Ibid., 2:742–43.

7. Thomas J. V. Owen to Atkinson, 11 June 1832, *BHW*, 2:574; Black Hawk, *Autobiography*, 153; Ogden, "Narrative of George W. Ogden," 42; Report of Oliver Emmell and White Crow, 27 June 1832, *BHW*, 2:695–96; Wakefield, *Black Hawk War*, 76–78.

8. Atkinson to Cass, 6 July 1832, *BHW*, 2:743; Johnston, Journal, 2 July 1832, Ibid., 2:1316; John Russell, "The Black Hawk War," Russell Family Papers, p. 22, Box 1, Folder 16; Charles Bracken, "Personal Narrative," *HOW*, 218; Johnston, Journal, 3–6 July 1832, *BHW*, 2:1316; Atkinson to Cass, 6 July 1832, Ibid., 2:743; Shaw, Journal, 6–7 July 1832, Ibid., 2:1334. For an argument that Atkinson approached Lake Koshkonong from the south, see Stark, *Along the Black Hawk Trail*, 97–99.

9. Thayer, *Hunting a Shadow*, 352, 410–11; James Justice, Journal, *BHW*, 2:1323; Peter Parkinson, Jr., "Notes on the Black Hawk War," *WHC*, 10:206–7; Atkinson to Jones, 19 November 1832, *BHW*, 2:1209–10.

10. Bracken, "Narrative," *HOW*, 218–19; Parkinson, "Notes," *WHC*, 10:206–7; Parkinson, "Pioneer Life," Ibid., 2:353–54; Shaw, Journal, 7 July 1832, *BHW*, 2:1334.

11. Johnston, Journal, 7–8 July 1832, *BHW*, 2:1317; Atkinson to Jones, 19 November 1832, Ibid., 2:1210; Wakefield, *Black Hawk War*, 81–83.

12. Johnston, Journal, 8 July 1832, *BHW*, 2:1317; Wakefield, *Black Hawk War*, 83; quoted from Shaw, Journal, 8 July 1832, *BHW*, 2:1334.

13. Atkinson to Dodge, 8 July 1832, *BHW*, 2:751; Johnston, Journal, 8 July 1832, Ibid., 2:1317; Wakefield, *Black Hawk War*, 82–84.

14. Johnston, Journal, 9 July 1832, *BHW*, 2:1317; Wakefield, *Black Hawk War*, 83–84; quoted from Armstrong, *Sauks and the Black Hawk War*, 443.

15. Wakefield, *Black Hawk War*, 84; Atkinson to Jones, 19 November 1832, *BHW*, 2:1210; quoted from [Backus], "A Brief History of the War with the Sac and Fox Indians," *MPHC*, 12:430.

16. Atkinson, Orders, 9 July 1832, *BHW*, 2:754; Atkinson, Orders, 9 July 1832, Ibid., 2:755; Atkinson, Orders, 10 July 1832, Ibid., 2:758; quoted from Johnston, Journal, 9 July 1832, Ibid., 2:1317.

17. Atkinson to Jones, 19 November 1832, *BHW*, 2:1210, 1212; Johnston, Journal, 9 July 1832, Ibid., 2:1317; Parkinson, "Notes on the Black Hawk War," *WHC*, 10:200.

18. Johnston, Journal, 10 July 1832, *BHW*, 2:1317; Menominee Indians in United States Service, 4–10 July 1832, Ibid., 1:562; Potawatomi Indians in United States Service, 22 June–22 July 1832, Ibid., 1:560–62; Atkinson to Scott, 9 July 1832, Ibid., 2:753; Gratiot, Journal, 10 July 1832, Ibid., 2:1304; Reynolds, *My Own Times*, 252; [Backus], "A Brief History of the War with the Sac and Fox Indians," *MPHC*, 12:430; Company of Jacob M. Early, 10 July 1832, *BHW*, 1:544–46; John T. Stuart to William H. Herndon, June 1865, *HI*, 64; George M. Harrison to Herndon, 1866, Ibid., 328–29.

19. Mayne, "The Old Fort," 197–201; Atkinson to Scott, 11 July 1832, *BHW*, 2:763; Johnston, Journal, 11–13 July 1832, Ibid., 2:1317–18; Johnston to Alexander, 4 July 1832, Ibid., 2:739; Atkinson to Nathan Clark, 12 July 1832, Ibid., 2:772.

20. Johnston, Journal, 7–11 July 1832, *BHW*, 2:1317–18; Justice, Journal, Ibid., 2:1323; Parish, *George Wallace Jones*, 149; Atkinson to Jones, 19 November 1832, *BHW*, 2:1209–10; quoted from [Backus], "Brief History," *MPHC*, 12:434.

21. Quoted from Atkinson to Scott, 9 July 1832, *BHW*, 2:753.

22. Harrison to Herndon, 29 January 1867, *HI*, 553–55; Atkinson to Scott, 11 July 1832, *BHW*, 2:763; quoted from Justice, Journal, Ibid., 2:1324.

23. Menominee Indians in United States Service, 4 July 1832, *BHW*, 1:562–63; Trask, "Settlement in a Half-Savage Land," 1–27; Samuel C. Stambaugh to George B. Porter, 7 June 1832, *BHW*, 2:545; George Boyd to Porter, 13 June 1832, Ibid., 2:581–82; Irwin to Porter, 18 June 1832, M-234, 421:70; quoted from Grizzly Bear's Talk, 22 June 1832, *BHW*, 2:650.

24. Atkinson to Boyd, 12 July 1832, *BHW*, 2:770–71; Boyd to Atkinson, 20 July 1832, Ibid., 2:834; Boyd to Daniel Whitney, 21 July 1832, *WHC*, 12:274–75; Boyd to Porter, 23 July 1832, Ibid., 12:277; Roll of Captain George Johnston's Company of Menominee Indians, 20 July–28 August 1832, Henry S. Baird Papers, Box 5 Folder 4, State Historical Society of Wisconsin, (hereafter cited as Baird Papers), Roll of Captain Augustin Grignon's Company of Menominee Warriors, 20 July–28 August 1832, Baird Papers, 5:4; Boyd to Stambaugh's staff, 24 July 1832, *WHC*, 12:281; Augustin Grignon, "Augustin Grignon's Recollections," Ibid., 3:294.

25. Jones, Orders, 16 June 1832, *BHW*, 2:599–601; Eby, *Black Hawk War*, 217; Scott, Orders, 3 July 1832, *BHW*, 2:735–36; Scott to Atkinson, 30 June 1832, Ibid., 2:717–18; Scott to William Whistler, 30 June 1832, Ibid., 2:718–19; William C. DeHart to Abraham Eustis, 28 June 1832, Ibid., 2:703–4.

26. Rosenberg, *Cholera Years*, 3–5, 13–17, 23–36 77–76.

27. Scott to Atkinson, 30 June 1832, *BHW*, 2:717–18; Scott to Cass, 11–12 July 1832, Ibid., 2:767–68; Scott to Atkinson, 12 July 1832, Ibid., 2:778; Walker, "Early Days on the Lakes," 310–12; Elijah Lyon, Journal, 21 July 1832, *BHW*, 2:1328; Scott to Reynolds, 15 July 1832, Ibid., 2:809; Eustis to Cass, 29 July 1832, Ibid., 2:906; Scott to Cass, 20 August 1832, Ibid., 2:1027.

28. Scott to Eustis, 29 July 1832, *BHW*, 2:904–5; Eustis to Cass, 29 July 1832, Ibid., 2:905–6; Scott to Cass, 24 July 1832, Ibid., 2:868–70; Scott to Atkinson, 1 August 1832, Ibid., 2:910–11; Scott to Atkinson, 4 August 1832, Ibid., 2:931–32; Eby, *Black Hawk War*, 240.

29. Dodge to Atkinson, 14 July 1832, *BHW*, 2:791; Henry to Atkinson, 14 July 1832, Ibid., 2:793; William Ewing to Atkinson, 14 July 1832, Ibid., 2:792; Justice, Journal, Ibid., 2:1323; Wakefield, *Black Hawk War*, 85–86.

30. Atkinson to Scott, 17 July 1832, *BHW*, 2:814–15; Dodge to Atkinson, 14 July 1832, Ibid., 2:791; Zanger, "Pierre Paquette," 298–303; Owen to Porter, 26 January 1832, M-1, 30:14; Jung, "Mixed Race Métis," 46–48.

31. John T. De La Ronde, "Personal Narrative," *WHC*, 7:350; Gratiot, Journal, 17 July 1832, *BHW*, 2:1304; quoted from Spoon Decorah, "Narrative of Spoon Decorah," *WHC*, 13:453.

32. Hagan, "Dodge-Henry Controversy," 377–84; Dodge to Atkinson, 18 July 1832, *BHW*, 2:820; Charles Bracken, "Further Strictures upon Ford's Black Hawk War," *WHC*, 2:402–6.

33. Johnston, Journal, 14–20 July 1832, *BHW*, 2:1318; Gratiot, Journal, 17 July 1832, Ibid., 2:1304; Atkinson to Scott, 17 July 1832, Ibid., 2:814; Cooke, *Scenes and Adventures*, 168–69.

34. Dodge to Atkinson, 18 July 1832, *BHW*, 2:820; Bracken, "Further Strictures," *WHC*, 2:408; Wakefield, *Black Hawk War*, 103–6; Justice, Journal, *BHW*, 2:1323–24.

35. Dodge to Atkinson, 19 July 1832, *BHW*, 2:825–24; Johnston, Journal, 20–21 July 1832, Ibid., 2:1318; quoted from Atkinson to Henry and Dodge, 20 July 1832, Ibid., 2:832.

36. Atkinson to Scott, 21 July 1832, *BHW*, 2:839–40; [Henry Smith], "Indian Campaign of 1832," 329.

37. Wakefield, *Black Hawk War*, 106; Black Hawk, *Autobiography*, 154. Secondary works that leave open the question of the British Band's location include Nichols, *Black Hawk and the Warrior's Path*, 128; Cole, *I Am a Man*, 199. Secondary works that argue the British Band went to Lac La Belle include Hagan, "Black Hawk's Route through Wisconsin," 22–26, and Eby, *Black Hawk War*, 231. Sources that suggest the British Band fled to Rock River Rapids are Barton, "Black Hawk Retreat," 61–62; Hagan "Dodge-Henry Controversy," 381; Decorah, "Narrative," *WHC*, 13:453; Bracken, "Further Strictures," *WHC*, 2:405; and Minutes of an Examination of Prisoners, 19 August 1832, *BHW*, 2:1030.

38. Black Hawk, *Autobiography*, 154; Street to Atkinson, 13 August 1832, *BHW*, 2:998; Council between Atkinson and the Winnebago and Menominee Indians, 6 August 1832, Ibid., 2:951; Porter's Grove Council, 4 June 1832, Ibid., 2:510; Minutes of an Examination of Prisoners, 20 August 2004, Ibid., 2:1035.

39. Bracken, "Narrative," *HOW*, 219–20; Wakefield, *Black Hawk War*, 106–8; Bracken, "Further Strictures," *WHC*, 2:408; Parkinson, "Pioneer Life, Ibid., 2:355–56; Justice, Journal, *BHW*, 2:1324.

40. Wakefield, *Black Hawk War*, 107–8; Henry to Atkinson, 23 July 1832, *BHW*, 2:858; Parkinson, "Pioneer Life," *WHC*, 2:358.

41. Peter Parkinson, Jr., "Strictures Upon Ford's Black Hawk War," *WHC*, 2:395; Parkinson, "Notes," Ibid., 10:208; Bracken, "Further Strictures," Ibid., 2:408; Parkinson, "Pioneer Life," Ibid., 2:356; *Atlas of Dane County, Wisconsin*, 56; Company of James W. Stephenson, 14 September 1832, *BHW*, 1:532; Wakefield, *Black Hawk War*, 109; *Galenian*, 1 August 1832; quoted from Magoon, "Memoirs," 431.

42. Wakefield, *Black Hawk War*, 109–10; Parkinson, "Pioneer Life," *WHC*, 2:356–67; Bracken, "Further Strictures," Ibid., 2:408; Ford, *History of Illinois*, 217; quoted from Parkinson, "Notes," *WHC*, 10:208.

43. Gleach, *Powhatan's World*, 48–51; Axtell and Sturtevant, "Unkindest Cut," 461–62, 471–472; Mooney, "Scalping," 2:482–83.

44. Osborn, *Wild Frontier*, 3–19, 38–40; quoted from Parkinson, "Pioneer Life," *WHC*, 2:356.

45. Parkinson, "Pioneer Life," *WHC*, 2:357; Minutes of an Examination of Prisoners, 19 August 1832, *BHW*, 2:1028–29, 1031; Minutes of an Examination of Prisoners, 20 August 1832, Ibid., 2:1035–37; Black Hawk, *Autobiography*, 155–57.

46. Thayer, *Battle of Wisconsin Heights*, 159; Clark, "Early Times at Fort Winnebago," *WHC*, 8:315; Roll of Prisoners, 27 August 1832, *BHW*, 2:1062–64; Black Hawk, *Autobiography*, 155–57; Tanner, *Atlas of Great Lakes Indian History*, 40, 93.

47. Bracken, "Further Strictures," *WHC*, 2:408–9; *General Regulations for the Army*, 124; Hagan, "Dodge-Henry Controversy," 382–84; Henry to Atkinson, 23 July 1832, *BHW*, 2:858; Dodge to Atkinson, 23 July 1832, Ibid., 2:842–43; Wakefield, *Black Hawk War*, 110–11; Bracken, "Narrative," *HOW*, 220; Dodsworth, *Battle of Wisconsin Heights*, 9–11.

48. Bracken, "Further Strictures," *WHC*, 2:409; Dodge to Atkinson, 23 July 1832, *BHW*, 2:842–43; Mahon, "Anglo-American Methods of Indian Warfare," 260, 273; Clark to Clark, 25 July 1832, *BHW*, 2:877; Dodge to Atkinson, 22 July 1832, Ibid., 2:843; Magoon, "Memoirs," 432; Black Hawk, *Autobiography*, 142–43, 155.

49. Dodge to Atkinson, 23 July 1832, *BHW*, 2:843; Henry to Atkinson, 23 July 1832, Ibid., 2:859; Parkinson, "Pioneer Life," *WHC*, 2:357; Bracken, "Further Strictures," Ibid., 2:409–10.

50. Mahon, "Indian Warfare," 260–61; Dodge to Atkinson, 22 July 1832, *BHW*, 2:843; Loomis to Atkinson, 31 July 1832, Ibid., 2:907; quoted from Black Hawk, *Autobiography*, 156.

51. Davis was definitely not at the battle. Clark's description of the battle has many fundamental errors that indicate he was not present. What he knew of the battle he most likely learned from Pierre Paquette. See Clark, "Early Times," *WHC*, 8:311, 315; P. L. Scanlan, "Military Record," 179; quoted from Cooke, *Scenes and Adventures*, 170–71.

52. Dodge to Atkinson, 22 July 1832, *BHW*, 2:843; Henry to Atkinson, 23 July 1832, Ibid., 2:859–60; Black Hawk, *Autobiography*, 155.

53. Black Hawk, *Autobiography*, 156–57, 160; Martin, *Physical Geography of Wisconsin*, 81–90, 271–81.

54. Wakefield, *Black Hawk War*, 113–15, 134; Justice, Journal, *BHW*, 2:1325; Parkinson, "Pioneer Life," *WHC*, 2:359–60; *Sangamo Journal*, 25 August 1832.

55. Johnston, Journal, 21 24 July 1832, *BHW*, 2:1318–19, 1319n; Justice, Journal, Ibid., 2:1325; Wakefield, *Black Hawk War*, 117–18; Parkinson, "Pioneer Life," *WHC*, 2:360–62; quoted from Atkinson to Scott, 25 July 1832, *BHW*, 2:875.

56. Black Hawk, *Autobiography*, 156–58.

CHAPTER SEVEN: THE THUNDERBIRDS' LAST FLIGHT

1. Henry Dodge to Gustavus Loomis, 22 July 1832, *BHW*, 2:845; Dodge to Henry Atkinson, 24 July 1832, Ibid., 2:863.

2. Return of Illinois Mounted Volunteers, 2 August 1832, *BHW*, 1:574; Albert S. Johnston, Journal, 27 July 1832, Ibid., 2:1319; James J. Justice, Journal, Ibid., 2:1325; quoted from William B. Archer to Jacob Harlan, 25 July 1832, Ibid., 2:873.

3. Atkinson to Winfield Scott, 27 July 1832, *BHW*, 2:891; Johnston, Journal, 24–28 July 1832, Ibid., 2:1319; Orin G. Libby, "Chronicle of the Helena Shot-Tower," *WHC*, 13:341–42.

4. Johnston, Journal, 28–30 July 1832, *BHW*, 2:1319–20; Wakefield, *History of the Black Hawk War*, 121–25; Cooke, *Scenes and Adventures*, 171–79; Decorah, "Narrative of Spoon Decorah," *WHC*, 13:453; [Smith], "Indian Campaign of 1832," 329–330.

5. Johnston, Journal, 1 August 1832, *BHW*, 2:1320; Cooke, *Scenes and Adventures*, 179–80; [Smith], "Indian Campaign," 330; quoted from Wakefield, *Black Hawk War*, 128.

6. Joseph Street to William Clark, 24 July 1832, *BHW*, 2:871–73; Loomis to Dodge, 25 July 1832, Ibid., 2:880–81; Atkinson to Scott, 5 August 1832, Ibid., 2:936; Loomis to Atkinson, 8 August 1832, Ibid., 2:962–63; Ferris, "Sauks and Foxes in Franklin and Osage Counties," 355, 384.

7. Thomas Burnett to Street, 26 July 1832, *BHW*, 2:883; Burnett to Street, 28 July 1832, Ibid., 2:898–99; Loomis to Atkinson, 30–31 July 1832, Ibid., 2:906–7; John Abercrombie to Loomis, 8 August 1832, Ibid., 2:960.

8. Tanner, *Atlas of Great Lakes Indian History*, 152; Cass to Clark, 19 June 1832, *BHW*, 2:630; Cass to George Gibson, 19 June 1832, Ibid., 2:631; John Kinzie to George B. Porter, 2 July 1832, M-1, 31:20; Clark to Gibson, 16 July 1832, William Clark Papers, vol. 4, p. 389.

9. Joseph Throckmorton, Report, 3 August 1832, *BHW*, 2:927–28; Reuben Holmes to Atkinson, 5 August 1832, Ibid., 2:938; Street to Clark, 2 August 1832, Ibid., 2:917.

10. Quoted from John H. Fonda, "Early Wisconsin," *WHC*, 5:261.

11. Throckmorton, Report, 3 August 1832, *BHW*, 2:927–28; Black Hawk, *Autobiography*, 158; Minutes of an Examination of Prisoners, 19 August 1932, *BHW*, 2:1029; Holmes to Atkinson, 5 August 1832, Ibid., 2:938; George Boyd to Porter, 9 August 1832, *WHC*, 12:287.

12. Quoted from Black Hawk, *Autobiography*, 159–60.

13. Throckmorton, Report, 3 August 1832, *BHW*, 2:928; Holmes to Atkinson, 5 August 1832, Ibid., 2:938–39; Minutes of an Examination of Prisoners, 19 August 1932, Ibid., 2:1029; Black Hawk, *Autobiography*, 159–60; Fonda, "Early Wisconsin," *WHC*, 5:261–62; [Smith], "Indian Campaign," 331; Wakefield, *Black Hawk War*, 136.

14. Black Hawk, *Autobiography*, 160; Cooke, *Scenes and Adventures*, 180; Johnston, Journal, 1–2 August 1832, *BHW*, 2:1320.

15. Atkinson to Scott, 9 August 1832, *BHW*, 2:965; Johnston, Journal, 1–2 August 1832, Ibid., 2:1320; Joseph Dickson, "Personal Narratives of Black Hawk War," *WHC*, 5:316; Robert Anderson to Larz Anderson, 5 August 1832, *BHW*, 2:933; Thayer, *Massacre at Bad Axe*, 166, 173–75.

16. *De Soto Chronicle*, 29 January 1887; *Vernon County Censor*, 10 August 1898; Eby, *The Black Hawk War*, 246, 252; quoted from Black Hawk, *Autobiography*, 160.

17. Minutes of an Examination of Prisoners, 19 August 1832, *BHW*, 2:1031; Johnston, Journal, 2 August 1832, Ibid., 2:1320–21; Black Hawk, *Autobiography*, 160–62; *De Soto Chronicle*, 29 January 1887.

18. Atkinson to Scott, 9 August 1832, *BHW*, 2:965; Johnston, Journal, 2 August 1832, Ibid., 2:1320–21; War News from Galena, 6 August 1832, Ibid., 2:954.

19. *Vernon County Censor*, 10 August 1898; Zachary Taylor, Report, 5 August 1832, *BHW*, 2:942; Anderson to Anderson, 5 August 1832, Ibid., 2:933; Johnston, Journal, 2 August 1832, Ibid., 2:1321; Wakefield, *Black Hawk War*, 132–33, 136–37.

20. *De Soto Chronicle*, 5 February 1887; Minutes of an Examination of Prisoners, 20 August 1832, *BHW*, 2:1035; Cooke, *Scenes and Adventures*, 186; Fonda, "Early Wisconsin," *WHC*, 5:261–62; Wakefield, *Black Hawk War*, 132–36.

21. Atkinson to Scott, 9 August 1832, *BHW*, 2:965; quoted from Cooke, *Scenes and Adventures*, 187.

22. Street to Clark, 3 August 1832, *BHW*, 2:927; Cooke, *Scenes and Adventures*, 187; Estes, "Battle of Bad Axe," *HOW*, 230–31.

23. Anderson to Anderson, 5 August 1832, *BHW*, 2:933; Atkinson to Scott, 9 August 1832, Ibid., 2:966–67; Thayer, *Massacre at Bad Axe*, 222–27; Eaton, "Returns of the Killed and Wounded of American Troops in Battles or Engagements with the Indians," p. 37; Black Hawk, *Autobiography*, 161. White casualty figures are taken from those mentioned throughout the text.

24. Fonda, " Early Wisconsin," *WHC*, 5:262–63; *Galenian*, 8 August 1832; Wakefield, *Black Hawk War*, 133; Estes, "Battle of Bad Axe," *HOW*, 231–32; Johnston, Journal, 2 August 1832, *BHW*, 2:1321; Shaw, Journal, 2 August 1832, Ibid., 2:1337–38; *De Soto Chronicle*, 12 February 1887; quoted from *Vernon County Censor*, 10 August 1898.

25. Quoted from Cooke, *Scenes and Adventures*, 185–86.

26. *De Soto Chronicle*, 12 February 1887; quoted from Perrin, *History of Crawford and Clark Counties*, 231–32.

27. Quoted from Wakefield, *Black Hawk War*, 132–33.

28. Street to Clark, 7 June 1832, *BHW*, 2:547–48; Owen to Atkinson, 6 June 1832, Ibid., 2:534; Potawatomi Indians in United States Service, 22 June–22 July 1832, Ibid., 1:560–62; Roll of Captain George Johnston's Company of Menominee Indians, 20 July–28 August 1832, Henry S. Baird Papers, Box 5, Folder 4, (hereafter cited as Baird Papers); Roll of Captain Augustin Grignon's Company of Menominee Warriors, 20 July–28 August 1832, Baird Papers, 5:4; Street to Clark, 2 August 1832, *BHW*, 2:917; George Walker to Atkinson, 10–11 October 1834, Ibid., 2:1287, 1291–92; Minutes of an Examination of Prisoners, 19 August 1832, Ibid., 2:1031.

29. Atkinson to Jones, 19 November 1832, *BHW*, 2:1211; Shaw, Journal, 3–4 August 1832, Ibid., 2:1338; Johnston, Journal, 3–5 August 1832, Ibid., 2:1321; Street to Clark, 3 August 1832, Ibid., 2:926; quoted from Wakefield, *Black Hawk War*, 140–41.

30. Scott to Cass, 10 August 1832, *BHW*, 2:980; [Smith], "Indian Campaign," 331; Minutes of an Examination of Prisoners, 27 August 1832, Ibid., 2:1056; Street to Scott, 22 August 1832, Ibid., 2:1042; Minutes of an Examination of Prisoners, 20 August 1832, Ibid., 2:1036.

31. Samuel Stambaugh to Boyd, 2 August 1832, *BHW*, 2:915–16; Johnston to Stambaugh, 7 August 1832, Ibid., 2:958–59; Stambaugh to Scott, 11 August 1832, Ibid., 2:987; Powell, "Recollections," 164–66; quoted from Stambaugh to Boyd, 28 August 1832, *BHW*, 2:1077.

32. Stambaugh to Scott, 11 August 1832, *BHW*, 2:987; Augustin Grignon, "Seventy-Two Years' Recollections of Wisconsin," *WHC*, 3: 294–95; quoted from Stambaugh to Boyd, 28 August 1832, *BHW*, 2:1071–78.

33. Street to Atkinson, 31 July 1832, *BHW*, 2:908; Street to Atkinson, 5 August 1832, Ibid., 2:940; Street to Atkinson, 13 August 1832, Ibid., 2:998; Street, Report of Prisoners and Casualties, 2 August 1832, Ibid., 2:918; Street to Clark, 3 August 1832, Ibid., 2:926; Street to Scott, 22 August 1832, Ibid., 2:1042.

34. Walking Cloud, "Narrative of Walking Cloud," *WHC*, 13:463–64; Lurie, "In Search of Chaetar," 170; Atkinson to Loomis, 13 July 1832, *BHW*, 2:783.

35. Decorah, "Narrative of Spoon Decorah," *WHC*, 13:450–53; Minutes of an Examination of Prisoners, 19 August 1832, *BHW*, 2:1028–29; Scott to the Winnebago Indians, 18 August 1832, Ibid., 2:1022; quoted from Scott to Cass, 19 August 1832, Ibid., 2:1024–25.

36. Stambaugh to Scott, 13 August 1832, *BHW*, 2:996; Gideon Low to Scott, 26 August 1832, Ibid., 2:1050; Low to Scott, 3 September 1832, Ibid., 2:1100.

37. Scott to Cass, 19 August 1832, *BHW*, 2:1025; Preliminary Roll of Prisoners, 27 August 1832, Ibid., 2:1058–61; Roll of Prisoners at Rock Island, 27 August 1832, Ibid., 2:1062–65; Street to Scott, 28 August 1832, Ibid., 2:1080; William Whistler to William Maynadier, 19 September 1832, Ibid., 2:1165.

38. Scott to Cass, 19 August 1832, *BHW*, 2:1025; Felix St. Vrain, Journal, 4 May 1832, Ibid., 2:1331.

39. Atkinson to Thomas J. Beall, 5 August 1832, *BHW*, 2:934; Scott to Taylor, 5 September 1832, Ibid., 2:1111; Council with the Sauk and Fox, 19 September 1832, Ibid., 2:1168; Roll of Prisoners at Rock Island, 27 August 1832, Ibid., 2:1062–64; *Galenian*, 5 September 1832.

40. Quoted from Black Hawk, *Autobiography*, 160–62.

41. *Ibid.*, 160–62; quoted from Minutes of an Examination of Prisoners, 27 August 1832, *BHW*, 2:1056.

42. Black Hawk, *Autobiography*, 160.

43. Quoted from Lurie, "In Search of Chaetar," 170.

44. Lurie, 163–83.

45. Quoted from Lurie, 171–77.

46. Black Hawk, *Autobiography*, 162–63; quoted from Street, Report of the Delivery of Black Hawk and the Prophet, 27 August 1832, *BHW*, 2:1065–67.

47. Lurie, "In Search of Chaetar," 172–78; quoted from Second Council with Representatives of the Winnebago Nation, 13 September 1832, *BHW*, 2:1144.

48. Anderson to Anderson, 9 September 1832, *BHW*, 2:1121–22; Scott to Cass, 9 September 1832, Ibid., 2:1124; Scanlan, "Military Record of Jefferson Davis," 174–82; *Galenian*, 5 September 1832; Black Hawk, Speech to Street, 4 September 1832, *BHW*, 2:1103.

49. *Galenian*, 5 September 1832; Black Hawk, *Autobiography*, 163–64; Scott to Cass, 9 September 1832, *BHW*, 2:1124, 1127; *Missouri Republican*, 11 September 1832; Patrick Galt to Osborne Cross, 28 August 1832, *BHW*, 2:1069–70; Atkinson to Scott, 16 September 1832, Ibid., 2:1157; quoted from Second Council with the Sauk and Fox, 20 September 1832, Ibid., 2:1175.

50. Scott and John Reynolds to Cass, 22 September 1832, *BHW*, 2:1188; quoted from Black Hawk, *Autobiography*, 1–18, 165–66.

51. Wallace, *Long, Bitter Trail*, 65–72, 105–8; Jung, "Forge, Destroy, and Preserve the Bonds of Empire," 404–5, 490–96.

52. Scott to the Winnebago Indians, 18 August 1832, *BHW*, 2:1022; Council with the Winnebago of Fort Winnebago Agency, 10 September 1832, Ibid., 2:1130–32; Council with the Rock River Winnebago, 11 September 1832, Ibid., 1133–34; Second Council with the Rock River Winnebago, 12 September 1832, Ibid., 2:1135.

53. Street to Scott, 9 September 1832, *BHW*, 2:1127–28; Council with the Winnebago from Fort Winnebago, Rock River, and Prairie du Chien Agencies, 12 September 1832, Ibid., 2:1136–39; Third Council with Representatives of the Winnebago Nation, 14 September 1832, Ibid., 2:150–51; Treaty with the Winnebago, 15 September 1832, *Indian Treaties*, 345–48; Royce, "Indian Land Cessions," 736–37; Kellogg, "Removal of the Winnebago," 23–29.

54. Quoted from Council with the Sauk and Fox, 19 September 1832, *BHW*, 2:1166–67.

55. Second Council with the Sauk and Fox, 20 September 1832, *BHW*, 2:1171–76.

56. Third Council with the Sauk and Fox, 21 September 1832, *BHW*, 2:1177–80; Kurtz, "Economic and Political History," 252–95; Treaty with the Sauks and Foxes, 21 September 1832, *Indian Treaties*, 349–51; Royce, "Indian Land Cessions," 736–37.

57. Quoted from *Missouri Republican*, 27 February 1835.

58. Kurtz, "Economic and Political History," 271–78; Black Hawk, *Autobiography*, 166–67; Talk between Atkinson, Black Hawk and the Winnebago Prophet, 28 December 1832, *BHW*, 2:1234–35.

CHAPTER EIGHT: THE CALM AFTER THE STORM

1. Treaty with the Sauks and Foxes, 21 September 1832, *Indian Treaties*, 350; Winfield Scott to Lewis Cass, 19 November 1832, *BHW*, 2:1212–13; Katharine Turner, *Red Men Calling*, 89; Catlin, *Letters and Notes*, vol. 2, 210–12.

2. Black Hawk, *Autobiography*, 1–10, 166–67; Nichols, *Black Hawk and the Warrior's Path*, 145; Elbert Herring to William Clark, 16 March 1832, M-21, 10:10:120–21; Henry Atkinson to Alexander Macomb, 5 April 1833, A51–1833, Letters Received by the Office of the Adjutant General, 1805–1899.

3. Nichols, *Black Hawk*, 146; quoted from Black Hawk, *Autobiography*, 167–68.

4. Katharine Turner, *Red Men Calling*, xiv-xv; Nichols, *Black Hawk*, 146; quoted from Black Hawk, *Autobiography*, 167–69.

5. Katharine Turner, *Red Men Calling*, 89–90; Treadway, "Triumph in Defeat," 7; *National Intelligencer*, 25 June 1833; Remini, *Andrew Jackson and His Indian Wars*, 22, 259; Scripps, *Memorials of the Scripps Family*, 118; quoted from Black Hawk, *Autobiography*, 170.

6. Turner, *Red Men Calling*, 91. For secondary sources that use this quotation, see Stevens, *Black Hawk War*, 259; Cole, *I Am a Man*, 246.

7. Eby, *Black Hawk War*, 275; *National Intelligencer*, 29 April 1833; quoted from Black Hawk, *Autobiography*, 171.

8. *National Intelligencer*, 25 and 29 April 1833; Roger Jones to Abraham Eustis, 25 April 1833, Letters Sent by the Office of the Adjutant General, 1800–1890, Microfilm Publication M-565, Reel 8, Frame 406; Treadway, "Triumph in Defeat," 8–12; Black Hawk, *Autobiography*, 171; Nichols, *Black Hawk*, 148.

9. Clark to Herring, 14 May 1832, M-234, 728:340–42; Atkinson to Herring, 20 May 1832, Ibid., 728:318; Treadway, "Triumph in Defeat," 14; quoted from *National Intelligencer*, 30 April 1833.

10. Nichols, *Black Hawk*, 148; Treadway, "Triumph in Defeat," 12–15.

11. *Ibid.*, 15.

12. Katharine Turner, *Red Men Calling*, 97; Treadway, "Triumph in Defeat," 15; quoted from *Niles Weekly Register*, 15 June 1833.

13. Turner, *Red Men Calling*, 96–97; Treadway, "Triumph in Defeat," 15; Black Hawk, *Autobiography*, 13–16, 171–72; quoted from Hone, *Diary*, vol. 1, 97–98.

14. Quoted from Black Hawk, *Autobiography*, 173.

15. Turner, *Red Men Calling*, 98; Treadway, "Triumph in Defeat," 15.

16. Turner, *Red Men Calling*, 100; Treadway, "Triumph in Defeat," 15–16; quoted from John Garland to Cass, 5 October 1832, M-234, 728:405–6.

17. Palmer, *Early Days in Detroit*, 155–56; Nichols, *Black Hawk*, 151; Garland to Cass, 5 October 1833, M-234, 728:406; Joseph Street to Herring, 1 August 1832, Ibid., 696:628; quoted from Black Hawk, *Autobiography*, 174–75.

18. Garland to Cass, 5 October 1833, M-234, 728:406–7; quoted from Black Hawk, *Autobiography*, 176–77.

19. Black Hawk, *Autobiography*, 83, 181; Nichols, *Black Hawk*, 154; quoted from Catlin, *Letters and Notes*, 217.

20. Treaty with the Sauk and Foxes, 28 September 1836, *Indian Treaties*, 474; Royce, "Indian Land Cessions," 762–63, 766–67; quoted from Black Hawk, *Autobiography*, 176.

21. Nichols, *Black Hawk*, 155; William R. Smith, "Black Hawk War," *HOW*, 164; quoted from William R. Smith, "Journal of William Rudolph Smith," 211–12.

22. Quoted from Black Hawk, *Autobiography*, 181.

23. *The Times* (London), 21 November 1838; Black Hawk, *Autobiography*, 182; Nichols, *Black Hawk*, 155; Beaman, "Black Hawk: Some Account," 126–31.

24. Kurtz, "Economic and Political History of the Sauk and Mesquakie," 277–78; Reinschmidt, *Ethnohistory of the Sauk*, 34; Berthrong, "John Beach," 316–19; quoted from Cutting Marsh, "Expedition to the Sauks and Foxes," *WHC*, 15:117.

25. Reinschmidt, *Ethnohistory of the Sauk*, 34–35; Berthrong, "John Beach," 323–33; Ferris, "Sauks and Foxes in Franklin and Osage Counties," vol. 11, 339–40; Royce, "Indian Land Cessions," 778–79; Green, "Mesquakie (Fox) Separatism," 134–38.

26. Reinschmidt, *Ethnohistory of the Sauk*, 34–38; Herring, *Enduring Indians of Kansas*, 70–100.

27. Ferris, "Sauks and Foxes," 381–83; quoted from Reinschmidt, *Ethnohistory of the Sauk*, 40–57.

28. Prucha, *Great Father*, 2:661–86; Reinschmidt, *Ethnohistory of the Sauk*, 57–64.

29. *Sangamo Journal*, 1 December 1832, 12 January 1833; *Niles Register*, 9 February 1833; Henry Gratiot to Cass, 19 November 1832, M-234, 696:395–98; Talk of Whirling Thunder to Gratiot, 16 December 1832, M-1, 31:344–46; George Boyd to George B. Porter, 31 March 1833, Ibid., 32:158; Gratiot to Porter, 12 April 1833, Ibid., 32:213–14.

30. Thwaites, "Territorial Census for 1836," *WHC*, 13:249; Alice E. Smith, *History of Wisconsin*, vol. 1, 189–90, 197, 466; Prucha, *Sword of the Republic*, 269–76; George Brooke to Zachary Taylor, 3 June 1836, *TPUS*,

27:58–59; Brooke to Jones, 16 June 1836, Ibid., 59–60; Cass to Henry Dodge, 25 June 1836, M-6, 16:16:159.

31. Cass to Atkinson, 24 October 1832, *BHW*, 2:1197; Andrew Jackson to the Congress, 4 December 1832, *Message from the President of the United States to the Two Houses of Congress . . .* , 22nd Cong., 2nd sess., 1832, Ho. Exec. Doc. 2 (Serial 233), 13 (hereafter this document cited as Ho. Exec. Doc. 2); Cass to Jackson, 25 November 1832, *Annual Report of the Secretary of War for 1832*, Ho. Exec. Doc. 2, 18–19; Stubbs and Connor, *Armor-Cavalry Part I*, 8–14; Report of R. M. Johnson, 3 March 1836, *Protect Western Frontier*, 24th Cong., 1st sess., 1836, Ho. Rep. 401 (Serial 294), 2.

32. Young, "United States Mounted Ranger Battalion," 458–61; Gratiot to Cass, 8 February 1833, M-234, 931:127; Talk of Whirling Thunder to Gratiot, 16 December 1832, M-1, 31:344–46; Macomb to Dodge, 14 March 1833, M-565, 8:394; Hughes, "First Dragoons," 15–18.

33. Joseph Plympton to the Acting Assistant Adjutant General, 3 November 1832, M-234, 696:421; Dodge to Atkinson, 10 December 1832, *BHW*, 2:1231; Thomas Burnett to Clark, 30 October 1832, M-234, 696:517–18; James D. Doty to Cass, 1 November 1832, Ibid., 696:528; Jung, "To Extend Fair and Impartial Justice to the Indian," 42–43.

34. Atkinson to John Reynolds, 31 October 1832, *BHW*, 2:1200–1; Atkinson to Jones, 19 November 1832, Ibid., 2:1212; Atkinson to Macomb, 31 January 1833, M-234, 728:315; George Wacker to Atkinson, 17 January 1833, Ibid., 728:316–18; La Salle County Circuit Court: Order for Discharge, 21 May 1834, *BHW*, 2:1283–84; La Salle County Circuit Court: Order for Discharge, 21 May 1834, Ibid., 2:1286–87.

35. Dowd, *Spirited Resistance*, 191–93; quoted from excerpt from *St. Augustine Herald*, 12 January 1836, *ASP: MA*, 6:22.

36. Jones to Macomb, 27 January 1838, *ASP:MA*, 7:993; John Missall and Mary Lou Missall, *Seminole Wars*, 221–22.

37. Quoted from Black Hawk, *Autobiography*, 41.

Bibliography

MANUSCRIPT COLLECTIONS

Baird, Henry S. Papers. State Historical Society of Wisconsin, Madison, Wisconsin.

Boilvin, Nicholas. Letters, 1811–1823. In Prairie du Chien, Wisconsin Papers. University of Wisconsin–Platteville Area Research Center, Platteville, Wisconsin.

Chouteau Family Papers. Missouri Historical Society, St. Louis, Missouri.

Clark, William. Papers. Kansas State Historical Society, Topeka, Kansas.

Dodge, Henry. Papers. State Historical Society of Iowa, Des Moines, Iowa.

Forsyth, Thomas. Papers. Series T, Lyman C. Draper Manuscript Collection. State Historical Society of Wisconsin, Madison, Wisconsin.

Michelson, Truman. Notes on Sauk Ethnography, MS 2735. National Anthropological Archives, National Museum of Natural History, Smithsonian Institution, Washington, D.C.

Taliaferro, Lawrence. Papers. Minnesota Historical Society, St. Paul, Minnesota.

UNPUBLISHED PUBLIC RECORDS

Adjutant General's Office. Letters Received by the Office of the Adjutant General, 1805–1899. RG 94, Records of the Office of the Adjutant General. National Archives, Washington, D.C.

———. Letters Sent by the Office of the Adjutant General, 1800–1890, Microfilm Publication M-565. RG 94, Records of the Office of the Adjutant General. National Archives, Washington, D.C.

————. Returns from U.S. Military Posts, 1800–1916, Microfilm Publication M-617. RG 94, Records of the Office of the Adjutant General. National Archives, Washington, D.C.

Bureau of Indian Affairs. Documents Relating to the Negotiation of Ratified and Unratified Treaties with Various Tribes of Indians, 1801–1869, Microfilm Publication T-494. RG 75, Records of the Bureau of Indian Affairs. National Archives, Washington, D.C.

————. Letters Received by the Office of Indian Affairs, 1824–1881, Microfilm Publication M-234. RG 75, Records of the Bureau of Indian Affairs. National Archives, Washington, D.C.

————. Letters Sent by the Office of Indian Affairs, 1824–1881, Microfilm Publication M-21. RG 75, Records of the Bureau of Indian Affairs. National Archives, Washington, D.C.

————. Letters Sent by the Secretary of War Relating to Indian Affairs, 1800 1824, Microfilm Publication M-15. RG 75, Records of the Bureau of Indian Affairs. National Archives, Washington, D.C.

————. Records of the Michigan Superintendency of Indian Affairs, 1814–1851, Microfilm Publication M-1. RG 75, Records of the Bureau of Indian Affairs. National Archives, Washington, D.C.

Eaton, J. H. "Returns of the Killed and Wounded of American Troops in Battles or Engagements with the Indians." RG 94, Records of the Office of the Adjutant General. National Archives, Washington, D.C.

Illinois Adjutant General. Black Hawk War Records, 1832–1891, RG 301.007, Illinois State Archives, Springfield, Illinois.

Indian Claims Commission. Docket 83, Sac and Fox Indians. RG 279, Records of the Indian Claims Commission. National Archives, Washington, D.C.

Inspector General's Office. Inspection Reports of the Office of the Inspector General, 1814–1842, Microfilm Publication M-624. RG 159, Records of the Office of the Inspector General. National Archives, Washington, D.C.

Quartermaster General's Office. Consolidated Correspondence File, 1794–1915. RG 92, Records of the Office of the Quartermaster General. National Archives, Washington, D.C.

Secretary of War. Letters Sent by the Secretary of War Relating to Military Affairs, 1800–1889, Microfilm Publication M-6. RG 107, Records of the Office of the Secretary of War. National Archives, Washington, D.C.

PUBLISHED PUBLIC RECORDS

American State Papers: Indian Affairs. 2 vols. Washington, D.C.: Gales and Seaton, 1832–1834.

American State Papers: Military Affairs. 7 vols. Washington, D.C.: Gales and Seaton, 1832–1861.

Carter, Clarence E., and John P. Bloom, eds. *The Territorial Papers of the United States.* 28 vols. Washington, D.C.: Government Printing Office, 1934–1975.

Commissary General of Subsistence. *Correspondence on the Subject of the Emigration of Indians.* 23rd Cong., 1st sess., 1834. Sen. Doc. 512. Serials 244–248.

Executive Office. *Message from the President . . . in Relation to the Lead Mines.* . . . 19th Cong., 2nd sess., 1826. Ho. Exec. Doc. 7. Serial 149.

———. *Message from the President. . . to the Two Houses of Congress . . .*, 22nd Cong., 2nd sess., 1832. Ho. Exec. Doc. 2. Serial 233.

General Regulations for the Army; Or, Military Institutes. Philadelphia: M. Carey and Sons, 1821.

Haswell, John H., ed. *Treaties and Conventions Concluded between the United States of America and Other Powers since July 4, 1776.* Washington, D.C.: Government Printing Office, 1889.

House of Representatives. *Protect Western Frontier.* 24th Cong., 1st sess., 1836. Ho. Rep. 401. Serial 294.

Kappler, Charles J., ed. *Indian Affairs: Laws and Treaties.* Vol. 2. Washington, D.C.: Government Printing Office, 1904.

Register of Debates in Congress. 14 vols. Washington, D.C.: Gales and Seaton, 1825–37.

U.S. Statutes at Large. 17 vols. Boston: Charles C. Little and James Brown, 1850–1873.

War Department. *Annual Report of the Secretary of War for 1827.* 20th Cong., 1st sess., 1827. Ho. Doc. 2. Serial 169.

———. *Annual Report of the Secretary of War for 1828.* 20th Cong., 2nd sess., 1828, Sen. Doc. 1. Serial 181.

———. *Annual Report of the Secretary of War for 1832.* 22nd Cong., 2nd sess., 1832, Ho. Exec. Doc. 2. Serial 233.

———. *Letter from the Secretary of War . . . In Relation to the Hostile Disposition of the Indian Tribes on the Northwestern Frontier.* 20th Cong., 1st sess., 1828. Ho. Doc. 277. Serial 175.

OTHER PUBLISHED PRIMARY SOURCES

Atwater, Caleb. *Remarks on a Tour to Prairie du Chien Thence to Washington City in 1829.* 1831; reprint, New York: Arno Press, 1975.

[Backus, Electus]. "A Brief History of the War with the Sac & Fox Indians." In *Collections of the Michigan Pioneer and Historical Society.* Vol. 12, 424–36. Lansing: Michigan Pioneer and Historical Society, 1888.

Basler, Roy P., ed. *Collected Works of Abraham Lincoln.* 9 vols. New Brunswick, N.J.: Rutgers University Press, 1953–1955.

Beaman, D. C. "Black Hawk: Some Account of his Life, Death, and Resurrection." Edited by Thomas Gregg. *Annals of Iowa* 13 (October 1921): 126–31.

Beouchard, Edward. "Beochard's Narrative." In *The History of Wisconsin. In Three Parts.* Vol. 3, 209–14. Edited by William Smith. Madison: Beriah Brown, 1854.

Black Hawk. *Black Hawk: An Autobiography.* Edited by Donald Jackson. 1833; reprint, Urbana: University of Illinois Press, 1955.

Blair, Emma Helen, ed. *Indian Tribes of the Upper Mississippi Valley and Region of the Great Lakes*. Vol. 2. Cleveland: Arthur H. Clark Co., 1912.

Bracken, Charles. "Further Strictures upon Ford's Black Hawk War." In *Collections of the State Historical Society of Wisconsin*. Vol. 2, 402–14. Madison: State Historical Society of Wisconsin, 1903.

———. "Personal Narrative of Charles Bracken." In *The History of Wisconsin. In Three Parts*. Vol. 3, 215–23. Edited by William Smith. Madison: Beriah Brown, 1854.

———, and Peter Parkinson, Jr. "Pekatonica Battle Controversy." In *Collections of the State Historical Society of Wisconsin*. Vol. 2, 365–92. Madison: State Historical Society of Wisconsin, 1903.

Bryant, William Cullen. *Prose Writings of William Cullen Bryant*. Vol. 1. Edited by Parke Godwin. New York: D. Appleton and Co., 1884.

Catlin, George. *Letters and Notes on the Manners, Customs, and Condition of the North American Indians*. Vol. 2. 1841; reprint, Minneapolis: Ross & and Haines, 1965.

Childs, Ebenezer. "Recollections of Wisconsin since 1820." In *Collections of the State Historical Society of Wisconsin*. Vol. 4, 153–95. Madison: State Historical Society of Wisconsin, 1906.

Clark, Satterlee. "Early Times at Fort Winnebago." In *Collections of the State Historical Society of Wisconsin*. Vol. 8, 307–21. Madison: State Historical Society of Wisconsin, 1908.

Cooke, Philip S. *Scenes and Adventures in the Army, Or the Romance of Military Life*. 1857; reprint, New York: Arno Press, 1973.

Decorah, Spoon. "Narrative of Spoon Decorah." In *Collections of the State Historical Society of Wisconsin*. Vol. 13, 448–62. Madison: State Historical Society of Wisconsin, 1895.

De La Ronde, John T. "Personal Narrative." In *Collections of the State Historical Society of Wisconsin*. Vol. 7, 345–65. Madison: State Historical Society of Wisconsin, 1908.

Dickson, Joseph. "Personal Narratives of Black Hawk War." In *Collections of the State Historical Society of Wisconsin*. Vol. 5, 315–17. Madison: State Historical Society of Wisconsin, 1907.

Draper, Lyman C., et al., eds. *Collections of the State Historical Society of Wisconsin*. 31 vols. Madison: State Historical Society of Wisconsin, 1855–1931.

———, ed. "Winnebagoes and the Black Hawk War." In *Collections of the State Historical Society of Wisconsin*. Vol. 5, 306–9. Madison: State Historical Society of Wisconsin, 1907.

Esarey, Logan, ed. *Messages and Letters of William Henry Harrison*. 2 vols. Indiana Historical Collections, vols. 7 and 9. Indianapolis: Indiana Historical Commission, 1922.

Estes, James B. "Battle of Bad Axe." In *The History of Wisconsin. In Three Parts*. Vol. 3, 230–32. Edited by William Smith. Madison: Beriah Brown, 1854.

Fonda, John H. "Early Wisconsin." In *Collections of the State Historical Society of Wisconsin*. Vol. 5, 205–84. Madison: State Historical Society of Wisconsin, 1907.

Ford, Thomas. *A History of Illinois.* Edited by Milo M. Quaife. 1854; reprint, Chicago: Lakeside Press, 1945.

Gorrell, James. "Lieut. James Gorrell's Journal." In *Collections of the State Historical Society of Wisconsin.* Vol. 1, 25–48. Madison: State Historical Society of Wisconsin, 1903.

Grignon, Augustin. "Seventy-Two Years' Recollections of Wisconsin." In *Collections of the State Historical Society of Wisconsin.* Vol. 3, 197–295. Madison: State Historical Society of Wisconsin, 1904.

Hollman, Frederick. "'My Long and Somewhat Eventful Life': Frederick G. Hollman's Autobiography." Edited by William Marten. *Wisconsin Magazine of History* 56 (Spring 1973): 202–33.

Holmes, J. C., et al., eds. *Collections of the Michigan Pioneer and Historical Society.* 40 vols. Lansing: Michigan Pioneer and Historical Society, 1877–1929.

Hone, Philip. *The Diary of Philip Hone, 1828–1851.* Vol. 1. Edited by Allan Nevins. New York: Dodd, Mead, and Company, 1927.

Iles, Elijah. *Sketches of Early Life and Times in Kentucky, Missouri, and Illinois.* Springfield, Ill.: Springfield Printing Co., 1883.

Lockwood, James H. "Early Times and Events in Wisconsin." In *Collections of the State Historical Society of Wisconsin.* Vol. 2, 98–196. Madison: State Historical Society of Wisconsin, 1903.

Magoon, R. H. "R. H. Magoon's Memoirs." In *History of Grant County, Wisconsin,* 427–35. Chicago: Western Historical Company, 1881.

Marsh, Cutting. "Expedition to the Sauks and Foxes." In *Collections of the State Historical Society of Wisconsin.* Vol. 15, 104–55. Madison: State Historical Society of Wisconsin, 1900.

Matson, Nehemiah. *Memories of Shaubena, With Incidents Relating to the Early Settlement of the West.* Chicago: D. B. Cooke and Co., 1878.

McKenney, Thomas L. *Memoirs Official and Personal, With Sketches of Travels . . .* 2nd ed. New York: Paine and Burgess, 1846.

Moore, Risdon. "Mr. Lincoln as a Wrestler." In *Transactions of the Illinois State Historical Society, 1904,* 433–34. Springfield: Illinois State Historical Library, 1904.

Ogden, George W. "Narrative of George W. Ogden." In *History of Rock County, and Transactions of the Rock County Agricultural Society and Mechanics Institute,* 41–43. Edited by Orrin Guernsey and Josiah Willard. Janesville, Wisc.: William M. Doty and Brother, 1856.

Parish, John C. *George Wallace Jones.* Iowa City: State Historical Society of Iowa, 1912.

Parkinson, Daniel M. "Pioneer Life in Wisconsin." In *Collections of the State Historical Society of Wisconsin.* Vol. 2, 326–64. Madison: State Historical Society of Wisconsin, 1903.

Parkinson, Peter, Jr. "Notes on the Black Hawk War." In *Collections of the State Historical Society of Wisconsin.* Vol. 10, 184–212. Madison: State Historical Society of Wisconsin, 1909.

———. "Strictures Upon Ford's Black Hawk War." In *Collections of the State Historical Society of Wisconsin.* Vol. 2, 393–401. Madison: State Historical Society of Wisconsin, 1903.

Powell, William. "William Powell's Recollections." In *Proceedings of the State Historical Society of Wisconsin, 1912*, 146–79. Madison: State Historical Society of Wisconsin, 1913.

Quaife, Milton M. ed. *The Early Day of Rock Island and Davenport: The Narratives of J. W. Spencer and J. M. D. Burrows*. Chicago: Lakeside Press, 1942.

Recollections of the Pioneers of Lee County. Dixon, Ill.: I. A. Kennedy, 1893.

Reynolds, John. *My Own Times: Embracing a History of My Life*. Chicago: Chicago Historical Society, 1879.

Rising, Marsha, ed. "White Claims for Indian Depredations: Illinois-Missouri-Arkansas Frontier, 1804–32." *National Genealogical Society Quarterly* 84 (December 1996): 274–304.

Scripps, James E. *Memorials of the Scripps Family: A Centennial Tribute*. Detroit. John F. Eby & Co., 1891.

[Smith, Henry]. "Indian Campaign of 1832." *Military and Naval Magazine of the United States* 1 (August 1833): 321–33.

Smith, William R., ed. *The History of Wisconsin. In Three Parts*. Vols. 1 and 3. Madison: Beriah Brown, 1854.

———. "Journal of William Rudolph Smith." Edited by Joseph Schafer. *Wisconsin Magazine of History* 12 (December 1928): 192–220.

Thayer, Crawford B., comp. and ed. *The Battle of Wisconsin Heights: An Eye-Witness Account of the Black Hawk War of 1832*. Menasha, Wisc.: Banta Press, 1983.

———. *Hunting a Shadow: An Eye-Witness Account of the Black Hawk War of 1832*. Menasha, Wisc.: Banta Press, 1981.

———. *Massacre at Bad Axe: An Eye-Witness Account of the Black Hawk War of 1832*. Menasha, Wisc: Banta Press, 1984.

Taylor, Zachary. "Zachary Taylor in Illinois." Edited by Holman Hamilton. *Journal of the Illinois State Historical Society* 34 (March 1941): 84–91.

Thwaites, Reuben G., ed. "Territorial Census for 1836." In *Collections of the State Historical Society of Wisconsin*. Vol. 13, 247–70. Madison: State Historical Society of Wisconsin, 1895.

Wakefield, John. *Wakefield's History of the Black Hawk War*. Edited by Frank Stevens. 1834; reprint, Madison, Wisc.: Roger Hunt, 1976.

Walker, Augustus. "Early Days on the Lakes, With an Account of the Cholera Visitation of 1832." In *Publications of the Buffalo Historical Society*. Vol. 5, 287–381. Edited by Frank H. Severance. Buffalo, N.Y.: Buffalo Historical Society, 1902.

Walking Cloud. "Narrative of Walking Cloud." In *Collections of the State Historical Society of Wisconsin*. Vol. 13, 463–67. Madison: State Historical Society of Wisconsin, 1895.

Washburne, Elihu B. "Col. Henry Gratiot." In *Collections of the State Historical Society of Wisconsin*. Vol. 10, 235–60. Madison: State Historical Society of Wisconsin, 1909.

Whitney, Ellen C., ed. *The Black Hawk War, 1831–1832*. 2 vols. *Collections of the Illinois Historical Library*, vols. 35–38. Springfield: Illinois Historical Library, 1970–78.

Wilson, Douglas L., and Rodney O. Davis, eds. *Herndon's Informants: Letters, Interviews, and Statements about Abraham Lincoln.* Urbana: University of Illinois Press, 1998.

BOOKS AND ARTICLES

Adams, George. *General William S. Harney: Prince of Dragoons.* Lincoln: University of Nebraska Press, 2001.
Allen, Robert S. *His Majesty's Indian Allies: British Indian Policy in the Defence of Canada, 1774–1815.* Toronto: Dundurn Press, 1992.
Armour, David A. "From Drummond Island: An Indian View of Michigan History." *Michigan History* 67 (May–June 1983): 17–22.
Armstrong, Perry A. *The Sauks and the Black Hawk War.* Springfield, Ill.: H. W. Rokker, 1887.
Atlas of Dane County, Wisconsin. Madison, Wisc.: Harrison & Warner, 1873.
Axtell, James, and William C. Sturtevant. "The Unkindest Cut, or Who Invented Scalping?" *William and Mary Quarterly* 37 (July, 1980): 451–472.
Barton, A. O. "Black Hawk Retreat in Dane County." *Wisconsin Archeologist* 24 (December 1943): 61–67.
Berthrong, Donald J. "John Beach and the Removal of the Sauk and Fox from Iowa." *Iowa Journal of History* 54 (October 1956): 313–34.
Birmingham, Robert. "Uncovering the Story of Fort Blue Mounds." *Wisconsin Magazine of History* 86 (Summer 2003): 47–57.
Callender, Charles. "Fox." In *Handbook of North American Indians.* Vol. 15, *Northeast,* 648–55. Edited by Bruce Trigger. Washington, D.C.: Smithsonian Institution, 1978.
———. "Great Lakes–Riverine Sociopolitical Organization." In *Handbook of North American Indians.* Vol. 15, *Northeast,* 610–211. Edited by Bruce Trigger. Washington, D.C.: Smithsonian Institution, 1978.
———. "Sauk." In *Handbook of North American Indians.* Vol. 15, *Northeast,* 636–47. Edited by Bruce Trigger. Washington, D.C.: Smithsonian Institution, 1978.
Calloway, Colin G. "The End of an Era: British-Indian Relations in the Great Lakes Area after the War of 1812." *Michigan Historical Review* 12 (Fall 1986): 1–20.
Clifton, James A. "Personal and Ethnic Identity on the Great Lakes Frontier: The Case of Billy Caldwell, Anglo-Canadian." *Ethnohistory* 25 (Winter 1978): 69–94.
———. *The Prairie People: Continuity and Change in Potawatomi Indian Culture, 1665–1965.* Lawrence: Regents Press of Kansas, 1977.
Cole, Cyrenus. *I am a Man: The Indian Black Hawk.* Iowa City: State Historical Society of Iowa, 1938.
Converse, Philip E. "The Nature of Belief Systems in Mass Publics." In *Ideology and Discontent,* ed. David A. Apter, 206–61. New York: Free Press, 1964.
Cummings, J. E. "The Burning of Sauk-E-Nuk: The Westernmost Battle of the Revolution." *Journal of the Illinois State Historical Society* 20 (April 1927): 49–62.

Dodsworth, Robert O. *The Battle of Wisconsin Heights and the Black Hawk War of 1832.* Spring Green, Wisc.: Wisconsin Department of Natural Resources, 1996.

Dowd, Gregory. *A Spirited Resistance: The North American Indian Struggle for Unity, 1745–1815.* Baltimore: Johns Hopkins University Press, 1992.

Drake, Benjamin. *Life and Adventures of Black Hawk, With Sketches of Keokuk, The Sac and Fox Indians, And the Late Black Hawk War.* Cincinnati: George Conclin, 1838.

Eby, Cecil. *"That Disgraceful Affair," The Black Hawk War.* New York: W. W. Norton and Co., 1973.

Edmunds, R. David. "Indian-White Warfare: A Look at Both Sides." *Northwest Ohio Quarterly* 61 (Spring–Fall 1989): 35–45.

————. "Main Poc: Potawatomi Wabeno." *American Indian Quarterly* 9 (Summer 1985): 259–72.

————. *The Shawnee Prophet.* Lincoln: University of Nebraska Press, 1983.

————. *Tecumseh and the Quest for Indian Leadership.* Boston: Little, Brown and Company, 1984.

————, and Joseph L. Peyser. *The Fox Wars: The Mesquakie Challenge to New France* (Norman: University of Oklahoma Press, 1993.

Eid, Leroy. "'National' War among Indians of Northeastern North America." *Canadian Review of American Studies* 16 (Summer 1985): 125–54.

Everhart, Duane. "The Leasing of Mineral Lands in Illinois and Wisconsin." *Journal of the Illinois Historical Society* 60 (Summer 1967): 117–36.

Ferris, Ida M. "The Sauks and Foxes in Franklin and Osage Counties, Kansas." In *Collections of the Kansas State Historical Society, 1909–1910.* Vol. 11, 333–95. Edited by George W. Martin. Topeka, Kans.: State Printing Office, 1910.

Fisher, Robert L. "The Treaties of Portage des Sioux." *Mississippi Valley Historical Review* 19 (March 1933): 495–508.

Foley, William. "Different Notions of Justice: The Case of the 1808 St. Louis Murder Trials." *Gateway Heritage*, 9 (Winter 1988–1989): 2–13.

Geertz, Clifford. "Ideology as a Cultural System." In *Ideology and Discontent*, ed. David A. Apter, 47–76. New York: Free Press, 1964.

Gibson, A. M. *The Kickapoos: Lords of the Middle Border.* Norman: University of Oklahoma Press, 1963.

Gilpin, Alec R. *The War of 1812 in the Old Northwest.* East Lansing: Michigan State University Press, 1958.

Gleach, Frederic. *Powhatan's World and Colonial Virginia: A Conflict of Cultures.* Lincoln: University of Nebraska Press, 1997.

Green, Michael D. "'We Dance in Opposite Directions': Mesquakie (Fox) Separatism from the Sac and Fox Tribe." *Ethnohistory* 30 (Summer 1983): 129–140.

Guha, Ranjit. *Elementary Aspects of Peasant Insurgency in Colonial India.* Delhi: Oxford University Press, 1983.

Hagan, William T. "The Dodge-Henry Controversy." *Journal of the Illinois State Historical Society* 50 (Winter 1957): 377–84.

———. "General Henry Atkinson and the Militia." *Military Affairs* 23 (Winter 1959–60): 194–97.

———. *The Sac and Fox Indians*. Norman: University of Oklahoma Press, 1958.

———. "The Sauk and Fox Treaty of 1804." *Missouri Historical Review* 51 (October 1956): 1–7.

Hamilton, Malcolm B. "The Elements of the Concept of Ideology." *Political Studies* 35 (March 1987): 18–38.

Harrington, M. R. *Sacred Bundles of the Sauk and Fox Indians*. 1914; reprint, New York: AMS Press, 1983.

Hauberg, John. "The Black Hawk War, 1831–1832." In *Transactions of the Illinois State Historical Society, 1932*, 91–134. Springfield: Illinois State Historical Society, 1932.

Herndon William H., and Jesse W. Weik. *Abraham Lincoln: The True Story of a Great Life*. Vol. 1. 1889; reprint, New York: D. Appleton and Co, 1923.

Herring, Joseph B. *The Enduring Indians of Kansas: A Century and a Half of Acculturation*. Lawrence: University of Kansas Press, 1990.

Hickerson, Harold. *The Chippewa and Their Neighbors: A Study in Ethnohistory*. New York: Holt, Rinehart and Winston, 1970.

Hughes, Willis B. "The First Dragoons on the Western Frontier, 1834–1846." *Arizona and the West* 12 (Summer 1970): 115–38.

Horsman, Reginald. *Expansion and American Indian Policy, 1783–1812*. East Lansing: Michigan State University Press, 1967.

———. "Wisconsin and the War of 1812." *Wisconsin Magazine of History* 46 (Autumn 1962): 3–15.

Jackson, Donald. "Old Fort Madison—1808–1813." *Palimpsest* 47 (January 1966): 1–62.

———. "William Ewing, Agricultural Agent to the Indians." *Agricultural History* 31 (April 1957): 3–7.

Jipson, N. W. "Winnebago Villages and Chieftains of the Lower Rock River Region." *Wisconsin Archeologist* 2 (July 1923): 124–39.

Jones, William. *Ethnography of the Fox Indians*. Washington, D.C.: Government Printing Office, 1939.

———. "Notes on the Fox Indians." *Iowa Journal of History and Politics* 10 (January 1912): 70–112.

Jung, Patrick J. "The Mixed Race Métis of the Great Lakes Region and Early Milwaukee." *Milwaukee History* 25 (Fall–Winter 2002): 45–55.

———. "To Extend Fair and Impartial Justice to the Indian: Native Americans and the Additional Court of Michigan Territory, 1823–1836." *Michigan Historical Review* 23 (Fall 1997): 25–48.

Kay, Jeanne. "The Fur Trade and Native American Population Growth." *Ethnohistory* 31 (Autumn 1984): 265–87.

Kellogg, Louise P. "The Removal of the Winnebago." In *Transactions of the Wisconsin Academy of Sciences, Arts and Letters* 21 (1924): 23–29.

———. "The Winnebago Visit to Washington in 1828." In *Transactions of the Wisconsin Academy of Sciences, Arts, and Letters* 39 (1935): 347–54.

Kuhm, Herbert W. "The Mining and Use of Lead by the Wisconsin Indians." *Wisconsin Archeologist* 32 (June 1951): 25–37.

Libby, Orin G. "Chronicle of the Helena Shot-Tower." In *Collections of the State Historical Society of Wisconsin.* Vol 13, 335–74. Madison: State Historical Society of Wisconsin, 1895.

Lurie, Nancy O. "In Search of Chaetar: New Findings on Black Hawk's Surrender." *Wisconsin Magazine of History* 71 (Spring 1988): 163–83.

Mahan, Bruce. *Old Fort Crawford and the Frontier.* Iowa City: State Historical Society of Iowa, 1926.

Mahon, John K. "Anglo-American Methods of Indian Warfare, 1676–1794." *Mississippi Valley Historical Review* 45 (September 1958): 254–75.

Martin, Lawrence. *The Physical Geography of Wisconsin.* 2nd ed. Madison, Wisc.: State of Wisconsin, 1932.

Mayne, D. D. "The Old Fort at Fort Atkinson." In *Proceedings of the State Historical Society of Wisconsin, 1898,* 197–201. Madison: Democrat Printing Co., 1899.

Metcalf, P. Richard. "Who Should Rule at Home? Native American Politics and Indian White Relations." *Journal of American History* 61 (December 1974): 651–65.

Missall, John, and Mary Lou Missall. *The Seminole Wars: America's Longest Indian Conflict.* Gainesville: University Press of Florida, 2004.

Mooney, James. "Scalping." In *Handbook of American Indians North of Mexico.* Vol. 2, 482–83. Edited by Frederick W. Hodge. Washington, D.C.: Government Printing Office, 1910.

Muldoon, Sylvan J. *Alexander Hamilton's Pioneer Son: The Life and Times of William Stephen Hamilton, 1797–1850.* Harrisburg, Pa.: Aurand Press, 1930.

Nasatir, A. P. "The Anglo-Spanish Frontier in the Illinois Country during the American Revolution, 1779–1783." *Journal of the Illinois State Historical Society* 21 (October 1928): 291–358.

Nichols, Roger L. *Black Hawk and the Warrior's Path.* Arlington Heights, Ill.: Harlan Davidson, 1992.

———. "The Black Hawk War in Retrospect." *Wisconsin Magazine of History* 65 (Summer 1982): 239–46.

———. "General Henry Atkinson and the Building of Jefferson Barracks." *Bulletin of the Missouri Historical Society* 22 (April 1966): 321–26.

———. *General Henry Atkinson: A Western Military Career.* Norman: University of Oklahoma Press, 1965.

Osborn, William M. *The Wild Frontier: Atrocities during the American-Indian War from Jamestown Colony to Wounded Knee.* New York: Random House, 2000.

Ourada, Patricia K. *The Menominee Indians: A History.* Norman: University of Oklahoma Press, 1979.

Palmer, Friend. *Early Days in Detroit.* Detroit: Hunt & June, 1906.

Pelzer, Louis. *Henry Dodge.* Iowa City: State Historical Society of Iowa, 1911.

Perrin, William H. ed. *History of Crawford and Clark Counties, Illinois.* Chicago: O. L. Baskin & Co., 1882.

Pratt, Harry E. "Abraham Lincoln in the Black Hawk War." In *The John H. Hauberg Historical Essays*, ed. O. Fritiof Ander, 18–29. Rock Island, Ill.: Augustana College, 1954.

Prucha, Francis Paul. *Broadax and Bayonet: The Role of the United States Army in the Development of the Northwest, 1815–1860*. Madison: State Historical Society of Wisconsin, 1953.

———. *The Great Father: The United States Government and the American Indians*. 2 vols. Lincoln: University of Nebraska Press, 1984.

———. *The Sword of the Republic: The United States Army on the Frontier, 1783–1846*. London: Macmillan Company, 1969.

Reinschmidt, Michael. *Ethnohistory of the Sauk, 1885–1995: A Socio-Political Study on Continuity and Change*. Göttingen, Germany: Cuvillier Verlag, 1993.

Remini, Robert. *Andrew Jackson and His Indian Wars*. New York: Penguin Books, 2001.

———. *Andrew Jackson and the Course of American Freedom, 1822–1832*. New York: Harper & Row, 1981.

Rosenberg, Charles E. *The Cholera Years: The United States in 1832, 1849, and 1866*. Chicago: University of Chicago Press, 1962.

Royce, Charles C. "Indian Land Cessions in the United States." In *Eighteenth Annual Report of the Bureau of American Ethnology*, 521–997. Washington, D.C.: Government Printing Office, 1899.

Rudé, George. *Ideology and Popular Protest*. New York: Pantheon Books, 1980.

Scanlan, P. L. "The Military Record of Jefferson Davis in Wisconsin." *Wisconsin Magazine of History* 24 (December 1940): 174–82.

Silver, James. *Edmund Pendleton Gaines: Frontier General*. Baton Rouge: Louisiana State University Press, 1949.

Skelton, William B. "The Commanding General and the Problem of Command in the United States Army, 1821–1841." *Military Affairs* 34 (December 1970): 117–22.

Skinner, Alanson. *Observations on the Ethnology of the Sauk Indians*. Milwaukee: Milwaukee Public Museum, 1923–25.

———. "War Customs of the Menomini Indians." *American Anthropologist* 13 (April–June 1911): 299–312.

Smith, Alice E. *The History of Wisconsin*. Vol. 1, *From Exploration to Statehood*. Madison: State Historical Society of Wisconsin, 1973.

Smith, Dwight L. "A North American Neutral Indian Zone: Persistence of a British Idea." *Northwest Ohio Quarterly* 61 (Autumn 1989): 46–63.

Smith, William R. "Black Hawk War." In *The History of Wisconsin. In Three Parts*. Vol. 3, ed. William R. Smith, 113–86. Madison: Beriah Brown, 1854.

Stark, William F. *Along the Black Hawk Trail*. Sheboygan, Wisc.: Zimmerman Press, 1984.

Starkey, Armstrong. *European and Native American Warfare, 1675–1815*. Norman: University of Oklahoma Press, 1998.

Stein, Gary C. "'And the Strife Never Ends': Indian-White Hostility as Seen by European Travelers in America, 1800–1860." *Ethnohistory* 20 (Spring 1973): 173–87.

Stevens, Frank. *The Black Hawk War*. Chicago: Blakely Printing Company, 1903.

———. "A Forgotten Hero: General James Dougherty Henry." In *Transactions of the Illinois State Historical Society, 1934*, 77–120. Springfield: Illinois State Historical Library, 1934.

———. "Illinois in the War of 1812–1814." In *Transactions of the Illinois State Historical Society, 1904*, 62–197. Springfield: Illinois State Historical Library, 1904.

Stocking, Amer Mills. *The Saukie Indians and Their Great Chiefs Black Hawk and Keokuk*. Rock Island, Ill.: Vaile Company, 1926.

Stubbs, Mary Lee, and Stanley Connor. *Armor-Cavalry Part I: Regular Army and Army Reserve*. Washington, D.C.: Office of the Chief of Military History, 1969.

Sugden, John. *Blue Jacket: Warrior of the Shawnees*. Lincoln: University of Nebraska Press, 2000.

Suppiger, Joseph. "Private Lincoln in the Spy Battalion." *Lincoln Herald* 80 (Spring 1978): 46–49.

Tanner, Helen Hornbeck, ed. *Atlas of Great Lakes Indian History*. Norman: University of Oklahoma Press, 1987.

Temple, Wayne C. "Lincoln's Arms and Dress in the Black Hawk War." *Lincoln Herald* 71 (Winter 1969): 145–49.

Thian, Raphael P. *Notes Illustrating the Military Geography of the United States, 1813–1880*. Washington: Government Printing Office, 1881.

Thwaites, Reuben G. "The Story of the Black Hawk War." In *Collections of the State Historical Society of Wisconsin*. Vol. 12, ed. Reuben G. Thwaites, 217–65. Madison: State Historical Society of Wisconsin, 1892.

Trask, Kerry. *Black Hawk: The Battle for the Heart of America*. New York: Henry Holt and Company, 2006.

———. "In the Name of the Father: Paternalism and the 1763 Indian Uprising at Michilimackinac." *Old Northwest* 9 (Spring 1983): 3–21.

———. "Settlement in a Half-Savage Land: Life and Loss in the Métis Community of La Baye." *Michigan Historical Review* 15 (Spring 1989): 1–27.

Treadway, Sandra G. "Triumph in Defeat: Black Hawk's 1833 Visit to Virginia." *Virginia Cavalcade* 35 (Summer 1985): 4–17.

Turner, Andrew Jackson. "The History of Fort Winnebago." In *Collections of the State Historical Society of Wisconsin*. Vol. 14, 65–102. Madison: State Historical Society of Wisconsin, 1898.

Turner, Katharine C. *Red Men Calling on the Great White Father*. Norman: University of Oklahoma Press, 1951.

Van der Zee, Jacob. "Early History of Lead Mining in the Iowa Country." *Iowa Journal of History and Politics* 13 (January 1915): 3–52.

———. "The Neutral Ground." *Iowa Journal of History and Politics* 13 (July 1915): 311–48.

Wallace, Anthony F. C. *Jefferson and the Indians: The Tragic Fate of the First Americans*. Cambridge, Mass.: Belknap, 1999.

————. *The Long, Bitter Trail: Andrew Jackson and the Indians.* New York: Hill and Wang, 1993.

————. "Prelude to Disaster: The Course of Indian-White Relations Which Led to the Black Hawk War of 1832." In *The Black Hawk War, 1831–1832*, Vol. 1, ed. Ellen M. Whitney, 1–51. *Collections of the Illinois State Historical Library*, Vol. 35. Springfield: Illinois State Historical Library, 1970.

Wentworth, John. *Fort Dearborn: An Address Delivered . . . May 21st, 1881.* Fergus' Historical Series No. 16. Chicago: Fergus Printing Company, 1881.

White, Richard. *The Middle Ground: Indians, Empires, and Republics in the Great Lakes Region, 1650–1815.* New York: Cambridge University Press, 1991.

Willig, Timothy D. "Prophetstown on the Wabash: The Native Spiritual Defense of the Old Northwest." *Michigan Historical Review* 23 (Fall 1997): 115–58.

Young, Otis E. "The United States Mounted Ranger Battalion, 1832–1833." *Mississippi Valley Historical Review* 41 (December 1954): 453–70.

Zanger, Martin. "Conflicting Concepts of Justice: A Winnebago Murder Trial on the Illinois Frontier." *Journal of the Illinois State Historical Society* 73 (Winter 1980): 263–76.

————. "Pierre Paquette, Winnebago Mixed-Blood: Profiteer or Tribal Spokesman?" In *Anthology of Western Great Lakes Indian History*, ed. Donald Fixico, 297–351. Milwaukee: University of Wisconsin–Milwaukee Indian Studies, 1987.

————. "Red Bird." In *American Indian Leaders: Studies in Diversity*, ed. R David Edmunds, 64–87. Lincoln: University of Nebraska Press, 1980.

NEWSPAPERS

De Soto Chronicle (De Soto, Wisc.), 1887.
Galenian (Galena, Ill.), 1832.
Illinois Herald (Springfield, Ill.), 1832.
Missouri Gazette (St. Louis), 1815–16.
Missouri Gazette and Illinois Advertiser (St. Louis), 1815.
Missouri Republican (St. Louis), 1832–35.
National Intelligencer (Washington, D.C.), 1832–33.
Niles Weekly Register (Baltimore), 1832–33.
Sangamo Journal (Springfield, Ill.), 1832–33.
The Times (London), 1838.
Vandalia Whig and Illinois Intelligencer (Vandalia, Ill.), 1832.
Vernon County Censor (Viroqua, Wisc.), 1898.

DISSERTATIONS, THESES, AND UNPUBLISHED ESSAYS

Hagan, William T. "Black Hawk's Route through Wisconsin." Unpublished MS, State Historical Society of Wisconsin, Madison, Wisconsin, 1949.

Jung, Patrick J. "Forge, Destroy, and Preserve the Bonds of Empire: Euro-Americans, Native Americans, and Métis on the Wisconsin Frontier, 1634–1856." Ph.D. diss., Marquette University, 1997.

Kurtz, Royce D. "Economic and Political History of the Sauk and Mesquakie: 1780s–1845." Ph.D. diss., University of Iowa, 1986.

Russell, John. "The Black Hawk War." Unpublished MS, Russell Family Papers, Abraham Lincoln Presidential Library, Springfield, Illinois.

Sims, Catherine A. "Algonkian-British Relations in the Upper Great Lakes Region: Gathering to Give and Receive Presents, 1815–1843." Ph.D. diss., University of Western Ontario, 1992.

Index